Rock Climbing
Lake Tahoe

Mike Carville

CHOCKSTONE

FALCON®
HELENA, MONTANA

A FALCON GUIDE®

Falcon® Publishing is continually expanding its list of recreational guidebooks. All books include detailed descriptions, accurate maps, and all information necessary for enjoyable trips. You can order extra copies of this book and get information and prices for other Falcon books by writing Falcon, P.O. Box 1718, Helena, MT 59624 or calling toll free 1-800-582-2665. Also, please ask for a free copy of our current catalog. Visit our website at www.FalconOutdoors.com or contact us by e-mail at falcon@falcon.com.

© 1999 by Mike Carville

Printed in Canada

05 04 03 02 01 00 99 TP 10 9 8 7 6 5 4 3 2 1

Falcon and FalconGuide are registered trademarks of Falcon® Publishing Inc.

Library of Congress Cataloging-in-Publication Data

Carville, Mike, 1963-
    Rock climbing Lake Tahoe / Mike Carville.
      p. cm.—(A FalconGuide)
    Includes indexes.
    ISBN 1-57540-088-X (pbk.)
    1. Rock climbing—Tahoe, Lake (Calif. and Nev.) Guidebooks.
    2. Tahoe, Lake (Calif. and Nev.) Guidebooks. I. Title.
    II. Series: Falcon guide.
    GV199.42.T16C37 1999
    796.52'23'0979438—dc21   99-25924
                                          CIP

CAUTION

Outdoor recreational activities are by their very nature potentially hazardous. All participants in such activities must assume responsibility for their own actions and safety. The information contained in this guidebook cannot replace sound judgment and good decision-making skills, which help reduce risk exposure, nor does the scope of this book allow for disclosure of all the potential hazards and risks involved in such activities.

Learn as much as possible about the outdoor recreational activities in which you participate, prepare for the unexpected, and be cautious. The reward will be a safer and more enjoyable experience.

♻ Text pages printed on recycled paper.

Table of Contents

Preface

The last climbing guide to the Tahoe area was published in 1991. That was eight years ago. Since that time, new route activity at existing crags and the development of new crags have increased steadily. This guide covers the new activity and has been expanded to include several popular crags in both the Reno and Carson Valley areas.

The introduction of each chapter includes a list of recommended routes that are considered, by general consensus, to be the most enjoyable and representative of the area. At the end of the book, there is a compilation of routes by grade. There is also a list of first ascents and an index of routes by name. On the last page of the book, there is a notice by the Access Fund. Please take a moment to read this. Like it or not, climbing has grown beyond an activity pursued by just a few individuals. Today, access is everyone's concern—please make it a priority before some government agency does.

The topo illustrations by artist Mike Clelland are another addition to the guide. Due to certain time constraints, some drawings were used from the last guide, and I drew a couple more at the last minute. Clelland's work is fantastic; his topos are the best I've ever seen. I hope you enjoy his work and that it makes negotiating the crags a little bit easier.

There will be errors in this book. Please send corrections, as well as any new route information, to the author in care of Falcon Publishing, P.O. Box 1718, Helena, Montana 59624.

Acknowledgments

Guidebooks are based on the cumulative efforts of many people—all of whom deserve acknowledgment. I wish to thank you all for your contributions, which have made *Rock Climbing Lake Tahoe* the most comprehensive climbing guide ever published for the Tahoe area. Several people were particularly significant to the production of this book, and I'd like to thank them for their notable contributions:

Mike Clelland—Mike is an artist from Driggs, Idaho, who drew the majority of topos in this guide. His work has appeared in *Climbing Magazine* and elsewhere, and it adds a new level of detail to the topos.

Brian Biega—Brian deserves much of the credit for getting this guide to press. He spearheaded the effort to supply the route information and many photographs that allowed Mike Clelland to begin drawing the topos. Brian continued to work in the field, sending additional topo information to Mike and me.

Graham and Terry Sanders—Wow! Graham, with the help of several South Shore climbers, pulled together all the information critical to Cave Rock, Space Invaders, and Mayhem Cove. Graham is also responsible for much of the new bouldering taking place on the South Shore. Terry has probably worked harder than anyone in the Tahoe area on access concerns and was instrumental in resolving critical issues at Cave Rock between climbers and the Washoe Indians. We hope that both groups can honor and respect each other and the area they hold special and sacred.

Dave Hatchett—Again, Dave has been a great source of quality information, especially with regard to Big Chief. Dave, his brother Mike, and several other climbers continue to develop Big Chief, which is becoming one of Tahoe's premier crags.

Petch Pietrolungo—Petch has been fueling the fires that have kept the new route scene burning bright at Lover's Leap and elsewhere. His energy and enthusiasm are contagious, and his help with new route information for this guide was much appreciated.

Jay Sell—Another tour de force around South Shore. Jay's new route activity at the Leap, Echo, and especially Luther Rock has added a significant number of new climbs to the Tahoe area. I also hear he pulls pretty hard for a big guy!

Gene Drake—Thanks again for your reviews of North Shore and your early guide to Donner, which has been such a great resource.

Victor Marcus and Angel—Your help sorting out Black Wall and Star Walls was much appreciated. I think I still owe you dinner and DRINKS?

Tom Herbert—You still pull hard for a dad. Thanks for the information on Donner and Pig.

Dave Nettle—Still lean and mean, and still doggin' the classics in his plastics. Thanks for getting things rolling again.

Lon and Kellé Harter—Your early research on the internet was so helpful and the drawings and information on River Rock and Dinosaur Rock were the BEST!

Rocco Spina—Many climbers enjoy Rocco's routes, and the development of Indian Springs provides a whole new crag for all to enjoy.

Roger Moreau—Roger supplied historical information and photographs for several sections of this guide. Thanks for helping preserve the history of climbing in the Tahoe area.

Ron Anderson, Christine Jenkewitz-Meytras, Rick Sumner, and Bob Sutton—Their fine guidebooks were such helpful references during the compilation of this guide.

Richard Leversee, Greg Epperson, and Jim Thornburg—Thanks for supplying some great photographs.

Additionally, I'd like to thank the following people for their contributions:

Bela and Mimi Vadez, John Hoffman, Scott Frye, Don Welsh, Bird Lew, Dan Pattituchi, Kenny, Brock Berry, Max Jones, Todd Worsfold, Hans Standteiner, Bill Sinoff, Tom Higgins, Mark Rogers, Brian Mibach, John Scott, Will Chen, John Robinson, David Weisman, Will Catrel, Doug Mishler, Steve Glotfelty, Rick Sylvester, Charles Downs, Al Swanson, Bill Serniuk, Joe Missick, Jim and Bonnie Zellars, Hank Ni, Dimitri Barton, Dan Osman, Paul Crawford, Jay Smith, Paul Teare, Dan Kumetat, Mick Keane, Jon Fox, Cliff Locks, Mark Nicholas, Jet, and Rebecca.

Safe and good climbing to all of you!

Lake Tahoe Overview

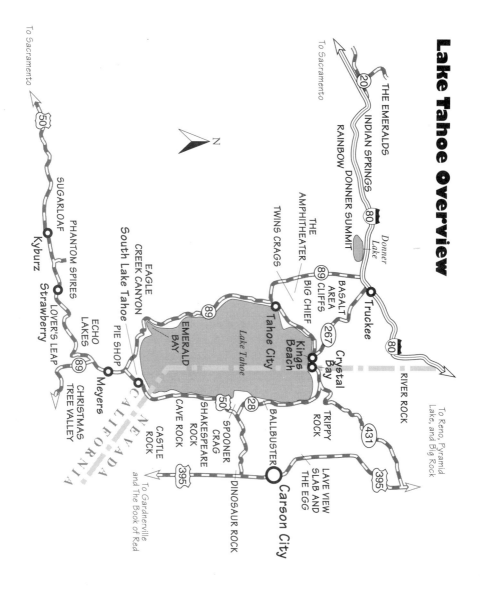

To Sacramento

To Sacramento

THE EMERALDS
INDIAN SPRINGS
RAINBOW
DONNER SUMMIT

Donner Lake

20

80

N

RIVER ROCK

To Reno, Pyramid Lake, and Big Rock

THE AMPHITHEATER
TWINS CRAGS

BASALT AREA
89 CLIFFS
BIG CHIEF

Truckee

267

Crystal Bay

Tahoe City

Kings Beach

Lake Tahoe

89

431

395

TRIPPY ROCK

LAVE VIEW
SLAB AND
THE EGG

50

SUGARLOAF

PHANTOM SPIRES

Kyburz   Strawberry

LOVER'S LEAP

ECHO LAKES

EAGLE
CREEK CANYON
South Lake Tahoe

PIE SHOP

EMERALD BAY

89

89

CHRISTMAS TREE VALLEY

Meyers

To Sacramento

CALIFORNIA
NEVADA

CAVE ROCK

CASTLE ROCK

SHAKESPEARE ROCK

SPOONER CRAG

50

28

BALLBUSTER

DINOSAUR ROCK

395

Carson City

To Gardnerville
and The Book of Red

xi

Introduction

Set in the alpine wilderness of the Sierra Nevada Mountains, Lake Tahoe offers a tremendous variety of climbing. You may choose to climb eloquent, multipitch classics on clean, compact granite, while climbers just a few miles away may spend the entire day feverishly working the moves on some radically overhanging sport route on metamorphic rock. Amid the splendor of the high country, all of Tahoe's climbing is scenic, yet the crags are only minutes from resort towns that offer all the necessary conveniences and amenities.

Lake Tahoe is the deepest high-altitude lake in North America and is renowned for its natural beauty. Resting in a mountain basin at 6,200 feet above sea level, the lake is encircled by rugged peaks that rise 3,000 feet higher. The lake was created when the basin sank between two uplifted fault blocks. The lake filled when the ancestral flow of the Truckee River, the basin's only drainage, was blocked at the north end, first by volcanic flows and then by glacial debris. The Truckee River eventually cut through those barriers and continues to flow today.

The Washoe Indians of western Nevada gave Tahoe its name, which means "a great, spiritually powerful body of water." The lake was a favorite summer retreat of the Washoe, who would winter at lower elevations in the valleys east of the Sierra. In spring, they returned to the mountains and stayed until late fall, living off the abundance of the lake and surrounding forests. The first historical visit to Lake Tahoe was made by John Freemont and Charles Preuss on Valentine's Day, 1844. The flow of emigrants to the area increased with the discovery of gold at Sutter's Creek in 1848. The ill-fated Donner party was among the early emigrants. Many from this group perished in the deep snows east of Donner Summit during the winter of 1846.

A SHORT CLIMBING HISTORY

The record of Tahoe's climbing history is sketchy at best. The earliest known records of roped climbs in the Tahoe Basin are those of the Sierra Club, whose members used Lover's Leap as a practice area for alpine ascents in the high Sierra. In the mid-1950s, Warren Harding and Sacramento climber John Ohrenschall climbed *Harding's Chimney* at Sugarloaf. Harding and Ohrenschall also teamed up to climb Upper and Lower Spire at Phantom Spires. News of their ascents spread. Roger Moreau and Russell Hoopes made a successful bid for the first ascent of Lower Spire on October 22, 1955. Moreau and friends were responsible for other first ascents at the Spires and Lover's Leap, as well as much of the early development of Shakespeare Rock. For a few years, Royal Robbins operated his climbing school, Rock Craft, at the Leap. In the 1967 issue of *Ascent,* Steve Roper published a guide to Lover's Leap; shortly thereafter, the exploration of the Leap's grand walls began in force.

In 1968, Tom Higgins and Frank Sarnquist free climbed *The Line* (5.9). This climb opened the doors to the possibilities of hard free climbing in the Tahoe area. In 1969, Jeff Lowe made what was surely one of the most impressive first ascents ever done at the Leap. Early one April morning, he set out alone under winter conditions and soloed the 600-foot-high *Hour Glass Wall* (5.9 A2).

Russ Hoopes and Bod Gaughram after an early
ascent of *Lover's Chimney*, Lover's Leap, October
15, 1956. Photo by Roger Moreau.

The 1970s ushered in a period of discovery in the quality and quantity of difficult climbing in the Tahoe area. Jim Orey was successful on *Hooker's Haven* (5.9 A4), a very technical traverse beneath a roof at Sugarloaf. A year later, Orey and Gene Drake climbed *Vanishing Point* (5.10). This sustained climb ascends a stunning dihedral devoid of the large dikes that so often offer easy passage up the Leap's steep walls.

In 1973, Royal Robbins climbed a somewhat obscure line that he named *Fantasia* (5.9). Many consider this route one of his finest efforts at the Leap. "More bold than hard," the beauty lies in its improbability. The following year, Bill Todd put up *E.B.'s Wall* (5.10b), bringing hard climbing to Echo Lakes. That same year, three classic lines on Eagle Lake Buttress (*Orange Sunshine* 5.9, *A Line* 5.9, and *Monkey Business* 5.10a) were climbed by Bill Todd, Rick Sumner, and John Taylor.

In 1975, Greg Dexter and Rick Sumner approached *Hour Glass* (5.11) with "light hearts and light racks" to make the first free ascent of the Leap's longest aid route. This was not only the hardest free route at Lover's Leap but also the first Tahoe route to have multiple 5.10 pitches.

By the late 1970s, climbers such as Max Jones and Mark Hudon were pushing the limits of free climbing with ascents including *Hooker's Haven* (5.12a), *Monkey Paws* (5.12a), and *Panic in Detroit* (5.12b/c). Rick Cashner came away with *Space Walk* (5.11c/d), one of the finest crack climbs in the Tahoe Basin. The most stunning climb of the decade, however, was Tony Yaniro's ascent of *Grand Illusion* (5.13b/c) at Sugarloaf in 1978. *Grand Illusion* was not only the hardest free route in the world at that time but also the world's first 5.13.

Yaniro, Jones, and Hudon were ahead of their time and received a lot of ridicule for their "progressive techniques," such as yo-yoing and hangdogging. However, these three individuals did more to raise the standards of difficult free climbing than anyone else at that time in Tahoe, and their practices, which are now commonplace, make complete sense when trying to work difficult moves and improve performance.

In the mid-1980s, Donner Summit, an area relatively open to a wide range of tactics, produced the greatest quantity of well-protected sport routes in the Tahoe Basin. As such, Donner's popularity grew immensely. Many people have shared in this development, but the most active have been Scott Frye, Don Welsh, Victor Marcus, John Hoffman, Gene Drake, Doug Mischler, and Steve Glotfelty.

During the past several years, a handful of new sport crags have been developed. Mike Carville developed the Emeralds, while Jay Smith, Paul Crawford, Dan Osman, and several others worked the dizzily steep walls of Cave Rock and Mayhem Cove. Rocco Spina and friends focused on Indian Springs. Dave Hatchett and Mike Hatchett made a record discovery when they began putting up new climbs at Big Chief. Todd Worsflod's routes extend across the Tahoe area including Donner Summit, Big Chief, the Amphitheater, and Eagle Creek Canyon. Al Swanson, along with the Hatchett brothers and other South Shore climbers, concentrated on Echo Lakes. Luther Rock and Lover's Leap have experienced a resurgence of new route activity led primarily by Jay Sell, Brock Berry, Petch Pietrolungo, Mark Nicholas, John Robinson, Graham Sanders, and Will Catrel.

At present, local ethics are relatively relaxed. During the mid-1980s, the introduction of rap bolting and sport tactics drove a wedge that split Tahoe's climbing community. To many climbers, the advent of sport climbing diminished the adventure of the ascent and undermined the very foundation of the sport. It was viewed (and still is to a certain degree) as overly consumptive of limited natural resources, meaning clean rock and new lines.

Climbers that support sport tactics feel it opens the door to new possibilities in an evolving sport. After many angry confrontations and several bolt chopping incidents, local climbers decided they would rather climb than whine; however, this does not imply that all of Tahoe's climbers embrace rap bolting. Climbers seeking first ascents should remain sensitive to the ethic of the area where they choose to climb.

FIRST ASCENTS

New routes seem to be all the rage today. For some climbers, to envision and link a series of movements formerly unexplored can renew a sense of adventure and discovery. It is not my intention to declare how you should put up a climb or to make it seem that climbing a new line is the only way that you can experience the driving elements of the sport. I do feel, however, that a couple of points should be addressed to reduce tensions and potential dangers in the future. Although much of the following may seem obvious, these suggestions are often disregarded.

Before putting up a new route, confer with locals to determine what methods are being used in that area.

Don't add or pull fixed gear from an established route without a big "OK" from the first ascent party.

If a climb is too hard or too scary, then toprope it.

Because most of the cracks at Tahoe have been climbed, the majority of new lines going in today are up smooth granite faces that require the use of protection bolts. Herein lies the controversy. The root of the problem lies in the indiscriminate use of fixed gear, especially when placed on rappel, and the creation of dangerous runouts due to lack of adequate protection.

Climbing has undergone quite a transition over the past couple of decades. Fifteen years ago, progression through the grades was a more deliberate process, in the sense that you were skilled in a particular grade before moving on to the next. As a consequence, falls were not nearly as common. Today, with better equipment and a general shift in perspective, more climbers are willing to risk a fall, and bolts take a pounding.

Today's new lines require the use of 3/8- or 1/2-inch diameter bolts, which are far more capable of withstanding repeated leader falls than 1/4-inch diameter bolts. If an old 1/4-inch bolt placed 15 or 20 years ago breaks on a runout—or just in a bad place—the result can kill someone. That kind of risk isn't acceptable on a bolted line. When old bolts start breaking—and they will—people will get hurt. Then someone will have to enforce certain regulations on where, when, and how we climb. If climbers don't get a grip on the situation, then the lawyers and bureaucrats will.

Descend or approach
from this direction

KEY TO TOPO SYMBOLS

Continue to the end of
pitch/top to ground

Left-facing ramp.

Left-facing corner.

Roof.

Knobs which can be slung.

Face climbing past a bolt.

Two bolt belay on ledge; line of rappel.

Crux rating.

Right-facing corner.

Straight-in corner.

Fixed piton (pin).

Straight-in crack.

Wide crack or chimney (chim.).

TALUS

From time to time, old bolts and pins need to be replaced. Try to consult the first ascent party, but if they are unavailable or unwilling, and the general consensus considers the existing fixed protection unsafe, it should be pulled and replaced with the current standard, a 3/8-inch bolt or a solid pin placement.

When putting in a line on rappel, figure out the safest and most logical clips for people of all heights. Use a toprope or whatever method works best. There is no excuse to blow placements or create unnecessary runouts when rap bolting. If you are not able to figure it out while hanging on the end of a rope, then consider leaving the line for someone who has more experience in bolt placement.

I feel that it is sometimes necessary to remove loose holds and blocks during a first ascent. Such extensive cleaning can produce a high-quality route and help prevent unnecessary injuries. However, blatant hold alteration is not accepted by the Tahoe climbing community. Also, be aware that it is illegal to place fixed protection in wilderness areas, such as the Desolation Wilderness.

If a short red sling is hanging from the lowest bolt on a face route, then the line is being worked. Please don't try the line on lead. It's not fair to rob the inspiration of the first ascent party. They most likely have a lot of time, energy, and money invested in their project.

SEASONS AND WEATHER

Although snow lies on the ground in Tahoe through April, the climbing season is usually well under way by this time. Summers in the Sierra are warmer and drier than in the Cascades and Northern Rockies. Even in the heat of midsummer, an afternoon breeze or shady exposure makes the climbing temperature "just right." Fall is considered by many to be the most beautiful season in the basin. After Labor Day, the number of visitors drops considerably. Mornings tend to be cool, followed by pleasant afternoons and mild evenings. Indian summer often continues into early October.

Although climbing is limited during the winter because of heavy snow, it is possible to climb on warm, sunny days at some crags. At Cave Rock, for instance, optimal redpoint conditions exist during early and late winter. Sometimes in December, you can walk into Pie Shop in tennis shoes, but other times, during the same month, the approach requires snowshoes or skis. Always pack warm clothes and wind protection, even on the warmest winter days, and bring a headlamp on longer approaches. Lastly, be extra careful when crossing snow-covered talus fields.

GETTING THERE AND STAYING THERE

The Tahoe Basin is located about 200 miles east of San Francisco and 45 miles west of Reno, Nevada. Two major highways service Tahoe. Interstate 80 runs east/west along the north edge of the Tahoe Basin, and U.S. Highway 50 enters the southern basin from the southwest. Several state roads also extend into the basin. Lake Tahoe also is accessible by bus service and airline.

INTERNATIONAL RATING SYSTEMS COMPARED

West German	YDS	British	Australian	East German	French
	5.0				
	5.1				
	5.2				
	5.3				
	5.4				
	5.5				
	5.6				
5+	5.7	4b / VS		VIIa	5a
6-	5.8	4c		VIIb	5b
6	5.9	5a / HVS	16 / 17	VIIb	5c
6+	5.10a		18	VIIc	6a
7-	5.10b	5b / E1	19	VIIIa	6a+
7	5.10c	E2	20	VIIIb	6b
7	5.10d		21	VIIIc	6b+
7+	5.11a	5c	22	IXa	6c
8-	5.11b	E3	23	IXb	6c
8	5.11c		24	IXb	6c+
8+	5.11d	6a	25	IXc	7a
9-	5.12a	E4	26	Xa	7a+
9	5.12b		27	Xb	7b
9	5.12c	6b / E5	28	Xb	7b+
9+	5.12d		29	Xc	7c
10-	5.13a	6c	30		7c+
10	5.13b	E6 / 7a	31		8a
10	5.13c		32		8a+
10	5.13d	E7	33		8b
10	5.14a		34		8b+

7

Overnight accommodations are readily available around Tahoe. The pleasant climate makes camping enjoyable during the summer, and many campgrounds have reasonable rates. Some of the facilities are run by the Forest Service, while others are private operations. Generally, campgrounds are open from May until early October. For more information, contact the appropriate United States government offices, the USDA Forest Service, or California State Parks and Recreation. State park campgrounds are on the Mistix Reservation System at (800) 444-7275.

You must have a permit to camp in wilderness areas, such as the Desolation Wilderness. The permits are free and available at Forest Service offices. Treat all stream and lake water in the Tahoe Basin before consumption because of *giardia lamblia,* a microscopic organism that causes a severe intestinal disorder.

You'll find many good restaurants around the lake—from low-budget Mexican fare. to fancy California cuisine. The Fire Sign on the west shore, the Squeeze in Truckee, and the Strawberry Lodge at Lover's Leap offer great home-style breakfasts. For those on a budget, the casinos have plentiful buffets. The Tahoe Community Store, with one location near Tahoe City and another one in Truckee, provides a wide range of health foods.

USING THIS GUIDE

This guidebook begins with the crags you encounter when driving Interstate 80 east from Sacramento. From Tahoe City, the layout moves south along California Highway 89 to U.S. Highway 50. From this point, the descriptions move north, reaching East Shore Crags, then backtrack southwest to Sugarloaf. The Reno Area and Carson Valley Crags follow, and the final two chapters cover bouldering and ice climbing.

The majority of routes in this guide are described using topo illustrations. These drawings are the most detailed and accurate method of representing cliffs and their climbs. Some remote formations and high-country peaks, which ascend broken or multifaceted faces, are too complex to be illustrated through topos and therefore are given narrative descriptions.

RATINGS/DISCLAIMER

The Yosemite Decimal System (YDS) is used in the Tahoe area. Although this system is relatively accurate, choosing a rating is subjective; thus two climbs of the same grade may not be exactly equal in difficulty. The rating scale for technical climbs that require a rope for safety begins at 5.0 and currently ends at 5.14. The letters a, b, c, and d are used to further define the degree of difficulty of grades 5.10 and up. A rating usually reflects the hardest technical move on a route. However, due to the sustained nature of some climbs, the rating may reflect the endurance needed to complete a certain section of the climb rather than the completion of any one move.

Some fixed protection in the area is getting old. A climber must be able to evaluate the condition of bolts and pins before clipping in. It's the climber's responsibility to determine the safety of protection, fixed or natural. An R or X in the rating indicates serious fall potential due to protection being far apart, poor, or unavailable. An R means runout, with a chance of a long fall. An X indicates the possibility of a very serious or fatal fall.

This is only a guidebook, merely a composite of opinions from many sources on the whereabouts and difficulties of various routes. It is not an instructional book on mountaineering technique or a substitute for good judgment. Rock climbing is a high-risk sport, and the user of this book assumes full responsibility for his or her own safety.

EQUIPMENT

A standard climbing rack includes a full range of protection from the smallest wired chock up to a 4-inch piece. Some climbs may require special types of protection or several pieces of the same size. Tahoe has many bolt-protected face climbs, and quickdraws are especially useful. A 165-foot/55-meter rope is sometimes necessary to reach belay points.

PRESERVING ACCESS

One of the toughest challenges facing the climbing community today is gaining and preserving access to the crags while maintaining the integrity of the natural environment. Many existing and future areas, including national parks and forest lands, could be closed to climbing if land managers feel climbers are unable to use the resources responsibly. Preserving the access to the rocks we climb is important, but the way that we treat the land as a whole is a greater concern. Trampling across a fragile meadow, pitching a tent or building a campfire in a sensitive area, upsetting wildlife (such as nesting birds), using live trees for firewood, cutting unnecessary trails, polluting water sources, or leaving trash behind are practices contrary to the preservation of the sport, and, more important, of the earth on which we all rely. A blatant disregard for the natural environment is the quickest way to lose access.

The Emeralds Overview

RECOMMENDED ROUTES

Indigo .8+
Three Minute Hero .9+
Buzz Saw .10a
Stone Fish .10b
Overflow .10c/d
Shadows on the Earth .11a
Apathy .11a
Atlantis .11c
Mono Dioght .11c
Radio Static .11c/d
The E-Ticket Ride .11+
Steel Monkey .12a
Chasing the Dragon .12b
Kudos .12b
Green Ice .12c
Voodoo Bliss .12d
Pimp the Ho .12d
Still Life .13a
Bustin' Rhymes .13a
Aqua .13b

Spaulding Lake

THE GORGE AND THE UPPER GORGE

KUDOS KLIFF

STEEL MONKEY WALL

SLABS

THE FORTRESS

RIDGE CANYON

Outwest

SLABS

N

Trees

RIVER

Gravel Pit

Campsites

Flume Pipe

THE FLUME FACE

To Bowman Lake

Emerald Pools (swimming)

Bowman Lake Road

1/2 mile

Campsites

South Yuba River

Dirt Entry Road

Bowman Lake Road

1.4 miles

To 80 exit

To 20

To 20

To Nevada City

P

The Emeralds

Hidden in a forested canyon above the South Yuba River, between Nevada City and Truckee, are several cliffs and a gorge similar to the great sport climbing arenas of Europe. The Emeralds are unique because the rock—a combination of highly metamorphosed sedimentary and igneous rock—is similar to limestone. The climbing requires intricate yet dynamic movement. The walls generally are well featured with positive square cuts and an occasional pocket. Some of the faces are so steep that a rope dropped from anchors 80 feet above the ground hangs free 30 feet from the base of the cliff.

The majority of the climbing at the Emeralds is divided into two areas. The Benches, a series of steep faces and buttresses, lie scattered along a west-facing ridge; and the Gorge, a rift in the forest floor a hundred feet deep and twice as wide, runs for 0.25 mile from Spaulding Lake to the Yuba River Canyon. The Emeralds also include two small cliffs, the Flume Face and Bowman Lake.

The climbing season extends from May to November, after which the area is covered with snow. Midsummer temperatures can be very high, and it is usually too hot to climb in late July and August. A standard rack for the area should include eight to twelve quickdraws, a couple of bail biners, and one rope. Only a few routes require supplemental protection. Many of the first bolts are difficult to reach and should be stick-clipped from the ground.

Camping is free and sites can be found by the river and in the trees along the dirt entry road. Please observe the "no open campfire" signs when they are posted. Grouse Ridge, a granite basin dotted with pristine lakes, is located just up Bowman Lake Road. This scenic area offers hundreds of miles of hiking and mountain biking trails and some of the finest fishing in the Sierra.

The Emeralds are located a few miles northeast of Emigrant Gap off Interstate 80. From I-80, exit onto California Highway 20 and drive west toward Nevada City for 4 miles. Turn north on Bowman Lake Road and continue for 1.4 miles. Just before the bridge across the South Fork of the Yuba River, cut right onto a dirt road that parallels the river. Continue along this dirt entry road through a shallow creek and up a small hill. If the main access gate is locked, you may have to park by the concrete bridge that spans the river and walk to the crags.

Stay on the main dirt road for 0.6 mile, passing through a quarry area and stretch of trees, until you reach some large boulders on the right. Behind the trees and boulders and to the right of a roof, you will find Steel Monkey Wall. The other crags at the Benches are above. The Gorge lies at the end of the dirt entry road and boulder outwash. The Flume Face and Bowman Lake are located at different points off Bowman Lake Road. For more detailed information, consult the overview map.

Warning: Extreme Flooding! During the spring and the early summer months, the Gorge and outwash areas often experience extreme flooding when the overflow gates of Spaulding Lake Reservoir are opened. The water level can rise quickly; and, at full release, the water can be fatal. The force of rushing currents, which generally takes several hours to rise to dangerous levels, can easily overturn cars and sweep away climbers. The flooding can change the terrain and routes, often stripping bolt hangers and features from the walls. Signs are usually posted each spring when the reservoir releases overflow water. Climb at your own risk, and move to higher ground at the first sign of high water.

11

THE FLUME FACE

This steep slab is visible from the bridge across the South Yuba River. To reach the routes, turn right off Bowman Lake Road 1.1 miles from California Highway 20. Follow the dirt road for several hundred yards and park on the side of the road just beyond a small creek atop a short hill. Walk east along the flume pipe, then hike up along the edge of the slab. Rappel to the base of the climbs.

THE FLUME FACE
A   Juluka .11c
B   The Cure .10c TR

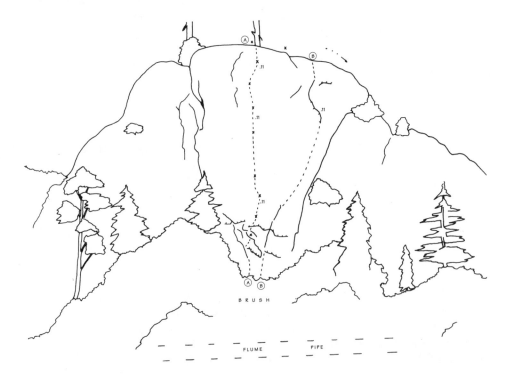

THE BENCHES

This low slabby ridge splits the Yuba River Canyon, and several excellent and steep cliffs are scattered along the northwest side. Steel Monkey Wall is located just off the dirt entry road. Above stands the Fortress and, to the left, Kudos Kliff.

Steel Monkey Wall

This short, overhanging wall is located 150 feet south of the dirt entry road to the right of a large roof and behind a group of trees and boulders. To reach the top of the crag, walk around the right side, then scramble up a third-class gully.

MOSQUITO COAST .11C (six bolts, two-bolt belay)
Not shown. Climb the steep slab left of the broken chimney that forms the left edge of Steel Monkey Wall. Enjoyable but dirty.

THE FLY .11B (three bolts, two-bolt belay)
Not shown. To the right of White Riot, climb the face to a crack and a belay.

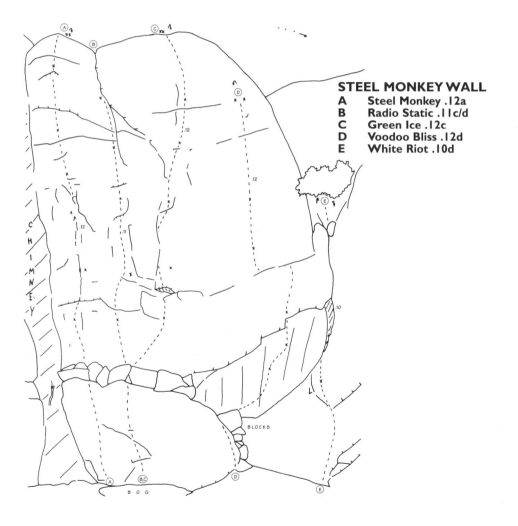

STEEL MONKEY WALL
A   Steel Monkey .12a
B   Radio Static .11c/d
C   Green Ice .12c
D   Voodoo Bliss .12d
E   White Riot .10d

SECOND TIME AROUND .8 R (pro: thin to medium)

Not shown. This route begins on a small ledge behind a twisted oak tree just right of the third-class gully that leads to the top of Steel Monkey Wall. Climb a hand crack to a small roof, then up the slab above. Some bolts protect the hardest moves. Just up and left of this wall, locate a short slab with two bolted lines (5.10–5.11).

The Fortress

This buttress stands a couple hundred yards above Steel Monkey Wall. From behind the top of Steel Monkey Wall, traverse right and up a third-class slab. The Fortress is visible from the top of the slabs. The blocky buttress is streaked with bright patches of green and orange lichen and is split halfway up by a roof system. Hike straight ahead through the trees and over a boulder field to the base. Reach the top of the crag via the fourth-class Approach Slab on the left side of the face.

THE FORTRESS

A   **Solar Wind .11 TR**
B   **Sun Burn .10 TR**
C   **Approach Slab (fourth class)**
D   **The Perils of Babylon .12b (rules problem, stay on arete)**
E   **Shadows on the Earth .11a (second pitch is loose, dirty, and rarely done)**

Kudos Kliff

This wall lies several hundred yards left of the Fortress. The face is on the left edge of a large section of slabs. To reach the top of the face, climb up the left side.

KUDOS KLIFF
A   Duppy Conqueror .11b/c (pro: thin to 1.5")
B   Kudos .12b
C   Ambushed in the Night .11d (pro: thin to 2")

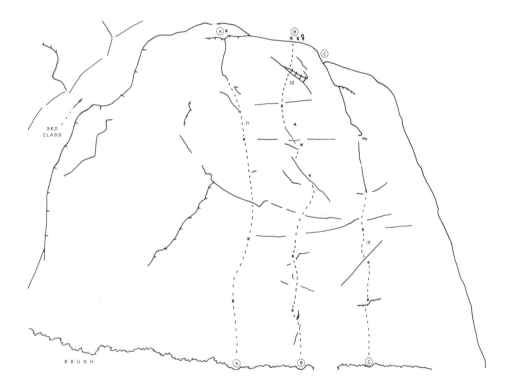

THE GORGE

This is a surreal place with small waterfalls, huge overhangs, and routes that are guaranteed to raise your blood pressure. The Gorge contains the majority of the area's test pieces. These steep lines demand power and finesse from the word "go" all the way to the anchor chains.

From the end of the dirt entry road, hike northeast through a large boulder outwash. Several minutes later, you can see the mouth of the Gorge on the right. The majority of the lines ascend the overhanging north (left) side of the Gorge. Some of these climbs may be radically altered or may no longer exist due to extreme flooding during the spring of 1997 and 1998. Rebolting may be necessary on some of the climbs.

THE E-TICKET WALL
A   **Emerald Staircase (project)**
B   **The E-Ticket Ride .11+ (pro: Friends 0.5" to 3")**
C   **The Dream Affair .11- (pro: thin to 2.5")**
D   **Toprope Wall .11 TR**

The E-Ticket Wall

This wall is located on the right side of the entrance to the Gorge. The huge, blocky roof overhangs 25 feet in 50 feet. This wall may have received severe damage from the release of water through floodgates at the top of the gorge. Some of the blocks may be loose as well.

The Bulge

The Bulge is a dark overhanging wall up and left of the Gorge's entrance. Route damage has been reported from the release of water through the floodgates. A large boulder may have shifted and blocked the starts of the right-side routes.

THE BULGE

A   Chicks Dig It! .11a
B   Still Life .13a
C   Narcada (project)
D   Pimp the Ho .12d
E   Bustin' Rhymes .13a

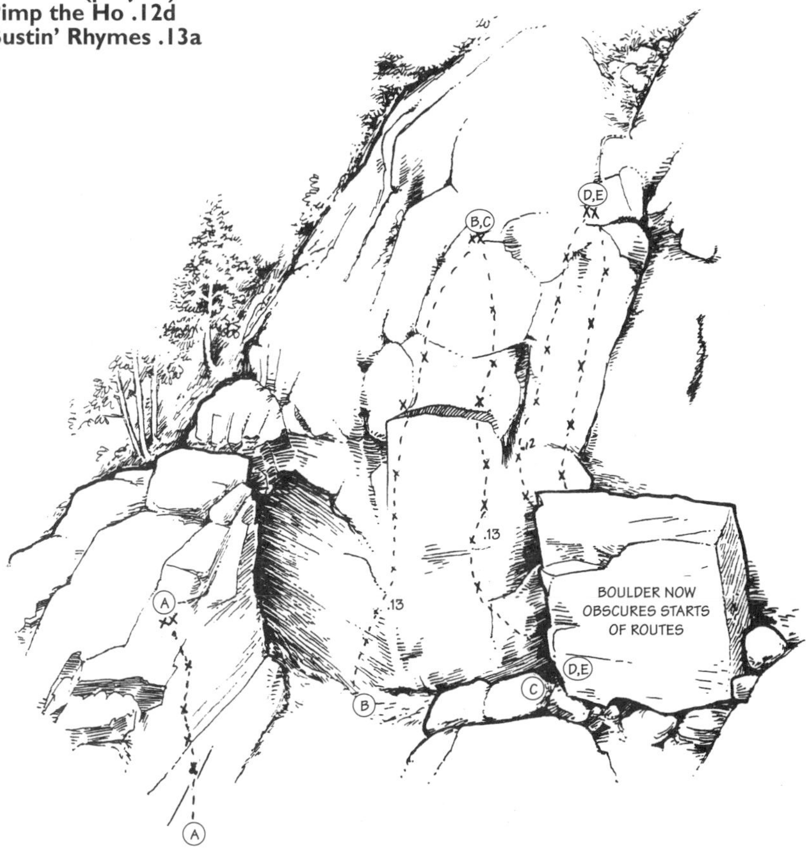

Don Welsh sending *Still Life*, 5.13a, on the Bulge.
Photo by M. Carville.

Higher and Lower Main Wall

This large overhanging wall forms the northwest side of the Gorge and extends from the huge boulder right of the Bulge to the second pool. Severe damage from the release of water through the floodgates has changed the starts of some climbs. The flood waters may have wiped out some starting holds and/or filled in the starts so that some of the routes are one to two bolts shorter.

LOWER MAIN WALL
A   **Big Green .13a (yet to be linked from eighth bolt to top)**
B   **Aqua .13b**
C   **Hundredth Monkey .12c (rating is to the top; .11c variation exists to first belay)**
D   **Project**
E   **Arid Oasis .12b**
F   **Atlantis .11c**

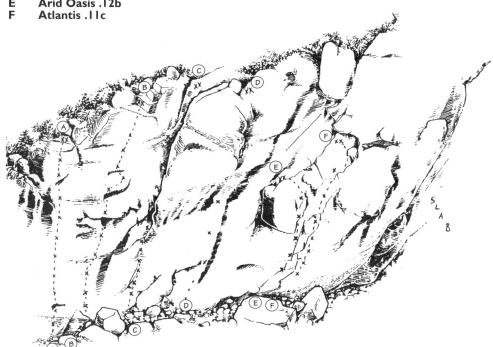

The Epitaph

This boulder is located directly across from *Aqua*. The climbs share the first two bolts and the top belay anchors.

JAWS .11B (four bolts)
Not shown. On the left, climb the face to a large edge, then cut left and up a crack.

BIG FOOT .12A (three bolts)
Not shown. On the right, climb straight up using the right arete near the top.

Higher Main Wall

This wall lies above the left side of the pool. From the Lower Main Wall, hike up the left edge (loose) of the large slab that separates the bases of these two walls to the second pool. Portions of this wall remain wet year-round.

THE INVISIBLE MAN .11+/.12- (12 bolts)

Not shown. This route ascends the center of the large, striking wall up and left of the second pool. Hike down to the top of the wall from the Upper Gorge and rappel to a bolted belay at the start of the route. Portions of this climb are loose.

THE GORGE, HIGHER MAIN WALL
A   Jail Break .12b
B   Cloud Factory .12c/d
C   Electric Chair (project)
D   Unnamed (project)

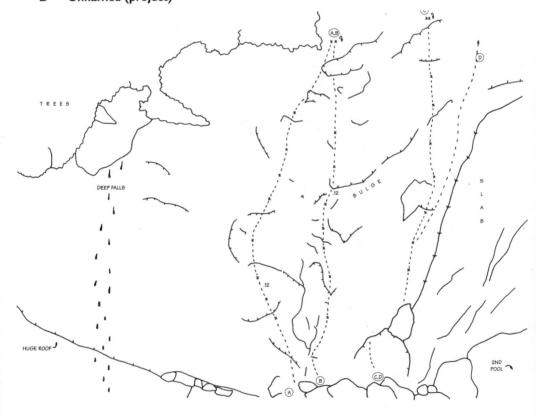

UPPER GORGE

To reach the Upper Gorge, exit the Gorge by the second pool from the top of a slab on the right. Follow a small trail that winds uphill close to the rim. The trail drops into the top of the Upper Gorge just before Spaulding Lake and the spillway. Severe flooding has damaged these routes.

Upper Wall

This obvious short wall forms the top south side of the Upper Gorge.

The following routes are on the face directly across (north) and left of Upper Wall. They are listed from left to right.

BUZZ SAW .10A (three bolts, two-bolt belay)

Not shown. Begin in the boulder cleft to the right of *Apathy*. 11a, which is on the Wishing Well—South. Climb the slab to the steep face above.

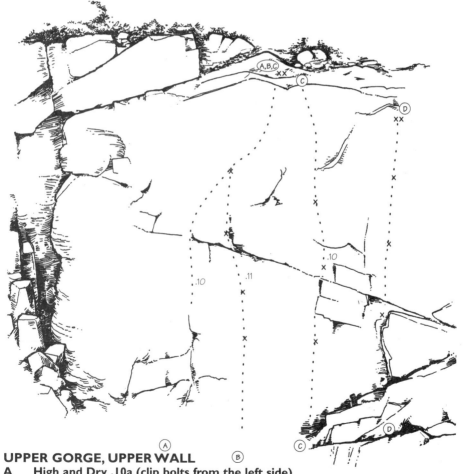

UPPER GORGE, UPPER WALL
A   High and Dry .10a (clip bolts from the left side)
B   Dam It .11b (clip bolts from the right side)
C   Overflow .10c/d
D   Chronic Fatigue Syndrome .10b

STRESS FRACTURE .9+ TR

Not shown. Ascend the prominent right-slanting crack. Supplemental gear is necessary for the anchors.

FIREBALL .11A (three bolts, two-bolt belay)

Not shown. Climb the steep face just left of a large boulder. Be careful clipping the second bolt.

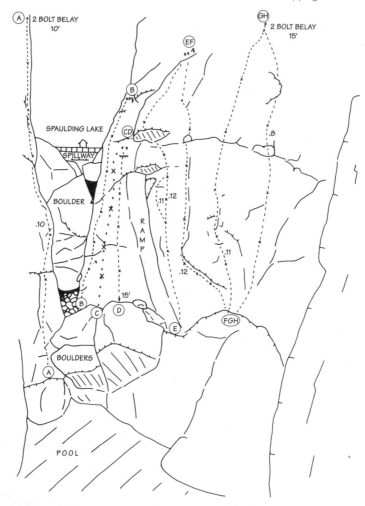

UPPER GORGE, THE WISHING WELL—SOUTH

A **Apathy .11a**
B **Three Minute Hero .9+**
C **Gypsy Moth .10a**
D **Sub-Zero .10c (start from the ground)**
E **Dynamic Panic .11d/.12b**
F **Chasing the Dragon .12b**
G **Maniac .11b**
H **Indigo .8+**
Fact or Friction .12a TR Climb the face between *Dynamic Panic* and *Chasing the Dragon*.

The Wishing Well

A short ways down the Upper Gorge, you will reach a spot blocked from above by a huge boulder. Below the boulder, high dark walls, known as the Wishing Well, surround a green pool. Several of the climbs traverse over the water before reaching the top. The easiest way to enter this area is to rappel from the anchors on *Apathy,* then climb one of the routes back out. A third-class escape traverses the south side to a talus slope that leads up to the rim.

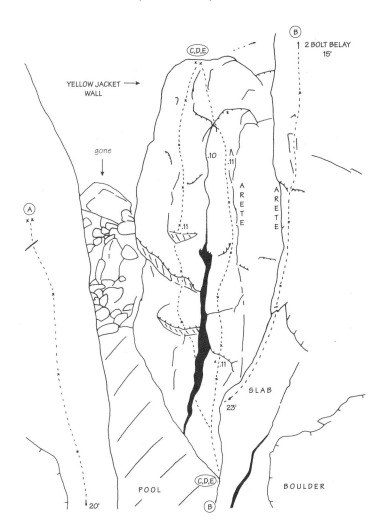

UPPER GORGE, THE WISHING WELL—NORTH

A   **Three Minute Hero .9+**
B   **Apathy .11a (blunt arete)**
C   **Mono Dioght .11c (face to arete)**
D   **Stone Fish .10b (chimney to thin crack)**
E   **Fish Face .11a (chimney to face)**

Yellow Jacket Wall

This wall is to the left of the Wishing Well—North. The right side of the face is overhanging and split by a T-shaped thin crack. To approach this wall, scramble down the talus slope from the rim on the opposite side (south) of Upper Gorge. These routes are 20 feet longer due to flood damage and may be more difficult than indicated.

FLAKE BAKE .10B (six bolts, two-bolt belay)
Climb the face on the left side.

YELLOW JACKET .11B (six bolts, two-bolt belay)
Climb the face in the center of the wall.

ULTRAVIOLET .11D (eight bolts, two-bolt belay)
Climb the T-shaped thin crack, then fade up and left.

BOWMAN LAKE

Bowman, also known as B! Word is a small but high-quality crag west and below Bowman Lake. From the dirt entry road turnoff, continue on Bowman Lake Road for 12.5 miles. After 9 miles, the road turns from pavement to dirt. At about mile 12, the road passes below a large cliff and then by a two-story building on the right. Finally, you will pass below Bowman Lake Dam. Once the road crosses over a small creek and begins to swing more sharply to the left, look below the road for a gently overhanging cliff. The cliff is about 100 feet high and is adjacent to the creek. A large pine tree stands in front of the face.

Approach the cliff by third classing down the gully from the road. There are also some rappel anchors on the top of the cliff. Please note that all the routes are bolted and end below the top of the cliff. The wall is a work in progress and several projects exist.

NICE FUCKIN' MODEL .12A
Climb from the ledge with a belay bolt above the log bridge.

BIO-EXORCIST .13A
Climb the big overhang.

HANDBOOK OF THE RECENTLY DECEASED .12c
Climb near the left-facing book.

JUNO YOUR CASE WORKER .11D
Climb the third route left of the chimney.

WE'VE COME FOR YOUR DAUGHTER, CHUCK .12A
Climb the second route left of the chimney.

BEETLEGEUSE .12B
Climb the first route left of the chimney.

LIVING WITH THE DEAD .11B
Climb the first route right of the chimney.

TROUBLED BY THE LIVING .11D
Climb the second route right of the chimney.

Photo by Jim Thornburg.

Indian Springs Overview

RECOMMENDED ROUTES
Fire Stone .9
Indian Springs .9
Joey's .10+
Lost Love .10d
Zephyr .10c/d

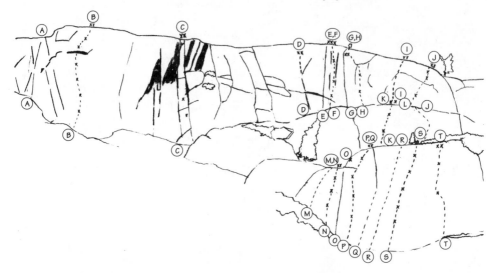

UPPER TIER
To access the climbs that start off the ledge, third-class the left side of Mid Tier.

A   Diamond .10 TR
B   Joey's .9+ (2 ropes to rap)
C   Lost Love .10d (pro: thin to medium)
D   Rocco's Corner .9
E   White Streak .11
F   Old Sea Hag .10
G   Super Doo .2
H   Fire Stone .9
I   Upper Puppy .9 TR
J   Country Bumpkin .10c (#4 Friend)

MID TIER
K   Pappy Smear 9+
L   Slick Dog .10 TR

LOWER TIER
M   Out of the Blue .10 TR
N   Captain Cheese Dog .9
O   Super Thin .9
P   Indian Springs .9
Q   RP 4 Me .9
R   Sundaze .9+ TR
S   Zephyr .10c/d
T   Arrow Head .10c/d R

Indian Springs

Indian Springs is a great spring and fall season crag. The climbing is located on a large south-facing, three-tiered slab. Indian Springs Campground lies just down the road, and the inviting waters of the South Yuba River give welcome relief from midsummer heat.

Indian Springs is located about 1 mile east of Cisco Grove on the north side of Interstate 80. To reach the crags, take the exit for Eagle Lakes off I-80 and drive northwest for about 0.5 mile on the frontage road. Park in a small pullout below the obvious slabs. Approach via a game trail and slabs to a brush-choked gully. From here, scramble up a short wall to the left end of Lower Tier. To descend the routes, walk off to the west through the brush, then circle back to the base. To avoid the brush, most climbers rappel the slabs.

The following three routes lie just above the road on a rounded face with a white steak. From the pullout, hike up and over to the right. These routes are listed from left to right. Also, the three cracks to the right of Soco have been toproped.

INTENGRATRON .10
Not shown. Traverse right across a crack past two bolts to a three-bolt anchor at the top of the wall.

SUPER DOG .10
Not shown. Climb the crack below the anchors of the previous route.

SOCO .9
Not shown. Climb the crack to the right of the previous route.

Rainbow Overview

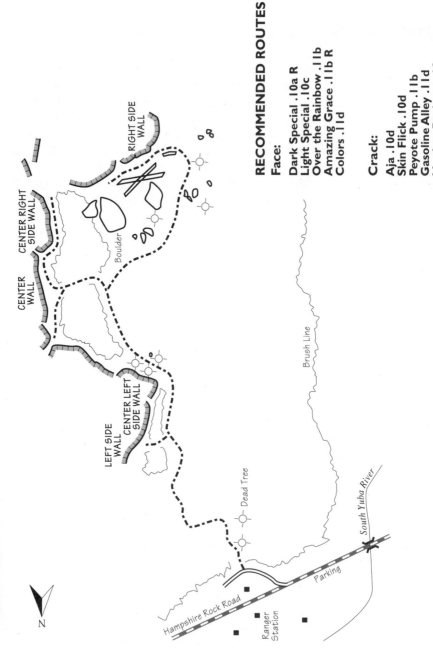

N

RECOMMENDED ROUTES

Face:

Dark Special .10a R
Light Special .10c
Over the Rainbow .11b
Amazing Grace .11b R
Colors .11d

Crack:

Aja .10d
Skin Flick .10d
Peyote Pump .11b
Gasoline Alley .11d
Monkey Business .12c

Rainbow

Rainbow is located on the west side of Donner Pass, about 17 miles west of Truckee and a few miles east of Cisco Grove. This small granite cul-de-sac lies above the tiny community of Big Bend. Seeing more than a couple climbing parties here, even on a weekend, is rare.

Rainbow lacks the long moderate routes that draw large weekend crowds to Tahoe's renowned climbing areas, but, nonetheless, it is a beautiful place and offers fine climbing. The majority of routes ascend thin edges or cracks on less-than-vertical, domelike walls. The climbs usually are no longer than half a pitch and yield nothing easier than about 5.10. With fewer than 30 routes, Rainbow may inspire the driven individual to tick most of the classics in a day.

The Rainbow Lodge has some great dinner specials and sometimes live music. Just a few miles of hiking to the south, the South Yuba River and Loch Levan Lakes offer fantastic swimming and picnicking. Camping is available at the east end of town off Hampshire Rock Road.

To find Rainbow, exit off Interstate 80 at Big Bend and turn onto Hampshire Rock Road. Continue to a roadside parking area just east of the South Yuba River. The climbing area is the obvious group of granite cliffs facing west. The approach trail begins behind a storage garage across the street from Big Bend Ranger Station and follows a narrow trail that winds through acres of manzanita to the base of the wall. The hike takes ten minutes.

Please consult the overview map to ensure that you do not trespass across the private properties west of the crag or become lost in the brush. Presently, the access policies are up in the air, and failure to respect private property could inhibit future access.

LEFT SIDE WALL

A Jousting with the Jackal .12a (pro: thin to medium)
B Lockbuster .9 (pro: thin to 2")
C Monkey Business .12c (pro: thin to medium)
D Aja .10d (pro: mostly thin to 2")
E Scarecrow .11b (grungy crack)
F Over the Rainbow .11b
G Colors .11d
H Drain Pipe .8 (pro: to 3")

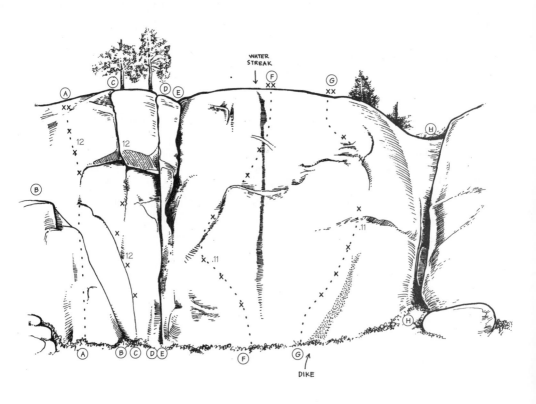

CENTER LEFT SIDE AND CENTER WALL

A   Gasoline Alley .11d (pro: RPs, small stoppers, and TCUs)
B   Malcolm's Route .9 (pro: thin to medium)
C   Sleeper .10c
D   Rainbow Bridge .10d (arete)
E   Walk and Don't Look Back A0 (start)/.10d R
F   Cheap Thrills A0 (start)/.11a R
G   Peyote Pump .11b (pro: thin to 3")
H   Jack the Ripper .11d After the fourth bolt, turn the left edge and belay on the slab in a corner. Continue to the top or descend the fourth-class slab below.
I   Jumping Jack Flash .10b
J   The Force (project)

The Force

CENTER RIGHT SIDE WALL

A   Light Special .10c Climb the crack to a ledge; or, for a better variation, climb the arete on *Dark Special,* then traverse left to the ledge.

B   Dark Special .10a R

C   38 Special .10c R

D   Amazing Grace .11b R (variation finishes through 5.9 roof crack)
      Assembled 5.10c (pro: thin to 1.5 ") Climb the crack up and to the right.

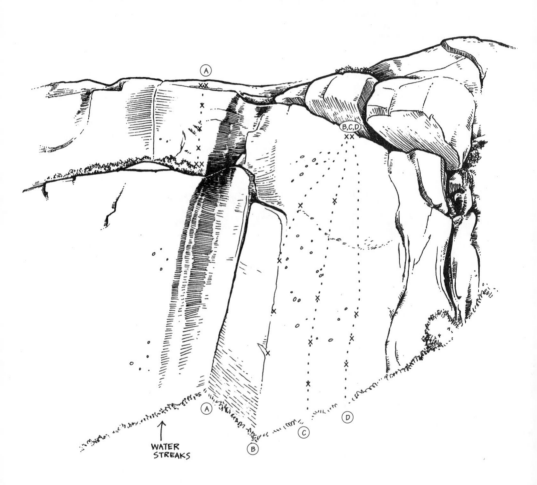

WATER STREAKS

RIGHT SIDE WALL
A   Dirty Deed .10b/c (a flared hand crack that is tricky to protect)
B   J.O.'s .10a (off-sized)
C   Black and Blue (project)
D   Project
E   Skin Flick .10d (pro: thin to 1.5")

Donner Summit Overview

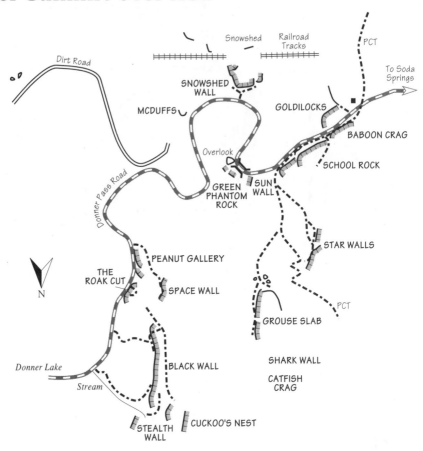

Dirt Road

Snowshed   Railroad Tracks   PCT

To Soda Springs

SNOWSHED WALL

MCDUFFS

GOLDILOCKS

BABOON CRAG

Overlook

SCHOOL ROCK

Donner Pass Road

GREEN PHANTOM ROCK

SUN WALL

STAR WALLS

THE ROAK CUT

PEANUT GALLERY

SPACE WALL

N

GROUSE SLAB

PCT

Donner Lake

BLACK WALL

SHARK WALL

Stream

CATFISH CRAG

STEALTH WALL

CUCKOO'S NEST

RECOMMENDED ROUTES

Face:

Phantom Staircase .8TR
Short Cake .9
Phantom Staircase .9TR
Eyes of Silver .10b/c
Bolt Run .10d
Europa .10d
Kwijiwabo .11a
Goldilocks .11a
Made in Japan .11a
Aerial .11b
Birdy .11b
Disciples of the New Wave .11b/c
Bark Like a Shark .11d
Neanderthal Dudes .11d
Rhythm Killer .12a/b
Brain Child .12b
Nice Dreams .12b
Puppet on a String .12c
Death Tongue .12d

Cannibals .12d
Warp Factor .13a
Pump Lust .13b
A Steep Climb Named Desire .13d

Crack:

Kindergarten Cracks .5
Junior High .6
Insidious Crack .6
Composure .6
Cannibal Gully .7
Rated X .7 (first pitch)
Jellyroll Arch .8 (tricky pro)
Eleventh Grade Corner .8+
One Hand Clapping .8 (first pitch)
Rated X .9 (variation)
Greener Pastures .9
Fine Line .9+
Nova Express .9+

Black September .9+
Bourbon Street .10a
Molar Concentration .10b (tricky pro)
Farewell to Arms .10b
Fire Cracker .10b
Karl's Gym .10d
The Thing .10d
Childhood's End .10d
Peter Principle .11a
Karl's Overhang .11a
Papa Bear .11b
Sky Pilot .11b
Welcome to My Nightmare .11b/c
Manic Depression .11d
Full Moon .11d
Monkey Paws .12a
Bliss Direct .12b
Panic in Detroit .12b/c
Star Wars Crack .13a

Donner Summit

Donner Summit, one of the most renowned climbing areas around Tahoe, offers a high concentration of routes and some of the finest rock in the Sierra. A wide variety of climbing, from short desperate lines to scenic multipitch cruises, is spread over many granite formations along Donner Pass Road (Old Highway 40). Traditional and sport climbing have coexisted in a relatively peaceful state here amid the panoramic splendor of the Donner Lake Basin.

Donner Summit is located a few miles west of Truckee. Nearby stores, restaurants, bars, and recreational opportunities help make Donner one of the most popular climbing areas in California. Summer weekends can be crowded and waiting lines often form at the base of routes; however, Donner has so many high-quality climbs that there are always a few spots where you can enjoy relative solitude.

A lot of new routes have been put up over the past few years. Many old bolts and belay anchors have been replaced with 3/8-inch bolts, maintaining the integrity of fixed gear on some older lines. You will find some of Tahoe's finest bouldering along the north shoulder of School Rock, near the base of Grouse Slab's southeast face, and atop Donner Peak. For more information on these areas, refer to the section on bouldering and toproping.

There are many camping and lodging facilities near Donner. The best camping is in the state park at the east end of Donner Lake. Spacious, well-maintained sites and hot showers are available for a nominal fee. It is illegal to camp along the big bend on Donner Pass Road below Snowshed Wall. Local law enforcement authorities may ask campers to move out. The Star Hotel and Hostel offers the least expensive rooms in downtown Truckee.

Donner Summit lies along Donner Pass Road, once the major link between the west and east sides of the Sierra Nevada Mountains. Donner is accessible off Interstate 80 from the west via Soda Springs, or from the east through the town of Truckee. Lake Tahoe is about 15 miles south of Donner, and Reno, "The Biggest Little City in the World," is 35 miles east. Note that Donner Pass Road is not plowed during the winter and usually is closed from November until April.

At 7,000 feet above sea level, Donner offers pleasant climbing even in August, when many of the lower areas become uncomfortably hot. The climbing season generally begins in May and ends by mid-November due to freezing temperatures and snow.

BLACK WALL

Black Wall is the largest formation at Donner Summit. Many of the routes are three and four pitches long. The dark-colored wall, which faces due east, is the first formation you encounter when driving up the highway from Donner Lake. You can approach Black Wall two different ways depending on the route location; both take about ten minutes.

For climbs on the left side of the wall, follow a well-established trail that begins below a small cliff and a prominent tree. From this point, head straight up the boulder field to the base of the wall. This puts you in the vicinity of *Rat's Tooth*. For climbs on the right side of the wall, follow the trail that begins just left of a small creek. The trail climbs up and across a small cliff and past another large tree, then it runs up a streambed (usually flowing until June). Near a group of scattered boulders, the trail veers left, leading to and then following along the base of the wall by *Rated X*. A faint trail continues along the base of the wall and connects with the other approach trail.

35

CANNIBAL GULLY

PORNO ROCK

Black Wall: 1. Last Tango. 2. Space Invaders,
3. Empty Overgo 4. Bliss, 5. One Hand Clapping,
6. Imaginary Voyage. 7. Flying Saucers, 8. Lightning
Bolt Roof. 9. Rated X.

Many of the routes on the left join on Lizard Ledge just below the summit of Black Wall. Two exit pitches leave the ledge, both are 5.6. The standard route is the 5.6 crack off the right edge of the ledge. Another option is the 5.8 corner off the left edge of the ledge. A 5.10 variation moves up the right crack, then traverses left and off. A final exit route takes you up a face pitch that turns the left corner down low, then continues past two bolts (5.6) to the top.

To descend Black Wall, walk southwest along a faint trail to the highway by the Road Cut, or cut left to the southeast ridge a short ways below the summit, then scramble down some third-class terrain to the base of Cannibal Gully. To descend from the routes that top out by *Rated X*, walk north along the slabs to a stream. Continue down the streambed, then cut right onto the approach trail.

The Primer Boulder is a large block just left of Cannibal Gully. *Primer* (5.9+) is the obvious green corner. *Lubrication* (5.9) follows the crack on the arete left of *Primer*. A short ways down and to the left of Primer Boulder is a thin crack called *The Last Tango* (5.11c).

Side Winder (5.11b/c) is between Primer Boulder and *The Last Tango*. Begin with an undercling and move right, then turn a corner and continue upward on a lie back. From a small ledge, climb the face via a seam past two fixed pins, then move back around the corner (left) to a hand traverse and crack system. This climb can be broken into two pitches if you belay on the ledge; otherwise, protect sparingly and runner all the protection.

The following four climbs are CLASSIC four-pitch routes on the left side of Black Wall.

BOURBON STREET .10A (standard rack)

Climb the first two pitches of *Inner Recess*. From the ledge, climb the crux pitch, which ascends the right crack on the looming wall above the belay. Start by climbing up, then out the chimney. Continue up the corner to the right and go between the two roofs to Lizard Ledge and a belay. Some parties belay below the roofs to reduce rope drag. From the right side of the ledge, climb the 5.6 crack to the summit.

TOUCH AND GO .9+ (standard rack)

Climb *Rat's Tooth*. From the bolted belay, move left into a corner (5.7) and continue to a ledge. From the ledge, ascend the dihedral and cracks until you can traverse right on a horizontal crack. Continue up the face and arete (5.7) and belay on Lizard Ledge. From the right side of the ledge climb the 5.6 slab to the summit.

EMPTY OVERGO .10 (standard rack)

Not shown. Climb *Rat's Tooth*. From the bolted belay, ascend the slightly overhanging hand crack called *Hung Over, Hang Over* (5.10a). The next pitch, called *Empty Sky*, heads left under a small roof and then follows bolts along the arete (5.10) to merge with the top of *Touch and Go*. This pitch is exposed and a little runout. From the right side of Lizard Ledge, climb the 5.6 crack to the summit.

ONE HAND CLAPPING .9 (standard rack)

This route begins from a ledge at the base of Black Wall up and right of *Rat's Tooth*. Climb the twin cracks through a slot (5.8) and continue to a bolted belay. Climb the thin crack above the belay and then go diagonal up and left through a steep flaring corner. Surmounting the bulge is the crux (5.9) on this exposed pitch. At this point, continue to Lizard Ledge or move right and belay at the bolts above a small ledge. From the ledge, climb up and left across the slab to Lizard Ledge and belay. From the right side of Lizard Ledge, climb the 5.6 crack to the summit.

INNER RECESS

Lizard Ledge

Rat's Tooth

BLACK WALL—LEFT

A   **Space Invaders .10b**
B   **Cannibal Gully .7**
C   **Inner Recess .8 (pro: 4")**
D   **Rambo Crack .12b**
E   **Bourbon Street .10a (standard rack)**
F   **Touch and Go .9 (pro: to 2.5")**
G   **Pinball Junkie .10d (.12a variation)**
H   **Rhythm Killer .12a/b**
I   **Empty Sky Direct .10**
J   **Empty Sky .10a**
K   **Hung Over, Hang Over .10a**
L   **Blow Ups Happen .10c**
M   **Rat's Tooth .9+ (pro: to 2.5")**
N   **Bliss Direct .12b**
O   **Bliss .10d**
P   **There Goes the Neighborhood .11b (pro: thin to 2.5")**
Q   **Skywalker .10a Climb halfway up the first pitch of *One Hand Clapping*, then traverse out of the corner past a bolt to the belay. Traverse left across the face from the belay.**
R   **Don't Try This at Home .11c (pro: thin to medium)**
S   **Can't Stop the Dance .11c (pro: thin to medium)**
T   **One Hand Clapping .9 (standard rack)**
U   **Firecracker .10b (pro: to 4")**
V   **New Moon .10d (pro: mostly thin to medium)**
W   **Next .10d R (pro: 2.5", first pitch runout)**
X   **Birdy .11b**

BLACK WALL—CENTER LEFT

A   Space Invaders .10b
B   Rhythm Killer .12a/b
C   Hung Over, Hang Over .10a
D   Blow Ups Happen .10c From the bolt, climb to thin crack and up a slab above.
       Hung Over, Hang Over.
E   Rat's Tooth .9+ (pro: to 2.5")
F   Bliss Direct .12b or C1
G   Bliss .10d
H   Skywalker .10a (see Black Wall—Left for topo description)
I   Don't Try This at Home .11c (pro: thin to medium, bolts)
J   Can't Stop the Dance .11c (pro: thin to medium, bolts)
K   There Goes the Neighborhood .11b (pro: thin to 2.5", bolts)
L   One Hand Clapping .9 (pro: to 3")
M   Fascination .10c (pro: tricky, thin to medium)
N   Hip to Be There .11c
O   Space Modulator .11a
P   Tulips .8
Q   Firecracker .10b (pro: to 4")
R   New Moon .10d (pro: mostly thin to medium)
S   Full Moon .11d (pro: thin)
T   Future Games .10b (pro: to 4")
U   Aqua Lung .10c (pro: to 4.5")
V   On Ramp .8
W   Next .10d R (pro: 2.5", first pitch runout)
X   Birdy .11b
Y   Slip Stream .11b (pro: to 1.5")
Z   No Stems, No Seeds .11a
       (pro: tricky, especially at start,
       thin to 1.5")
1   Pebble Beach .10d TR
2   Protection Difficult .8R

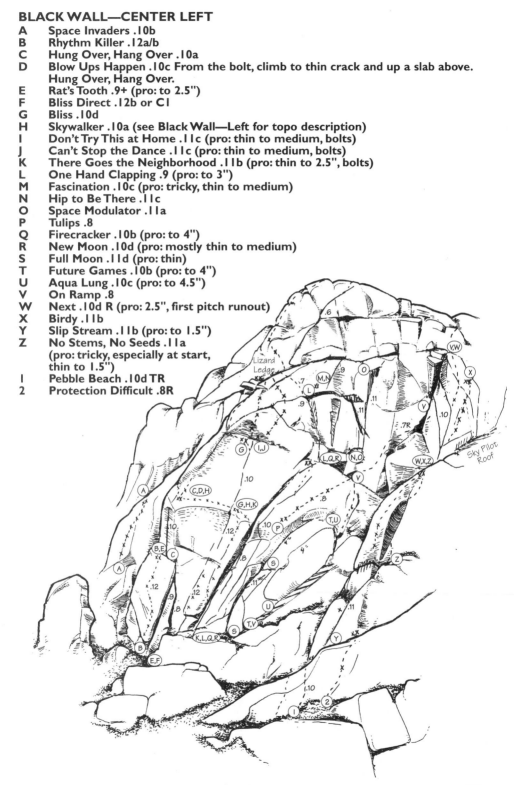

BLACK WALL—CENTER RIGHT

A One Hand Clapping .9 (pro: to 3")
B Fascination .10c (pro: tricky, thin to medium)
C Hip to Be There .11c
D Space Modulator .11a
E On Ramp .8
F Next .10d R (pro: 2.5", first pitch runout)
G Birdy .11b
H Slip Stream .11b (pro: to 1.5")
I No Stems, No Seeds .11a (pro: tricky, especially at the start, thin to 1.5")
J Pebble Beach .10d TR
K Protection Difficult .8R
L Sky Pilot .11b (pro: to 2.5")
M Headstone .11c (pro: to 1.25")
N The Fuse .10d

O Give Me Slack .7
P Torture Chamber .11b
Q Mr. Clean .10c
R Ajax .11d
S Flying Saucers .12a R (pro: difficult, thin to medium)
T Inside Out .8+ (pitch third: chimney behind block)
U Super Slide .10b R
V Donner Delight .8
W 1984 .10c R
X Silver Book .7
Y Tilt .10a
Z Full Tilt .11a
1 The Voyeur .9
2 Porno Book .8
3 Mushroom Madness .9

NEW FASCINATION .10D (standard rack to 4")

Not shown. A great four-pitch route. Climb the thin crack *New Moon* (5.10d) through the roof of *Firecracker* (5.10b) and belay at the top of the first pitch of *One Hand Clapping* (5.9). Climb the short second pitch of *One Hand Clapping* and belay at the bolts above the small ledge to the right. Move up and right to the stellar thin crack called *Fascination* (5.10c). Climb to the summit.

IMAGINARY VOYAGE .11C (pro: thin to 2.5")

Not shown. A truly brilliant climb. Every pitch is 5.11 and superb. The climb links *Slip Stream* (5.11b), *No Stems, No Seeds* 5.11a, the airy *Sky Pilot* (5.11b), and the awkward and thin *Headstone* (5.11c). If you climb at this level, then this is a climb not to miss.

BLACK WALL—RIGHT

A	Mushroom Madness	.9 (dirty)
B	Lightning Bolt Roof	.11c/d (.12a/b variation; pro: to 4")
C	Thunder Bolt Roof	.12a
D	Rolling Thunder	.12
E	Black September	.9+
F	Summer Breeze	.10c
G	Indian Summer	.11c
H	Rated X	.7 (.8/.9+ variation; pro to 3.5")
I	Finger Licker	.11a (pro: thin to medium)
J	The Hook	.11d
K	Labyrinth	.6
L	Minotaur	.7

Hans Standteiner climbing *Birdy*, 5.11b, at Black Wall. Photo by M. Carville.

CUCUMBER SLUMBER .10B

Not shown. Begin from the right edge of the third terrace. Follow a zigzagging crack up a vertical wall on the right side of *Porno Book*.

CHECKMATE .11

Not shown. This toprope problem ascends a slanting crack just right of *Cucumber Slumber*.

HIGH ENERGY .11A

Not shown. This overhanging, left-slanting crack is above the stream on the far right and lower edge of Black Wall.

STEALTH WALL

This small, well-developed formation is located down and to the right of Black Wall, north of the stream.

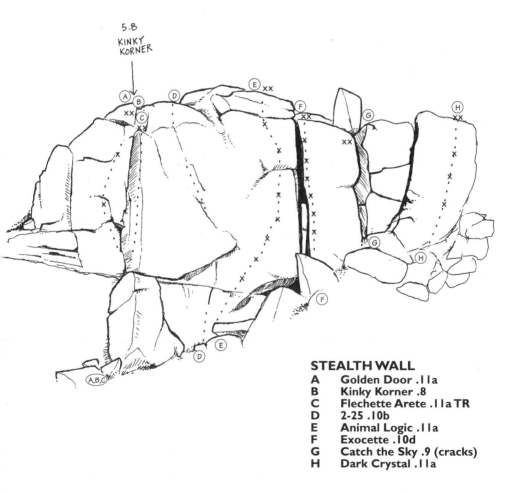

STEALTH WALL

A	Golden Door .11a
B	Kinky Korner .8
C	Flechette Arete .11a TR
D	2-25 .10b
E	Animal Logic .11a
F	Exocette .10d
G	Catch the Sky .9 (cracks)
H	Dark Crystal .11a

CUCKOO'S NEST (Not shown)

This cliff lies to the west and high above the north edge of Black Wall. The approach requires some hearty bushwhacking. No trail exists.

COMFORTABLY NUMB .12A
Follow the bolt line left of *Placid Hallucination.*

PLACID HALLUCINATION .9+
This 40-foot crack is just left of center.

ELECTRIC KOOL-AID ACID TEST .10B
Ascend a right-slanting crack, then traverse back left to finish near the previous route.

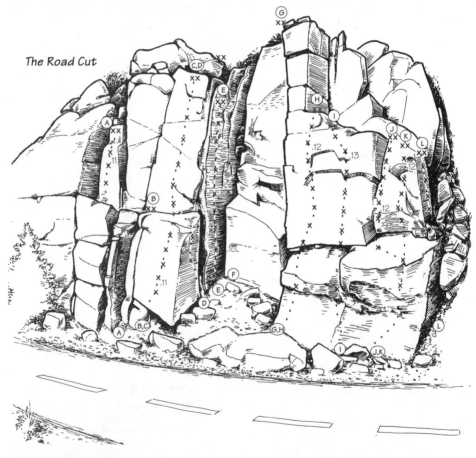

The Road Cut

THE ROAD CUT

A	Escargot .11a	G	Totem Pile .10 R (arete, difficult to protect, loose, and dirty)
B	Crack A No Go .10a	H	Transmoggnifier .12d
C	Big Shot .11d	I	Spaceman Spiff .13a
D	Hit and Run .11b	J	Itchy and Scratchy .12b
E	Penguin Lust .12c	K	Far Side .12d
F	Herring Breath .10a	L	Easy Street .10c

STARK REALITY .9

Locate this off-width crack downhill and around the corner of *Electric Kool-Aid Acid Test.*

DRAGON SLAYER .10a

Locate this cliff below Cuckoo's Nest. It follows a slanting corner.

THE ROAD CUT

The Road Cut appears unsightly at first, but upon closer inspection, the quality of rock becomes apparent. The faces are steep and well-featured with positive edges and pockets. To the left of the crag, a slabby gully and a short traverse up and right lead past some trees to the top.

GOLD FINGER .11c

Not shown. This climb is located around the corner from *Spaceman Spiff* on the north face. It follows a left-slanting crack. The bolts to the right are a project.

SPACE WALL

Space Wall has some of the best bolted face climbs at Donner. To approach this cliff, park by the southeast face of Peanut Gallery and hike up a steep gully on the left. From the top of the gully, follow a faint trail across and right to the base of Space Wall.

SPACE WALL

A	**Kwijiwabo .11a**
B	**Alien Sex .12a**
C	**Neanderthal Dudes .11d**
D	**Purple Toupee .12a/b**
E	**Made in Japan .11a**
F	**Dark Side of the Moon .10b (pro: to 3")**
G	**Moon Shadow .10d**
H	**Black Hole .6 (chimney)**
I	**Sun Spots .9 (B1 start)**

PEANUT GALLERY—SOUTHEAST FACE

A Shoot Out .8
B Change Up .8
C Scratchin' Nails .10b TR
D Finger Graffiti .11c
E Bolt Run .10d
F The Heckler .11a
G Eyes of Silver .10b/c
H Middle Ages .8

PEANUT GALLERY—NORTHEAST FACE

A Jack of Hearts .10a R (pro: to 1.5")
B Bluff .7 (crack system right of *Jack of Hearts*)
C Free Falling .9
D Spring Fever .10a
E A Face in the Crowd .9
F Tumbling Turmoil .10a
G X Files (pro: thin) 5.10-

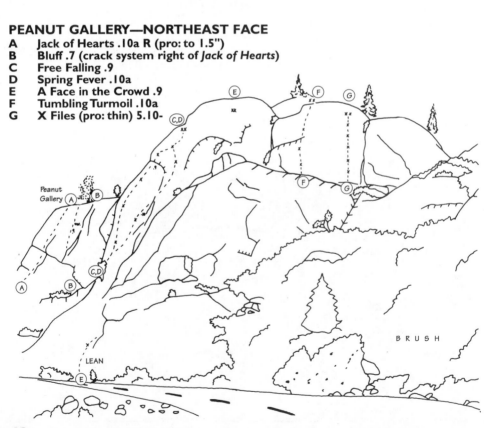

PEANUT GALLERY

At the Peanut Gallery, slab climbing is the name of the game. The rock is clean and compact, and many of the old bolts have been replaced with new larger bolts. The slabs are right alongside the road. The southeast face gets sun almost all day and is relatively sheltered from the wind.

SNOWSHED WALL

Snowshed Wall has a very high concentration of intermediate and advanced routes. The east face catches morning sun; and the main cliff, which faces north, gets afternoon sun. The short approach and great climbing make Snowshed Wall one of the most popular crags at Donner Summit.

To descend Snowshed, hike toward the east past some large boulders and then down the slabs behind *Brain Child,* or head west into a gully with a large boulder wedged at the top. The gully runs along the west side of the wall to *Aerial.*

There are several fine climbs up and left of the east edge of Snowshed Wall. *Animal Magnetism* (5.11d) is a short, thin crack. It is located just before the snowshed that covers the railroad tracks. Above the snowshed, on a face marked by a white dike, you will find *Off White* 5.10d (pro: to 1", bolts). Train Time Crag, a short and fun wall, lies farther east adjacent to the snowshed train tunnel.

Tunnel Rock, a jumbled series of corners and slabs, is located a short ways up and to the right of the face of *Telegraph Crack. The King of Pain* (5.11c) begins on the left and climbs a crack in an overhanging corner to a slab. You will need thin to medium protection. A short ways to the right is a bolted arete called *The Texas Two-Step* (5.11a). Around the arete locate *Painted Spider* (5.11c), which ascends a steep face, brightly colored with lichen, and past five bolts.

Snowshed Wall—East Face

Many variations link the routes on the left side of the gully. There are three short climbs on the top and upper right side of the gully left of *Conform or Be Cast Out.*

RICK AND ERIC'S .10B
Not shown. The obvious crack on the upper left side of the gully.

SIDE EFFECT .9+
Not shown. The steep corner on the right wall.

NIGHT COUNTRY .11B
Not shown. The thin crack on the right wall.

Snowshed Wall—North Face (left)

BERTHA BUTT BOOGIE .10C
Not shown. Climb a slanting crack around the corner to the left from *Karl's Gym.* Continue up a crack that leads to face climbing and ends at the belay bolts shared with *Karl's Gym.* The *Northwest Passage* (5.9+) is a 300-foot girdle traverse that begins at *Split Pea* and finishes at *Devaluation.*

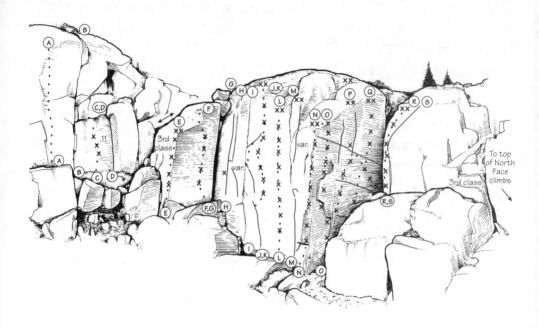

SNOWSHED WALL—EAST FACE

A   The Stranger Within .11c/d
B   Telegraph Crack .8 (pro: to 3")
C   Laser Treatment .11c (pro: to 1.25) Finish with a hand traverse to the right or up the thin crack (5.10) above.
D   Mole's Corner .8 (pro: to 2")
E   Missing Mind .11b
F   Brain Child .12b
G   Rage Reduction .6
H   Drop Out .10d (.11a variation)
I   Nova Express .9+
J   Welcome to My Nightmare .11b/c Follow the arching crack system on left.
K   Nice Dreams .12b
L   Death Tongue .12d
M   Farewell to Arms .10b
N   Little Feat .10d R
O   Cannibals .12d
P   Pump Lust .13b
Q   Puppet on a String .12c (.13a direct start variation)
R   Conform or Be Cast Out .11c/d
S   Sanitation Crack .10b/c

SNOWSHED WALL—NORTH FACE (LEFT)

A	Hans and Franz .12b
B	Karl's Gym .10d (pro: to 2.5")
C	Split Pea .8 (pro: to 2")
D	Pea Soup .9 (pro: to 1.5"; tricky)
E	Tip Bitter Blues .12a/b TR
F	Bell Bottom Blues .12a
G	Manic Depression .11d
H	Monkey Paws .12a
I	Bottomless Topless .10a (chimney)
J	Panic in Detroit .12b/c
K	Peter Principle .11a
L	Peter Panic .11d (pro: thin to 2.5")
M	The Thing .10d (.11a variation)
N	Two Fingers Gold .11c TR
O	The Boys Are Back .11c
P	Walk Away .11d TR
Q	Seams to Me .11d
R	Devaluation Direct .9+
S	Devaluation .7 (tricky placements, easy to backward zipper gear)
T	Crack of the Eighties .13a (.12d toprope)
U	Aerial .11b
V	The Drifter .11c/d
W	Pangalactic Gargle Blaster .11d
X	Disciples of the New Wave .11b/c
Y	On the Edge .11c R
Z	Hair Lip .10d
1	Hair Shirt .8 (off-width)
2	Palsy .9 (.10a/b direct start)

Bird Lew jamming the stellar thin crack *Panic in Detroit*, 5.12b/c, on the north face of Snowshed Wall. Photo by M. Carville.

Snowshed Wall—West Gully (left)

McDuff's .10c

Not shown. This 25-foot toprope problem is on a small, north-facing wall across from the first big bend in the highway below Snowshed Wall.

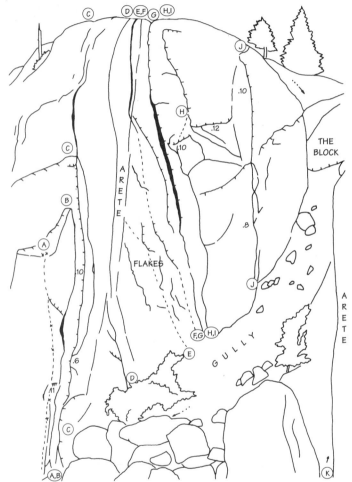

SNOWSHED WALL—WEST GULLY (LEFT)

A   Aerial .11b
B   Molar Concentration .10b (pro: thin to 2")
C   Composure .6 (corner)
D   Alvin's Toprope .9
E   Rapid Transit .8R (flakes are difficult to protect)
F   Shake It Out .10b TR
G   Break Out .8 (chimney)
H   Bypass .11a
I   Turoid .12c (roof crack)
J   Jam Session .10b
K   Disciples of the New Wave .11b/c

GREEN PHANTOM ROCK

A   Unknown
B   Phantom Staircase .8/.9/.10 TR
C   Yellow Jacket .10+

D   Roccocater .10
E   Road Kill .10
F   Undercling Thing .10
G   Great Escape .10b
H   Fine Line .9+

BRUSH

SUN WALL

A   Twin Cracks .9+
B   Dominoes .11
C   Unknown .11
D   Rocking Chair .11
E   Take It Easy .8
F   Gun Smoke .10
G   Smoke .8

H   Smoke Screen .10
I   Sundance .10+
J   Between the Lines .10
K   Pistol Grip Pillar .10
L   Day Dream Drummer .9
M   Survival of the Fattest .12 TR

PROW
SYSTEM

Uphill to
Double
Cracks

DOWNHILL
to
SUN WALL

GREEN PHANTOM ROCK

To reach Green Phantom Rock, park at the overlook, cross the highway, and hike beneath the old bridge. The trail leads to the top of the wall, and the routes are accessible and good.

POWER STRUGGLE .10+

Not shown. Hike up the gully toward Star Walls. On a steep face below some powerlines, climb a 30-foot-high flared, left-slanting crack. A bolt protects the first moves.

SUN WALL

This tiny cliff band faces southwest and lies in a shallow gully, which provides shelter when poor weather makes climbing difficult elsewhere. Some of the routes on the left side are very short. The wall is located just uphill past the bridge and above the road.

MYSTIC TRAVELER .11 (girdle traverse)

Not shown.

BIRD BRAIN A3

Not shown. Ascend the face above the highway via seams.

GROUSE SLAB

Grouse Slab is a great place to escape on a crowded weekend. Park by School Rock and begin hiking north on the Pacific Crest Trail (PCT). After a small rise in the trail, veer right off the PCT and hike across a shallow gully on a faint trail that gradually becomes more defined. Stay on this trail, which heads toward Grouse. There is some great bouldering just before the south face. To descend Grouse Slab, walk southwest from the top, following the path of least resistance. Once down, contour along the base.

Grouse Slab—Southwest Face

MISS PRINGLES .10B/C

Not shown. This route is on a slab about 150 yards left of the southwest face routes. Start just right of the center and follow three bolts up friable flakes to a bolted belay.

THE WHOLE TRUTH .12A (four bolts)

Not shown. This super technical face climb is on a short, steep slab below the approach ledge, which leads to the routes on the right.

Grouse Slab—East Face (right)

PIE IN THE FACE .9

Not shown. This poor-quality route is on a short, rotten face up and right of *Slowhand*. There are a couple of bolts and a gnarled tree on top.

SUCK FACE .10

Not shown. Another poor-quality route that lies to the right of *Pie in the Face*.

MITIGATE .7

Not shown. Begin about 150 yards left of *Slowhand* at the top of a talus gully. Climb a left-leaning crack system for two pitches (5.6/5.7). The route ends on the ridge about 150 feet left of the summit.

Grouse Slab: 1.Greener Pastures, 2. Jellyroll Arch, 3. Insidious Crack, 4. Mitigate, 5. Anxiety Attack, 6. Slowhand

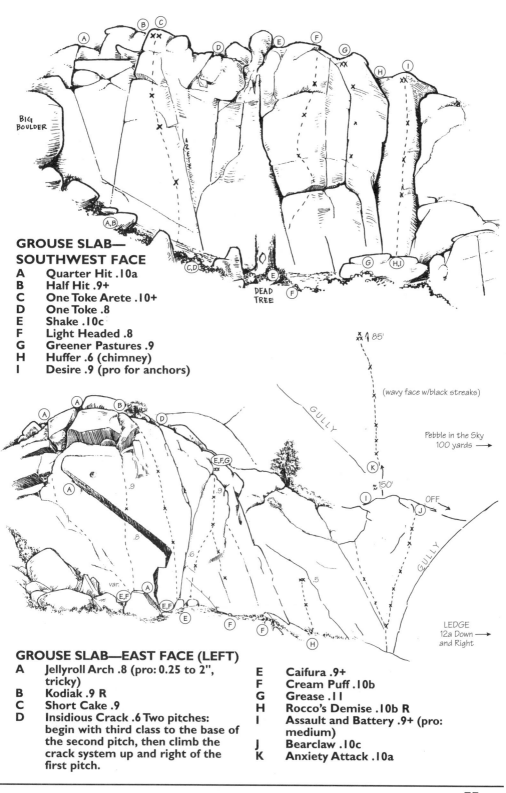

GROUSE SLAB— SOUTHWEST FACE

A Quarter Hit .10a
B Half Hit .9+
C One Toke Arete .10+
D One Toke .8
E Shake .10c
F Light Headed .8
G Greener Pastures .9
H Huffer .6 (chimney)
I Desire .9 (pro for anchors)

GROUSE SLAB—EAST FACE (LEFT)

A Jellyroll Arch .8 (pro: 0.25 to 2", tricky)
B Kodiak .9 R
C Short Cake .9
D Insidious Crack .6 Two pitches: begin with third class to the base of the second pitch, then climb the crack system up and right of the first pitch.

E Caifura .9+
F Cream Puff .10b
G Grease .11
H Rocco's Demise .10b R
I Assault and Battery .9+ (pro: medium)
J Bearclaw .10c
K Anxiety Attack .10a

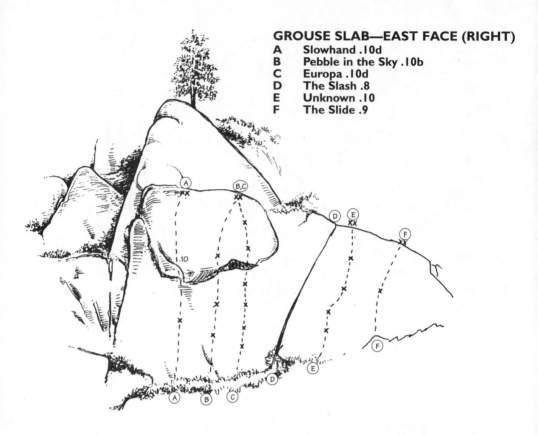

GROUSE SLAB—EAST FACE (RIGHT)

A	Slowhand .10d
B	Pebble in the Sky .10b
C	Europa .10d
D	The Slash .8
E	Unknown .10
F	The Slide .9

SHARK WALL (Not shown)

Shark Wall is on the bushy hillside between Grouse Slab and Black Wall. Two routes exist on this cliff. Both climbs are interesting and worth the hike.

BARK LIKE A SHARK (5.11D)

Follow the bolts up the central portion of the face.

SQUEAL LIKE A SEAL (5.11C)

To the right of *Bark Like a Shark*. Ascend a flake to a bolted face.

CATFISH CRAG (Not shown)

This small crag lies about 100 yards right of Shark Wall.

THE TEXORCIST (5.11A)

This steep bolted face is split by a horizontal crack.

COTTONTAIL CRACK (5.10A)

To the right of *The Texorcist*. This route ends at a tree.

STAR WALLS

Star Walls harbors the highest concentration of difficult sport routes at Donner. The approach trail branches left off the PCT just north of School Rock. A faint trail wanders up a shallow depression and across some slabs to the huge overhanging face of South Star Wall. From this point, the trail continues along the base to North Star Wall, then rejoins the PCT at the switchbacks.

SOUTH STAR WALL

A   Cookie Mix .12a
B   Slim Pickens .12c
C   Pot Licker .13a
D   Puma .13b
E   Bronco .12d
F   Taste the Pain .13c
G   Noah's Arc .13a
H   Project
I   Warp Factor .13a
J   A Steep Climb Named Desire .13d
K   Star Wars Crack .13a
L   Father's Day .14a
M   On the Outskirts of Hope .12b (pro: TCUs to 1" for final crack)

Scott Frye finishing *A Steep Climb Named Desire*;
5.13d, on South Star Wall. Photo by M Carville.

GEMSTONE WALL

A   The Pearl .11c/d
B   Fire Opal .11b
C   Caffeine Club .12c/d
D   Diamond in the Rough .12a

ARETE

Gemstone Wall

Gemstone Wall is the left portion of North Star Wall.

North Star Wall

FREE AND EASY .6

Not shown. About 100 feet right of *Childhood's Beginning*, climb up a face to a left-facing corner near the top.

LOOK MA NO HANDS .11A

Not shown. Climb past two bolts on a slab to a bolted belay.

NORTH STAR WALL
A **Diamond in the Rough .12a**
B **Break It Out .9+**
C **Ice Pirates .11b**
D **Black Magic .10a (black corner)**
E **Rhinestone Desperado .11b/c**
F **Childhood's End .10d**
G **Childhood's Beginning .8**

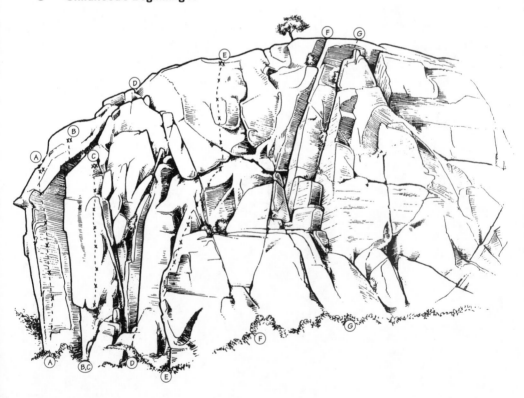

SCHOOL ROCK

A Kindergarten Crack Left .5 (pro: medium and large)
B Kindergarten Crack Right .5 (pro: medium and large)
C Mary's Crack .8 (pro: to medium and large)
D Junior High .6 (pro: to medium and large)
E Unknown .10
F Teacher's Pet .10b (pro to 3")
G Senior Prom .9
H Metal Shop .11a (pro: thin to medium, bolts)
I Eleventh Grade Corner .8+
J Front Point .11a X (no pro, best to toprope)
K Karl's Overhang .11a (15-foot hand crack in roof)
L Bimbo Roof .12+ (hard)
M Short Subject .11d

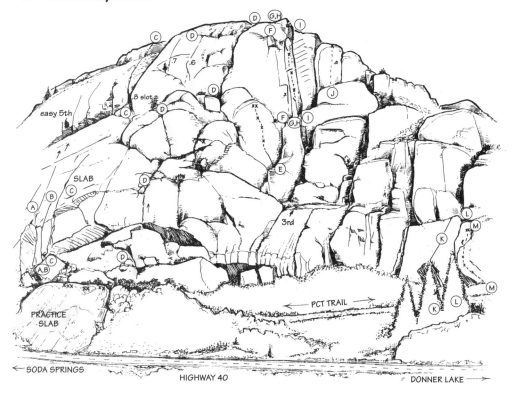

SCHOOL ROCK

School Rock is a large, domelike formation that dominates the western skyline above the overlook near the top of Donner Pass Road (Old Highway 40). There are several multipitch routes that offer great beginner and intermediate terrain. The routes generally are slabby and punctuated by short steep bands. School Rock has some of the best views of Truckee Basin. To descend, walk southwest along the ridge until you reach the PCT, or third class the slabs right of *Eleventh Grade Corner*.

A gully lies to the right of *Junior High,* and *Chalkboard* (5.8) lies on a short wall to the right of the gully. On the prow to the right of *Chalkboard,* locate some toprope cracks called *Pop Quiz* (5.9). Around and down the backside of the summit ridge above *Front Point,* there is a small wall with two excellent cracks. This little cliff is called There Is No God. Both cracks are 5.10, but the right one is more difficult. Several face climbs have been done to either side of these cracks.

School Rock: 1.Kindergarten Cracks, 2. Mary's Crack, 3. Junior High, 4. Eleventh Grade Corner

The area above and along the ridge is a favorite bouldering circuit. Almost every face and crack has been soloed or toproped. The routes are easy fifth class and have bolt anchors on top. This is a great place for first-time climbers to try things out.

Varmint .10

Not shown. Ascend the face up and to the right of *Short Subject.*

BABOON CRAG (Not shown)

Baboon Crag is south of School Rock at the very top of Donner Pass Road (Old Highway 40). This long narrow cliff lies just above the north side of the road and runs alongside the PCT. There are several short climbs, a good bouldering traverse, and some small roofs and bulging sections.

Primate .10d (pro: to 2.5")

Pull two small roofs and finish on a ledge left of the alcove.

Orang-U-Hang .10c

Go right along a hand traverse and then up a flared, thin hand crack.

Strung Out .8 (pro: to 2.5")

This route is to the right of the alcove. Traverse right below a ledge and finish on top.

Jungle Book .11a (pro: small to medium)

This route is on the far right side and climbs an overhanging face up edges to a left-facing corner.

Ape Fire .10c

This route is right of *Jungle Book.*

Gecko .10b

The next route farther right.

GOLDILOCKS

Goldilocks lies below Donner Pass Road (Old Highway 40) just shy of the pass. The approach is easy and short, but be careful not to trespass on the private property around the lodge, which is just west of the crag. Good bolts and convenient anchors combined with fantastic climbing makes this an extremely popular crag.

Mimi's .12

Not shown. Begin left of *Mama Bear* and climb the right-slanting, thin crack that shares anchors with *Hot Shit.*

GOLDILOCKS

A	**Over the Top .11a** Climb the crack through the left side of the roof.	
B	**Gold Dust .10d**	
C	**Goldilocks .11a**	
D	**Wolf Crack .12a**	
E	**Mama Bear .11a/b**	
F	**Hot Shit .10b**	
G	**Green Hornet .11b TR**	
H	**Papa Bear .11b (thin crack)**	
I	**Baby Bear .10a**	

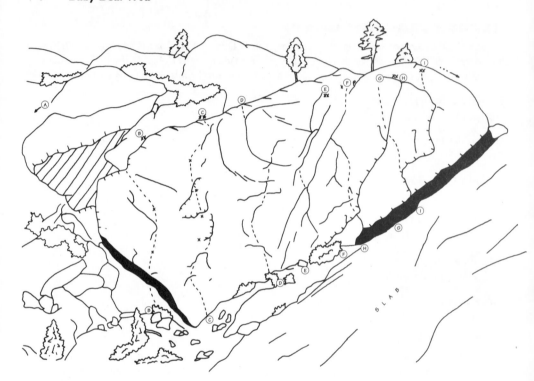

BABYLON (Not shown)

The infamous *Babylon* (5.12c) is about a mile east of Donner Pass on the south side of Interstate 80. Parking along the interstate may result in a ticket. It is better to approach the crag via a long hike uphill from Black Wall or downhill from the PCT.

BABYLON .12c

This stunning crack is on an overhanging face marked by a light-colored streak.

THE RIGHT STUFF .11A

This route is farther south on a huge slab.

Photo by Brian Biega.

Truckee River Canyon Overview

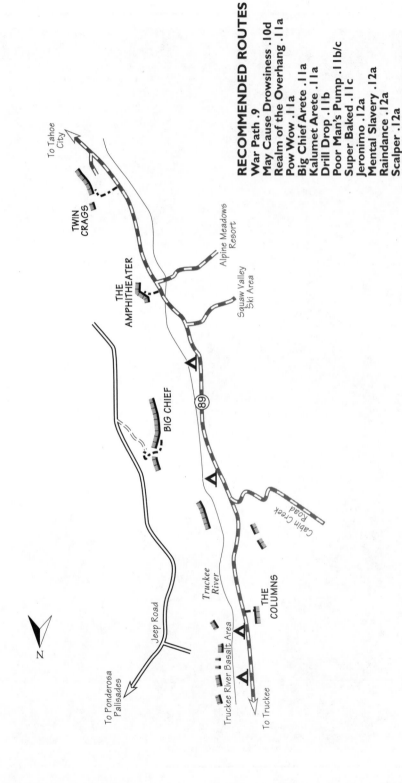

To Tahoe City

TWIN CRAGS

THE AMPHITHEATER

Alpine Meadows Resort

Squaw Valley Ski Area

BIG CHIEF

89

To Ponderosa Palisades

Jeep Road

Truckee River

Truckee River Basalt Area

THE COLUMNS

Cabin Creek Road

To Truckee

N

RECOMMENDED ROUTES

War Path .9
May Cause Drowsiness .10d
Realm of the Overhang .11a
Pow Wow .11a
Big Chief Arete .11a
Kalumet Arete .11a
Drill Drop .11b
Poor Man's Pump .11b/c
Super Baked .11c
Jeronimo .12a
Mental Slavery .12a
Raindance .12a
Scalper .12a
Copper Feather .12a/b
All Guns Blazing .13a

Truckee River Canyon

There are several climbable volcanic cliffs in the Truckee River Canyon, a geologic feature that extends from Tahoe City north to the town of Truckee. Most of the rock is fine-grained basalt and typically features clean cracks, smooth faces, and angular holds. Secure protection can be difficult to place because the gear tends to skate out of the smooth interior of the cracks. The shorter crags are usually toproped. Be cautious even though many of the routes have bolts at the crux. Some of the cliff tops are shattered, so be careful not to dislodge any loose blocks. All of these crags are climbable throughout the winter.

TRUCKEE RIVER BASALT AREA

A series of basalt cliffs stand above the Truckee River on the east side of California Highway 89, just south of Truckee. The two most developed cliffs, located above the south end of the campground, are described below.

For the most direct approach to the crags, wade across the river and hike up the talus slope to the base. An alternative approach, which avoids fording the river, begins from the east end of Truckee. Drive west on South River Drive, off CA 267, just past the bridge. Continue beyond the pavement until the road ends. Walk along the river until you are below the cliffs. Hike up the talus to the base of the routes.

TRUCKEE RIVER BASALT AREA—CLIFF #4
A   Ham Sandwich .11c TR
B   Silent Victory .11c
C   Totally Board .9
D   Clear the Bridge .10c
E   Farmboy .7
F   Homeboy .10a
G   Tommy Knockers .10a
H   Peace Maker .7

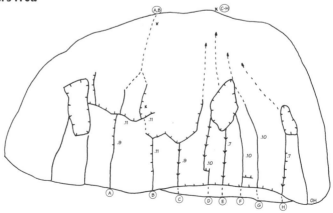

TRUCKEE RIVER BASALT AREA—CLIFF #5

A Objection Overruled .10d
B Secret Witness .10c
C Tremors .7
D Impact is Imminent .11b
E Practice What You Preach .12a TR
F Perilous Nation .10c
G Greenhouse Effect .9+
H Ozone .9

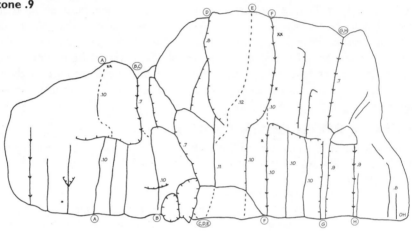

THE COLUMNS

This cliff is comprised of basalt columns creating perfectly formed cracks of various sizes. This 25-foot-high crag is easily toproped, and the routes range from 5.8 to 5.11. To find the Columns, park on California Highway 89 north of Cabin Creek Road and near the south end of the campground. Hike west a few hundred feet up the slope. The cliff is hidden in the trees.

BIG CHIEF

This prominent red wall is over 250 feet high, making it the largest formation in the canyon. It stands on a ridgeline above the east side of the Truckee River, a couple miles north of Squaw Valley. The majority of the rock is solid and steep with positive holds. Most of the lines are protected by bolts, although supplemental gear is sometimes necessary. Big Chief offers the best sport climbing in the Truckee River Canyon.

To approach Big Chief, turn south off California Highway 267, less than a mile from Truckee, onto Ponderosa Palisade Road. Drive to the top of the hill and turn right on Silver Fir, then left on Thelin Street. After a short distance, bear right just past a gate onto a well-established dirt road. Set your odometer and continue for 5.2 miles on this dirt road, then turn right onto a bumpy side road and continue for 0.6 mile to the end. Hike west through the forest on a faint trail that soon carves its way through a slope of manzanita to a notch near the north end of the formation. Descend the notch, contouring to the left along the base of the west face and the majority of the routes. The approach hike takes about 15 minutes.

Big Chief Overview

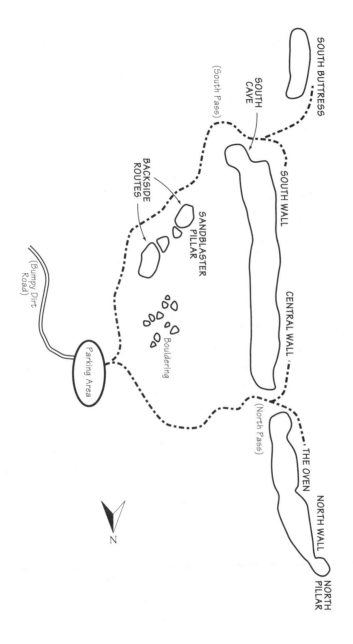

SOUTH BUTTRESS

(South Pass)

SOUTH
CAVE

SOUTH WALL

BACKSIDE
ROUTES

SANDBLASTER
PILLAR

CENTRAL WALL

Bouldering

(Bumpy Dirt
Road)

Parking Area

(North Pass)

THE OVEN

NORTH WALL

NORTH
PILLAR

N

SOUTH WALL

COPPER FEATHER

CENTRAL WALL

1

Big Chief, Truckee River Canyon:
I. Copper Feather 12a

BACKSIDE ROUTES I
A The Accused .11a
B Morning Sweater .11c
C Countdown .11a

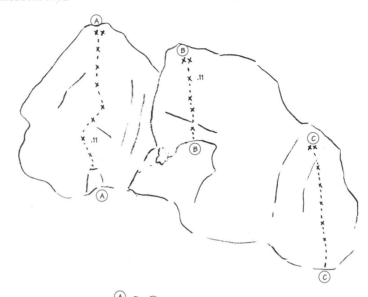

BACKSIDE ROUTES II
A Sandblaster Arete .12a/b
B Jungle Preacher .11a/b
C Junior Knows Best .11b/c
(short route up and right)

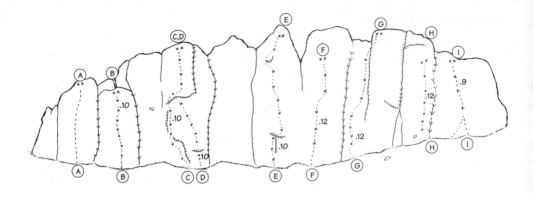

SOUTH BUTTRESS
A   Aunt Martha's Mustache .11
B   Sugar Fix .10d
C   7-11 Burrito .10a
D   Slurpee Headache .10d
E   Junk Food Junkie .10c
F   Class Moon .12a
G   Quick Stop .11d
H   Milking a Dead Cow .12c
I   Community Service .9

SOUTH CAVE
A   Realm of the Overhang .11a
    (.11c variation)
B   Louisiana Lip Lock .12a
C   Flying High Again .11b

South Wall

TIMES UP .10A

Not shown. One of two routes left of *Sweat Hog.* A line of seven bolts ascends the right side of a faint corner to a two-bolt belay.

SWEATING BULLETS .11A

Not shown. Just left of *Times Up.* Climb past two bolts to a ledge, then follow another six bolts to a two-bolt belay.

SOUTH WALL

A	**Sweat Hog .11b/c**
B	**Drill Drop .11b**
C	**Live Wire .11c**
D	**Pain Killer .10d**
E	**May Cause Dizziness .11a**
F	**Festus .10a**
G	**May Cause Drowsiness .10d**
H	**Glass Eye .10**
I	**Donkey Show .10**

CENTER WALL—LOWER RIGHT

A   Eat the Worm .11b
B   Early Bird .12a TR
C   Unknown .10a
D   Wampum .7
E   Route Stealers From Hell
     .10a
F   Force Feed .11a
     (.10 variation)
G   Too Light to Wait .10b

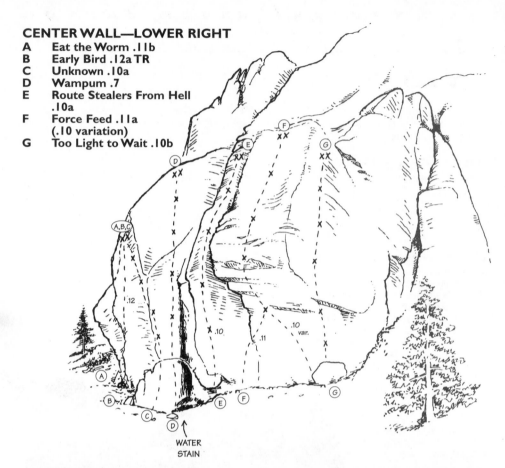

Center Wall—Cave Area: 1. Killer Bee, 2. Scalper, 3. War Path, 4. Copper Feather

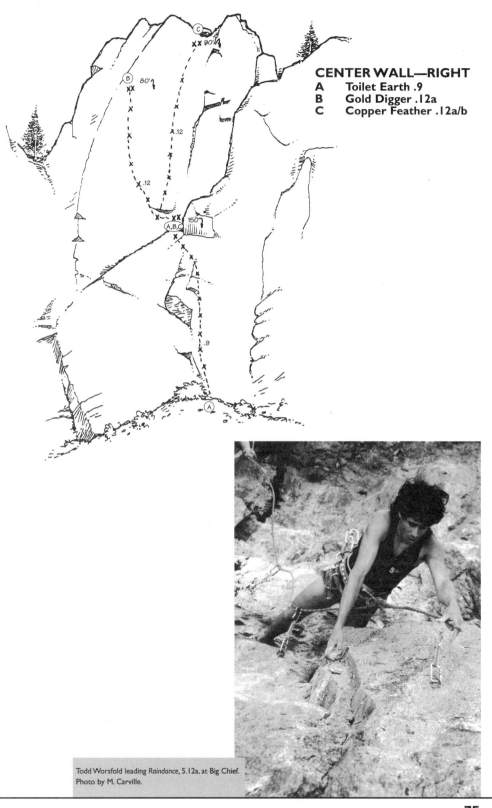

CENTER WALL—RIGHT
A   **Toilet Earth .9**
B   **Gold Digger .12a**
C   **Copper Feather .12a/b**

Todd Worsfold leading *Raindance*, 5.12a, at Big Chief.
Photo by M. Carville.

CENTER WALL—CAVE AREA

A	Head Rush .11a	F	Blazing Buckets .13b	L	Ghost Dance .12a
B	Big Chief Arete .11a	G	All Guns Blazing .13a	M	Scalper .12a
C	Killer Bee .10c	H	Mudshark .13c	N	Raindance .12a
D	Wicked Quickie .12c	I	Totally Chawsome .12a	O	Mohawk .10b
E	Vulgar Display of Power	J	Pow Wow .11a	P	Witch Doctor .10c
	.13b/c	K	Peace Pipe .11d	Q	War Path .9
				R	War Paint .9

CENTER WALL—LEFT

A   Travail Buttress .11a (pro: thin to medium)
B   Eye of the Beholder .11c
C   Headband .11b
D   Sitting Bull .11c
E   Flame Thrower .10d
F   Running Bull .11c
G   Green Hornet .10d
H   Kalumet Arete .11a
I   Thrash under Pressure .10

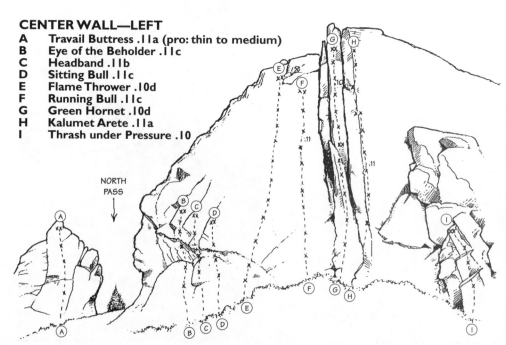

NORTH WALL AND THE OVEN

A North Pillar .10a
B High Tide .11c
C Laas Rocket .10a
D Jeronimo .12a
E Jeronimo Drinking Firewater .12b
F Firewater .12c
G Medicine Man .12a
H Freak of Nature .12a
I Climb against Nature .12b
J Under Cooked .11b
K Half Baked .10a
L Over Cooked .11d
M Super Baked .11c
N Bun in the Oven .11b
O Sundance .10a
   (.11a variation)

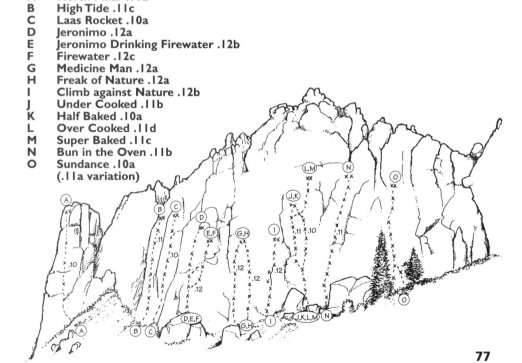

North Wall and The Oven: 1. North Pillar,
2. Medicine Man, 3. Over Cooked, 4. Sundance

THE AMPHITHEATER

This cul-de-sac of rock faces southwest and is sunny most of the day. It lies on the hillside above California Highway 89 and across from the entrance of Alpine Meadows. The rock is solid and the routes range in height from 40 to 100 feet.

To approach the area, park near the entrance of Alpine Meadows. Walk north along CA 89 for about 0.25 mile until you are beneath the Amphitheater. The hike up to the base takes about 30 minutes.

The Amphitheater—Main Wall (Not shown)

Main Wall is the large cliff face that forms the left side of the Amphitheater. Supplemental gear is necessary for these climbs. To descend the routes, rap from the belay anchors.

SLEEPER .11A/B

This climb begins on the left side of the wall. Clip a bolt, then move left and up a flake and corner system with three bolts and a pin. Continue to a two-bolt belay near the top of the wall.

SHINING PATH .11B

Clip the first bolt of *Sleeper*, then move right to a second bolt and up a corner to an arete. Climb straight up past a pin and some bolts to the belay shared with *Sleeper*.

BAT EJECTOR .11A

This route climbs the prominent corner with bolts, then traverses left to a bolted belay. The rock is rotten on the short face section below the corner.

SINNER .12A

Follow the thin crack up a smooth bulge between *Shinning Path* and *Bat Ejector*. When possible, mantle and move left to *Bat Ejector*.

The Amphitheater—Center Wall

This is the short, steep wall at the head of the Amphitheater.

THE AMPHITHEATER—CENTER WALL
A   **Finger Felon .12b**
B   **Mental Slavery .12a**
C   **Poor Man's Pump .11b/c**
D   **As You Like It .10b**
E   **Finger Fuck .12b/c TR**
F   **Rising Star .10d**

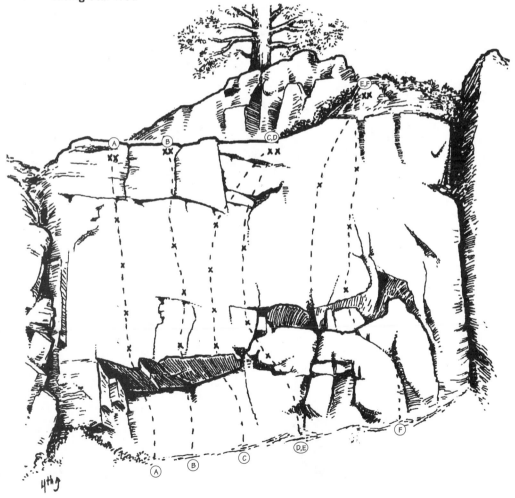

Twin Crags—Right Side: A. Dangerous Dan—10c.
B. Rap Attack .12a—C. Rurp Lim .7

TWIN CRAGS

This outcrop of symmetrical basalt columns is located above the east side of California Highway 89, about 1 mile northeast of Tahoe City. It is the only developed crag in the immediate area. The quality of the rock is excellent, although the top of the crag is broken into many loose blocks, so be careful. Protection tends to skate out of the cracks due to the fine-grained texture of the rock.

Twin Crags offers a wide variety of climbing from aretes and cracks to faces and roofs. The views of Lake Tahoe are fantastic, especially in spring when the thunderheads build over the lake. The crag receives sun from midmorning until sunset and is often climbable during the winter.

Park at the Twin Crag Summer Home Tract on CA 89 (about 1 mile east of Tahoe City), then follow the trail that begins just left of a small shed and meanders uphill. Diagonal up and left through the forest to a long talus field. From near the top of the talus, a narrow trail leads through the manzanita brush to the left edge of the crag. Descents can be made from rappel anchors, which exist at many points along the top of the cliff.

Twin Crags—Center (Not shown)

These routes are in the broken section between the left and right sides of the crag. Climbs are listed from left to right.

TWIN FAGS .7

Ascend a dark face in a gully between two opposite-facing corners.

DON'T SKATE MATE .10a

This route begins 25 feet right of *Twin Fags* and climbs a broken crack past an overhanging block to the top of the cliff.

JOHAN'S .8

Climb a broken gully 30 feet right and around the corner from *Don't Skate Mate*.

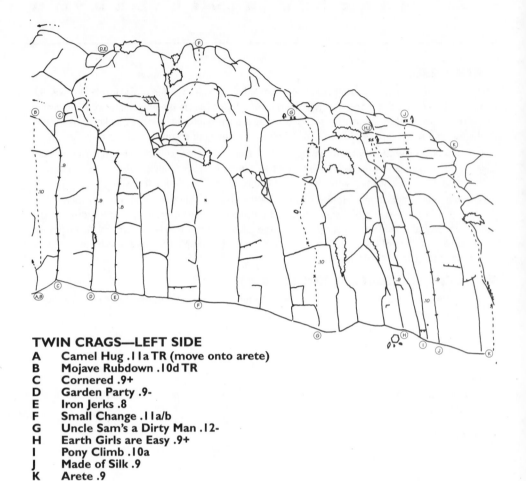

TWIN CRAGS—LEFT SIDE

A   Camel Hug .11a TR (move onto arete)
B   Mojave Rubdown .10d TR
C   Cornered .9+
D   Garden Party .9-
E   Iron Jerks .8
F   Small Change .11a/b
G   Uncle Sam's a Dirty Man .12-
H   Earth Girls are Easy .9+
I   Pony Climb .10a
J   Made of Silk .9
K   Arete .9

Twin Crags—South Wall

This is the far right side of the crag about 30 yards right of *Slam Dunk*. The first three routes may use the same two-bolt belay. Climbs are listed from right to left.

MADE IN THE SHADE .9

Crack to a right-facing corner with a bolt near the top.

JUST LEFT .11A

Hand crack through the right side of a small roof to a left-facing corner.

DON'T BE AFRAID OF THE DARK .10A

Follow faint Y-shaped crack, then fade left near the top.

JUST RIGHT .11A

Crack to a left-facing corner with one bolt below the top.

TWIN CRAGS—RIGHT SIDE

A Tahoe Bolt Murder .10b
B Club Toe .11c
C The Ghost .9

D
E Nipples That Cut Glass .10b
F Jamolator .12b/c
G By Fair Means .10a
H Chris Toe .8
   Flirting' with Disaster .10b
   (flaring crack)

I Wild Bull Rider .11a
J The Dihedral .11a/b
K Scissor Kick .12a
L Dangerous Dan .10c
M Rap Attack .12a
N Throne of Gold .11d

O Rurp Line .7
P Unknown
Q The Dagger .9
R A Fine Line .10b
S Slam Dunk .12b

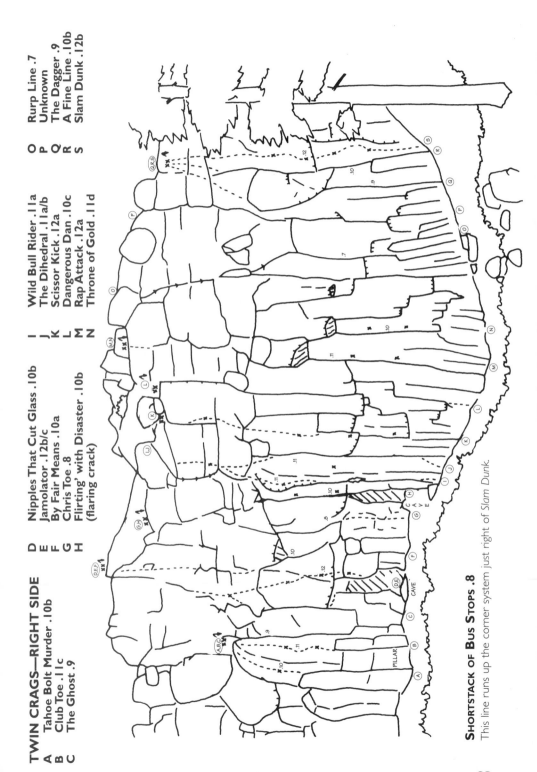

SHORTSTACK OF BUS STOPS .8

This line runs up the corner system just right of *Slam Dunk.*

83

Eagle Creek Canyon Overview

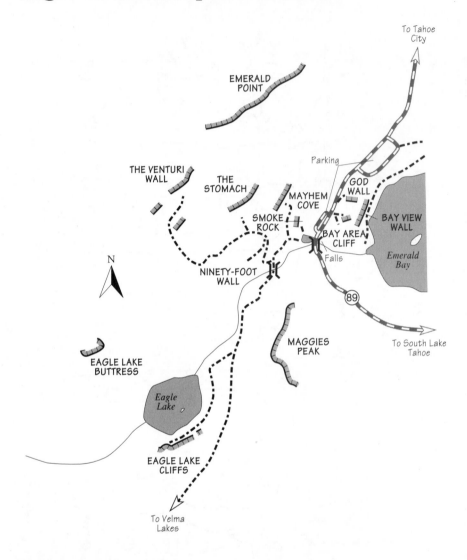

EMERALD POINT

THE VENTURI WALL

THE STOMACH

Parking

GOD WALL

MAYHEM COVE

SMOKE ROCK

BAY AREA CLIFF

BAY VIEW WALL

Emerald Bay

Falls

N

NINETY-FOOT WALL

89

To Tahoe City

To South Lake Tahoe

MAGGIES PEAK

EAGLE LAKE BUTTRESS

Eagle Lake

EAGLE LAKE CLIFFS

To Velma Lakes

RECOMMENDED ROUTES

Holdless Horror .6
Rentier .7
Shuman the Human .7
Section 20 .7
East Ridge Route .7
Strontium 90 .8
All American Finger Crack .9
Block Buster .9
Space Truckin' .10a
Monkey Business .10a
The Diamond .10b
Lightning Bolt .10b
The Nagual .10c

Lost in Space .11a
The Guillotine Direct .11a
Polar Circus .11b
Sandbagged .11b/c
High Velocity .11c
Riddler .11c
Space Walk .11c/d
The Coroner .11d
Huntin' Gator .12b
Mandatory Suicide .12a
Wild at Heart .12b
Drinkin' White Lightning .12c
Cajun Hell .13a

Eagle Creek Canyon

This deep granite canyon lies above Emerald Bay and California Highway 89 on the west shore of Lake Tahoe. There is climbing around the mouth of the canyon, as well as 1 mile west at Eagle Lake. Craggy peaks, alpine landscape, and splendid lake vistas make this area the most celebrated natural setting in the Tahoe Basin.

Several crags are within a ten-minute walk of the parking area. Below CA 89 and overlooking Emerald Bay, you will find God Wall, Bay View Wall, and Bay Area Cliff; west of the parking area, Smoke Rock, Mayhem Cove, and Ninety-Foot Wall.

A parking area and trailhead for the Desolation Wilderness is located on the west side of the highway by Eagle Creek. To reach the climbing areas in the canyon, hike west up the canyon on a trail that parallels the creek. In summer, this area becomes extremely popular with hikers and sightseers. Lock valuables in the trunk or take them with you. And, unfortunately, *giardia* is always a possibility, so treat drinking water accordingly.

Camping is allowed almost anywhere in the canyon. A wilderness camping permit is necessary and can be obtained at no charge from the Forest Service in South Lake Tahoe.

BAY VIEW WALL

This slabby face is up and right of the Vikings Home, a historical landmark located at the southwest end of Emerald Bay. Not much has been done on this cliff. A few lines—various crack systems linked by bolts—are visible from the ground. Supplemental gear is necessary. Approach the wall by bushwhacking down and across from Eagle Falls, or by walking down the easier but less direct visitor path from Viking Home, which begins at a parking area a few hundred yards north up California Highway 89 from the Eagle Lake trailhead.

GOD WALL

This wall is just below California Highway 89, a couple hundred yards north of Eagle Creek Falls. A large roof traverses the face about a third of the way up. The rock is coarse grained and the cracks are sometimes difficult to protect. Many variations of these lines exist.

BAY AREA CLIFF (Not Shown)

This cliff is located several hundred feet below the highway and about 80 yards north of Eagle Creek Falls. Walk down a gully near the falls. Identify the wall by a large, right-facing corner with three overhanging cracks about 70 feet long.

THE JESTER .6 (pro: to 3")
This line runs up the center of the cliff to the left of the prominent corner. Climb a short chimney in a left-facing book to a platform. Follow a shallow corner to the top.

THE EMERALD BEYOND .9 (pro: to 3")
This route follows the first of three cracks right of the corner. Broken rock and a short corner lead to an overhanging hand crack.

THIN FINGERS .10B (pro: to 1.5")
This is the center crack, which is thin and overhanging.

SANDBAGGED .11B/C (pro: to 2.5")

Ascend the overhanging crack on a small buttress about 25 feet right of the corner.

DELBERT'S DIAGONAL .9 (pro: to 2")

This is the obvious left-diagonal crack on a small cliff to the east of *Emerald Beyond*.

DELBERT'S DIRECT .9+ (pro: to 2")

This is the corner just left of *Delbert's Diagonal.*

SMOKE ROCK

This large boulder is 100 yards northwest of the parking area at Eagle Creek. The 50-foot-high wall is slightly overhanging and the rock is excellent. There are bolt anchors on top for setting up topropes, although some additional gear may be needed.

GOD WALL
A	Unknown .11
B	Holy Moses .11c
C	Light Years .12a
D	Hail Mary .11d
E	Godsend .11d
F	Race with the Devil .10d

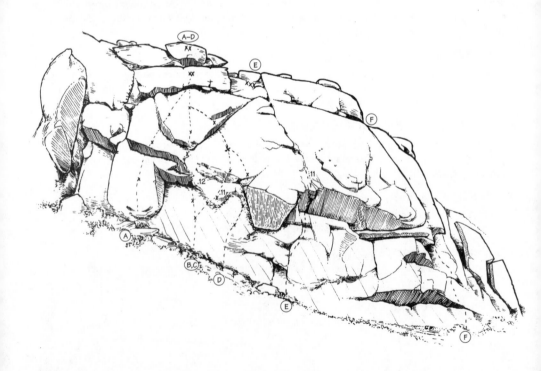

SMOKE ROCK

A	.11+
B	.11+
C	.7
D	.10
E	.11a
F	.10c
G	.11b

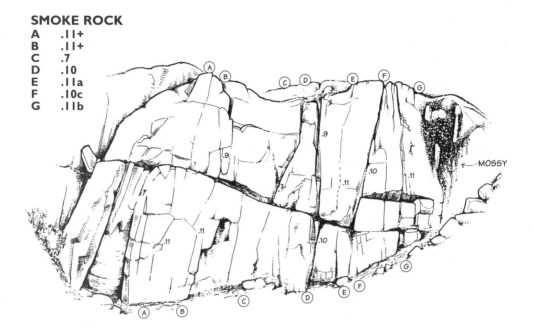

Mayhem Cove: 1. India Ink. 2. Cajun Hell. 3. The
Guillotine Direct. 4. Disturbing the Priest. 5.
Coma Sutra

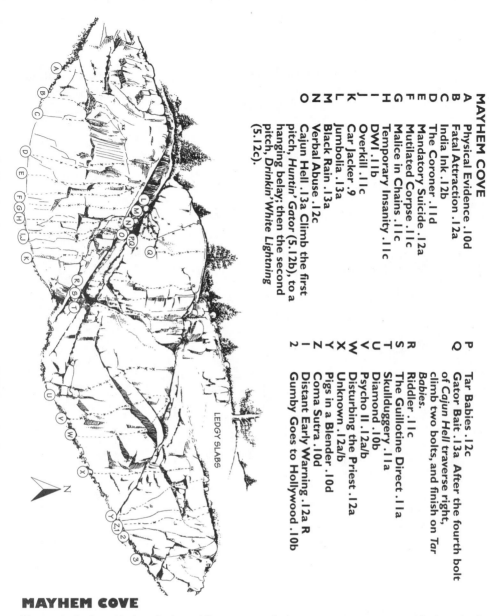

MAYHEM COVE

A Physical Evidence . 10d
B Fatal Attraction . 12a
C India Ink . 12b
D The Coroner . 11d
E Mandatory Suicide . 12a
F Mutilated Corpse . 11c
G Malice in Chains . 11c
H Temporary Insanity . 11c
I DWI . 11b
J Overkill . 11c
K Car Jacker . 9
L Jumbolia . 13a
M Black Rain . 13a
N Verbal Abuse . 12c
O Cajun Hell . 13a Climb the first pitch, *Huntin' Gator* (5.12b), to a hanging belay; then the second pitch, *Drinkin' White Lightning* (5.12c).

P Tar Babies . 12c
Q Gator Bait . 13a After the fourth bolt of *Cajun Hell* traverse right, climb two bolts, and finish on *Tar Babies*.
R Riddler . 11c
S The Guillotine Direct . 11a
T Skullduggery . 11a
U Diamond . 10b
V Psycho II . 12a/b
W Disturbing the Priest . 12a
X Unknown . 12a/b
Y Pigs in a Blender . 10d
Z Coma Sutra . 10d
1 Distant Early Warning . 12a R
2 Gumby Goes to Hollywood . 10b

LEDGY SLABS

MAYHEM COVE

This junky-looking black-and-white cliff was originally known as a scary crag with dicey leads. Mayhem is now the premier sport crag in the canyon. The routes are fantastic, ascending steep, featured faces protected by closely spaced bolts. A low-angle ramp splits the left side of the cliff and includes a shallow cave that harbors the most difficult routes in the canyon. Mayhem lies a few hundred yards northwest of the trailhead at Eagle Lake parking area. An old road above Smoke Rock traverses below Mayhem. From the road, wander up to the center of the cliff along a faint trail through boulders and manzanita brush.

LIZARD MAN . 10B

Not shown. Climb a face right of *Spontaneous Combustion* to a crack that splits a roof.

SLANDER . 13A

Not shown. This popular link-up climbs *Verbal Abuse* and then continues up *Tar Babies* to the anchor.

Todd Wordsfold pulling through the lower crux on
Cajun Hell, 5.13a, at Mayhem. Photo by M. Carville.

NINETY-FOOT WALL

This cliff is about 70 feet tall and a couple hundred feet long. It has a high concentration of good climbs on solid and compact rock. The wall features crack systems and square-cut holds. The majority of the routes can be easily toproped from anchor bolts along the rim. Access the top of the crag from the left side via a casual scramble. Most of the lines are toproped because the wall is short and some of the cracks are bottoming, making protection placements marginal. Long slings and supplemental gear should be used to back up the bolt anchors. Ninety-Foot Wall is very popular and can be crowded. Due to its southern exposure, you can climb here from early spring until late fall.

To reach the wall, walk up Eagle Lake Trail from the parking area. After 0.25 mile, reach a small bridge over the creek. Instead of crossing the bridge, stay to the right of the creek, following it upstream for 50 yards. The cliff stands directly to the right and about 25 yards uphill.

NINETY-FOOT WALL (LEFT)

A   Shuman the Human .7
B   Rentier .7
C   Lost in Space .11a
D   Strontium 90 .8
E   Bastille .11b
F   Relativity .10b (arete)
G   Casual Observer .2 (chimney)
H   Alias Emil Bart .10c
I   Rip-off .10
J   Never Ending Story .11
K   Fallout .9
L   Bachar's Line .11
M   Holdless Horror .6
N   Vintage 85 .9
O   Lightning Bolt .10b

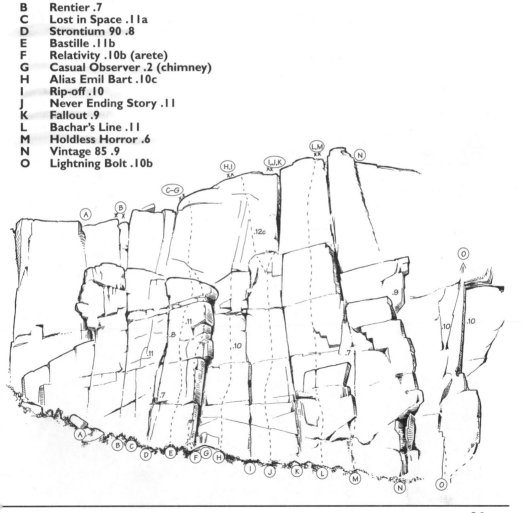

Niney-Foot Wall: 1. Strontium 90 .8. 2. Fallout 9. 3. Holdless Horror .6

NINETY-FOOT WALL (RIGHT)

A   **Lightning Bolt .10b**
B   **Ice Nine .10a**
C   **Polar Circus .11b**
D   **Ti-si-ack .10d**
E   **Dave's Run .11b**
F   **One More for the Road .10d (many variations)**

THE STOMACH (Not shown)

This is a whitish granite dome several hundred feet above and to the east of Ninety-Foot Wall. Hike up ledges and terraces above Ninety-Foot Wall to a large pine tree, then bushwhack to the base of the dome, which is about 50 yards away. Only a couple routes have been climbed here.

STOMACH ACHE .9 TR

Begin near the left side of the wall about 20 feet right of a scary flake. Climb straight up for one full pitch following the path of least resistance.

REGULAR ROUTE .11 (pro: to 2.5")

Begin in a right-facing dihedral on the right side of the face. Climb the corner until it is possible to traverse right to a large ledge. From here, climb a short, knobby wall, then continue up ledges and short walls to the top.

THE VENTURI WALL

This cliff stands high above Ninety-Foot Wall. From Ninety-Foot Wall, hike up ledges and terraces below a large pine tree, then wander a good ways up and left. The hike takes at least 45 minutes.

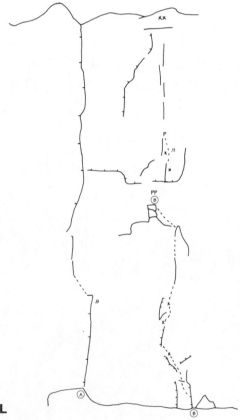

THE VENTURI WALL
A   Venturi .9+
B   High Velocity .11c (pro: draws, TCUs, and RPs)

EMERALD POINT

The summit pinnacle (9,195 feet) of this long and craggy ridge is the second highest point on the Rubicon Crest. The crest extends from above the parking area at Emerald Bay to Grouse Lakes Valley. The west face rises 2,000 feet above Eagle Creek Canyon and is comprised of many pinnacles, cliffs, and multipitch faces. Numerous first ascent possibilities exist for adventurous climbers.

Warning: The following routes are only for the adventurous! Serious approaches and route-finding skills are necessary. To reach the base of the established routes, follow Eagle Creek for 0.5 mile past Ninety-Foot Wall. Locate a large round boulder at the bottom of a shallow ravine, which heads toward the peak. A talus field located a short ways up and right of the ravine leads to the base of the wall and a huge white dihedral called White Walls. The simplest descent from the top is down the west ridge (third class). When it becomes possible, descend a long narrow gully to the creek.

Lower Section Routes (Not shown)

WHITE WALLS .8 (pro: to 2.5")

This route climbs the huge white dihedral noted in the approach description. Climb 40 feet up the face to a ledge, right of the main corner. From the ledge, face climb up and right to a bolt on a smooth bulge. Move past the bulge (5.8), then up and left to a sloping belay ledge in the main corner. Continue up the corner past a loose block on the right to the flat summit platform.

DIVERSIONS .8 (pro: to 2")

Climb up an off-width to the base of a chimney, 50 feet right of *White Walls*. Traverse 40 feet on positive face holds to a thin crack system. Ascend the crack right, then up about 100 feet to an arete with a belay ledge farther to the right. Continue up the arete to the summit platform.

ALL AMERICAN FINGER CRACK .9 (pro: to 2")

This route ascends an exquisite thin crack that splits a rounded buttress between *Section 20* and the two previous routes. What looks like a 5.11 finger crack goes at 5.8 due to a sea of small knobs dotting the face. Climb the finger crack (5.8) for 100 feet to a belay ledge beneath a triangular roof. Move left and up a thin jam crack through some bulges (5.9) to the top of the buttress. This is a quality climb.

SECTION 20 .7 (pro: small to large; .8–.10 variations)

This route is about 900 feet long and is the most popular line on the face. It begins 0.25 mile right and uphill from *White Walls* and *Diversions*, and below the summit. Climb a low-angle chimney on the left wall of a knobby arete. From the top of the fourth pitch, walk up and left for 0.25 mile to the Russet Wall, a reddish-brown face with a tree at its base. From the summit of Emerald Point, you'll find the best views in the Tahoe Basin.

The Plectrum (Not shown)

This is the sharpest and most exposed pinnacle on the summit of Emerald Point. It stands about 50 yards right of the top of *Section 20* and is reached via an easy fifth-class traverse.

EAST FACE A1 (pro: to 2")

This route follows a thin crack on the east face. Someday it will go free.

WEST FACE .6 A1 (pro: to 2")

Climb up the moderate cracks on the west face. Just below the top, move to a pedestal on the north face where a single aid bolt is used to reach the summit.

EMERALD POINT, SECTION 20

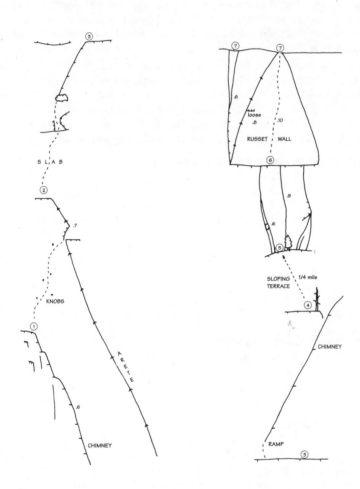

MAGGIES PEAK

This peak forms the left side of Eagle Creek Canyon and rises 800 feet above the southeast side of Eagle Lake. The main face has broken ledges and some of the rock is poor quality. Several routes have been done, ranging from 5.8 to 5.11. Under favorable winter conditions, the gullies on the north face offer some of the best mixed ice routes in the area.

To approach Maggies Peak, hike up Eagle Lake Trail to its junction with Velma Lakes Trail. Continue for 0.25 mile on the left fork toward Velma Lakes. The cliff is visible on your left and a third-class scramble leads to the base. To descend from the upper wall, traverse west along some ledges to a long and narrow talus field that forms the west side of the face. Continue down to the trail.

EAGLE LAKE CLIFFS

Eagle Lake Cliff

This superb cliff is worth the half-hour approach hike. It has some of the best moderate crack climbing in the basin. The cliff lies above the south side of Eagle Lake in a spectacular granite basin with stunning views of Emerald Point and its massive west wall.

To reach this area, take Eagle Lake Trail from the parking area to the lake, which is about 1 mile. Continue along the south shore to the far end of the lake. The cliff is obvious and stands above the boulder field. To descend, walk south to some gullies and ramps that lead to a third-class section dropping toward the lake, or downclimb an easy fifth-class chimney inside the boulder cave below the belay for *Changeling* and *The Buzzard*.

EAGLE LAKE CLIFF

A	Wild at Heart .12b Left of upper arete. (bolts)
B	The Criterion .11a (pro: thin to medium)
C	Thrust is a Must .10d (pro: to 3", mostly medium)
D	Seams to Me .10c (pro: to 1.5")
E	The Nagual .10c (pro: to 2.5")
F	Barney Rubble .10a
G	Quest for Power .11a
H	Space Truckin' .10a (pro: to 2.5", mostly medium)
I	Space Walk .11c/d Crack on side wall. (pro: to 2", mostly thin to medium)
J	Separated Reality .8
K	Off the Wall .10c (face climb past four bolts)
L	Polecat A3 (pro: mostly thin; inside chimney formed by the pillar, new bolts)
M	The Vulture .10a
N	The Buzzard .11b (bolt to thin crack on side wall)
O	Changeling .8+ (pro: to 2"; crack on left side of boulder cave)
P	Cracula .10a (pro: to 2"; crack on right side of boulder cave)
Q	Buster Brown .10b (pro: to 4")
R	Block Buster .9 (pro: to 3.5")
S	Master Race .11c TR
T	Der Fuhrer .11d TR
U	Master of Disaster .10a

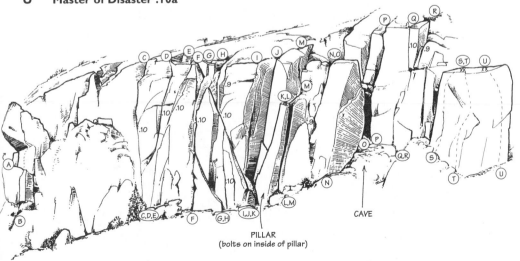

Eagle Lake Cliff. 1. The Criterion, 2. The Nagual,
3. Space Truckin', 4. Space Walk, 5. The Buzzard,
6. Buster Brown, 7. Der Fuhrer

Punk Rock (Not shown)

This small wall is up and right of Eagle Lake Cliff. A thin, right-leaning flake lies in the center of the face.

MOON RAKER .10A
Climb an obvious left-facing corner on the left side of the cliff.

LOST AND FOUND .9
Ascend the flake.

ATOMIC PUNK .10C
Climb the corner and roof on the right side of the cliff.

Upper Eagle Creek Cliff (Not shown)

These cliff bands extend west up the canyon on either side of the creek flowing into Eagle Lake. The routes range from 5.9 to 5.12.

GOLD METTLE .11D/.12A
This climb is located on the right side of the canyon on a bulging golden wall split by a 2- to 4-inch crack.

Three Stooges Wall (Not shown)

This wall is located on a plateau high above the southwest shore of Eagle Lake. From the junction with Eagle Lake Trail, walk up Velma Lakes Trail for about 1 mile. Walk west across the plateau to a rock wall slightly hidden in the trees. The following three lines are on the right side of the cliff. Several climbs have been done to the right, around the corner.

THE MANNY .12A
Crack on the left side.

THE MO CRACK .10A
Crack in the center.

THE JACK CRACK .10D
Crack on the right side.

EAGLE LAKE BUTTRESS

This prominent granite buttress (8,640 feet) towers distinctly at the south end of a high ridge about 1 mile west of Eagle Lake. The approach hike takes about 1.5 hours from the parking area by Emerald Bay. To reach the buttress, cross the outlet at Eagle Lake and follow a ravine to a ridge, which leads to the base. Excellent rock, sweeping views, and a sunny southern exposure make these climbs a great adventure. For the easiest descent from the summit, go down the *Mountaineer's Route*.

MOUNTAINEER'S ROUTE FOURTH CLASS
From the southwest edge, wander up some low-angle slabs and then up some steeper fourth-class slabs to a notch between Eagle Lake Buttress and a subsidiary pinnacle on the west side. Continue along the ridge to the summit.

Eagle Lake Buttress: 1. Mountaineer's Route, 2. A Line, 3. Wind Tree, 4. Eagle Route, 5. Monkey Business, 6. Orange Book, 7. Orange Sunshine, 8. East Ridge Route

A LINE .9 (pro: to 2.5")

This route follows a left-leaning crack system from the bottom to the top of the buttress. The route becomes obvious when viewed from below and to the right of the buttress. The initial pitch is about 100 feet long, half of which is fourth class, followed by two roofs and a jam crack. From a belay ledge, climb up past another roof to a large belay ledge beneath a bulge. The crux pitch is the off-width crack above, which ends at a small ledge on the left. An easy gully leads to the summit.

I'M A GUMBY DAMMIT .9

Not shown. This route goes up the overhanging crack just to the right of *A Line*. Belay at the base of a clean corner. Climb to the top of the corner, then move across to a ramp and up a thin crack to the top.

WIND TREE .9 (pro: to 3")

A solitary juniper called Wind Tree stands high on the spine of the buttress. This route ascends the left-facing crack system to the tree. Begin on a ledge about 40 feet above the ground and climb up broken cracks to a small ledge where two cracks form a V. Move up the left crack, which is a right-facing corner, to a large belay ledge 70 feet higher. Climb a steep section and a big arch until just before a dihedral covered with vegetation. Wander right on knobs to a 5.9 off-width crack. Climb up and right to Wind Tree. Finally, traverse left to an arete and jam crack, which is followed by easier climbing to the summit.

EAGLE ROUTE .5

Follow *Wind Tree* to the V mentioned above. From here, ascend the right side of the crack system. Another similar pitch leads to a belay just above a groove. Move left to a flared chimney containing a flake. Follow *East Ridge Route* to the top.

MONKEY BUSINESS .10A (pro: to 2.5", mostly thin)

This excellent route lies in the center of an obscure buttress just left of *Orange Book*. Rope up at the big juniper tree at the base of the wall. Climb a short jam crack and chimney, then go up a long broken gully to a large belay area a few feet left of *Orange Book*. Ascend a short, jam and lie-back crack (5.9) with poor protection up to the right side of the triangular overhang. Move left out a wide crack that passes the lip of the overhang and follow a thin crack that splits a slab. From some ramps, head back left to a small ledge on an exposed arete. Low-angle rock joins the *East Ridge Route* to the summit.

ORANGE BOOK .8

This climb follows a prominent left-facing orange dihedral. Stem up a 5.7 corner to a good ledge 90 feet up. Continue climbing the corner to a belay where the corner begins to overhang. Climb the cracks and chimneys through the overhangs to *East Ridge Route* and follow it to the top. A 5.6 variation exists. From the top of the second pitch, move right and down to a hole. Slide through the hole and then up an increasingly steep lie-back crack to the East Ridge.

ORANGE SUNSHINE .9 (pro: to 2.5")

This great line ascends some parallel vertical cracks on the right side wall of the orange dihedral about 120 feet above the ground. Climb the first pitch of *Orange Book* and belay beneath the cracks. Move up and right past an overhang and up the left-hand crack. Belay on a broken terrace known as King Henry. Follow *East Ridge Route* to the top.

EAST RIDGE ROUTE .7 (pro: to 2")

The beautiful panoramas of Lake Tahoe, Eagle Creek Canyon, and the pinnacle ridge that stretches northwest from the buttress make this climb the most scenic route on the face. Climb up some easy slabs on the north side of the ridge to a ledge at the bottom of a steep crack. A short, curving crack joins the main crack, which leads to some sloping ledges. From here, head right to a belay platform on the prow of the ridge. Ascend the pair of wide cracks farthest right to a broken terrace, King Henry. Jam a curving crack and scramble up blocks until the ridge becomes third class. Continue along the ridge to some 5.5 cracks that split the final wall. The summit lies just above.

CRAG PEAK (Not shown)

This backcountry peak (9,045 feet) is located near the eastern boundary of the Desolation Wilderness. Due to the long and arduous approach, it is seldom visited by climbers. Begin hiking from Meeks Bay on the west shore of Lake Tahoe. After 7.5 miles, you can see the 400-foot-high triangular northeast face of Crag Peak above the south end of Hidden Lake. Wander up a U-shaped valley for 0.5 mile to the base of the wall. You can camp at one of the lakes below.

Although the rock is good, many of the cracks are shallow and solid protection can be difficult to place. The climbs that reach the notch left of the summit have dangerously loose rock. With a northeast exposure, the face is often wet from snowmelt until midsummer. To descend from the summit, walk along the northwest ridge until you can cut back along the peak's base.

BLACK ABYSS .8 (pro: to 2.5"; three pitches)

Climb a series of dark caves about 120 yards left of *Ivory Book*. A poorly protected pitch cuts up and left across a low-angle slab to a right-facing corner. The corner leads to the first cave and a belay. Continue to the end of the corner and up a loose ramp, moving left to the second cave and a belay. The last pitch heads left, then right, and finally finishes straight up on easy rock.

IVORY BOOK .9 (pro: to 3"; three pitches)

This route ascends an obvious, left-facing white corner. Climb the corner to a belay on top of a pillar. Climb some easy rock to an overhanging 5.9 chimney called the Quarter Moon. Belay above the corner on ledges to the right. A short pitch leads right under an arch to another belay ledge. Continue straight up to some fourth-class rock and the top.

VARIATION .7 A1

From the top of the second pitch, traverse left along the lip of an overhang to a right-facing corner. Move 40 feet up the corner and belay. Nail the A1 crack out right to the top.

POOP-OUT PINNACLE .7 (pro: to 2.5")

Begin 25 yards left of *Coney Corner*. Jam and stem a left-facing dihedral to a pinnacle beneath a large white overhang. Rappel the route (165 feet).

CONEY CORNER .8 (pro: to 2.5"; three pitches)

This route starts 100 yards right of *Ivory Book* in a smaller but still prominent left-facing corner. The first pitch (5.8) ends on a tiny belay stance. The second pitch heads up moderate but broken rock. The final pitch has one 5.7 move.

INDIAN ROCK (Not shown)

This is the largest cliff in the Tahoe Basin, and although it lies several miles southeast of Eagle Creek Canyon, it is still considered part of the area. The wall forms the northwest face of Angora Peak. The heavily fractured face is a thousand feet high and divided by three huge terraces, all of which are accessible via third-class scrambles. Sections of superb, 400-foot-high granite rise between the terraces. Hundreds of crack systems await first ascents. The length of the approach has curbed the popularity of this high and wild alpine wall.

Two formations on the face serve as good reference points. The Tahoe Wall is a smooth, monolithic section of rock on the right side of the second terrace. The Treasure Chest is a square, 300-foot-high wall near the center of the face.

To find Indian Rock, head south on Fallen Leaf Lake Road, which is off California Highway 89. The intersection is about 3 miles west of the Y in South Lake Tahoe. Follow the road around the south shore of Fallen Leaf Lake to a resort on the west end. Instead of crossing the bridge, take the left fork to Lily Lake. Park off the road and follow the Triangle/Tamarack Lakes Trail for 1 mile. Hike up a loose and sometimes scary talus slope to the base of the wall. Allow an hour to reach the face from the end of the road.

To descend, walk north until you can cut back left down the edge of the rock (third class). Exit to the north from any of the terraces.

WHITE LIGHTNING .9 (pro: to 2.5"; 200 feet)
Climb an aesthetic, lightning-bolt-shaped crack on the center of a smooth white face near the left upper edge of the wall. The crack doesn't quite reach the ground, so traverse in from the right on some blocks. The crack begins as a 1.25-inch flaring corner and finishes as a beautiful jam crack.

DOOLAGOGA DIHEDRAL .7 (pro: to 3"; 270 feet)
Begin in a left-facing chimney/crack corner on the left side of the highest terrace. Belay on a good ledge. Move up 10 feet, then hand traverse left. As soon as possible, continue straight up to a group of trees at the top.

ORANGE MARMALADE .10B (pro: to 2"; 120 feet)
Begin a couple hundred feet below the start of *Doolagoga Dihedral*. Climb a sustained, right-leaning crack that splits an orange wall halfway up the face and left of center.

RARE GEM .10B (pro: to 3.5"; 1,000 feet)
This route takes a fairly direct line just to the right of the center of the face from the second terrace. After climbing the first three pitches of *Indirect Route*, scramble to a pinnacle-shaped wall. Climb the wall just right of center; then climb an easy chimney to a belay ledge (right) below a short vertical wall. An unprotected 5.9 face reaches a finger crack in a left-facing corner. From the top of the corner, walk up 100 feet to Treasure Chest. Traverse from the right to reach the second crack system. A fist crack leads to a V slot, through an overhang, and to a belay ledge 30 feet higher to the right. Move farther right and climb a long steep crack that varies from fingers to off-width (5.10). The final terrace is blocked by overhangs and roofs. From here, tricky route finding leads to the top. Head up a yellow slab and a very thin, left-slanting crack to a gully and a belay above an overhang. Continue up the gully to the summit.

INDIRECT ROUTE .10B A3 (pro: to 3", thin pins and hooks; 1,000 feet)

Begin by a juniper tree near the center of the face and a couple hundred feet left of a prominent nose-shaped roof. Climb a 20-foot-high, left-facing corner to a dirt ramp. Scramble right, up the ramp and then back left up another ramp to a short left-facing corner. From the top of the corner, step right to a triangular belay ledge. Move right to a finger crack, then over a roof on the left to a smooth slab in a shallow slot. Continue up 50 feet to a belay on top of a pillar. Step right off the pillar and climb a steep and flared thin crack (5.10). Belay on the first terrace.

Walk a couple hundred feet up and right. The fourth pitch begins in the first flared corner on the left side of a smooth, monolithic face, Tahoe Wall. Pass the overhangs above on the right and belay at a ledge. From the left side of the ledge, a crack leads to the top of Tahoe Wall. Pitch six takes some A3 thin cracks and a 5.8 mantel followed by more nailing in the obvious open dihedral above. From the left side of a sloping belay ledge, climb on blocks left and up to a large terrace. The eighth pitch aid climbs the large left-facing corner on the overhanging wall above. When the nailing becomes thin, pendulum left to a big loose flake. From the top of the flake, a 1-inch crack can be aided to a loose belay ledge. Continue up and left to a long narrow ledge, then walk 30 feet left and belay at the base of an easy gully that leads to the summit.

INDIAN HEAD .9 (pro: to 2.5")

This route begins on Tahoe Wall 50 yards right of a striking, parallel flake system that merges a hundred feet above the ground. Climb the face on the outside of a left-facing corner for about 30 feet, then move back into the corner and follow it to a good belay ledge. From here, the climb finishes on a third-class section to the right.

Rick Picket clips the draw after the crux of *Karncave*, 5.13a/b, at Cave Rock. Photo by Brian Biega

East Shore Crags

RECOMMENDED ROUTES
Over the Falls .11a
Asylum .12a
Rip Curl .12a
Port of Entry .12a
Concave .13a (to upper anchors)
Shut up and Climb .13a (to upper anchors)
Psycho Monkey .13a
Phantom Lord .13c/d
Slayer .13d/.14a

While the majority of rock in the Lake Tahoe area is granite, most of the developed crags along the east shore of the lake are tuff, andesite, and rhyolite. This type of rock generally features positive holds that sometimes are loose. Although most of the lines are bolt protected, some routes require supplemental gear, which can be tricky to place securely.

Due to its sunny eastern exposure, this side of the lake is known as the banana belt. Because volcanic stone tends to feel greasy when it is hot, the most popular time to climb here is in the fall, winter, and spring, when the combination of cool temperatures and sun give the rock a better feel.

TRIPPY ROCK

Trippy Rock is an andesite plug about 75 feet high and 100 feet across. Although most of the rock is steep or overhanging, the top can be reached easily via a third-class climb up the backside. There are bolt anchors on top for convenient toproping. The northwest face has cracks up a slab. Many variations exist.

To reach Trippy, drive about 3.2 miles north of Incline Village on Nevada Highway 431. Just before the vista point, turn left onto a dirt road and continue for about 200 yards. The rock is 100 yards up and right on the hillside.

TRIPPY ROCK—SOUTH FACE
A First Dose .10b
B Crimper Overdose .11a
C Leisure Suit .11b
D Pootang .11c
E Roto Arete .9

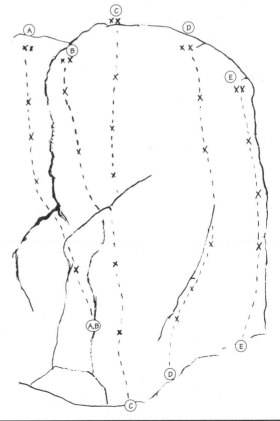

Trippy Rock—Northwest Face (Not shown)

TWEEDLE DEE .5

TWEEDLE DOO .5

BALLBUSTER ROCK

Ballbuster Rock is a giant granite boulder about 50 feet high with over a dozen routes and many more variations. There are good natural anchor placements for toproping. Travel 3 miles north from the junction of U.S. Highway 50 and Nevada Highway 28 at Spooner Summit. The rock is 50 yards west of NV 28.

Ballbuster Rock—South Face (Not shown)

The climbs are listed left to right.

THE MANTLE .10c

Mantle and then climb the seam, finishing on the arete up top and a bolt anchor.

KNOB JOB .10D

From the gray knob, face climb to the large knob and then to a bolt anchor.

CORNER CRACK .9

Climb the corner/crack in the center of the wall.

BALLBUSTER ROCK—EAST FACE
A   The Arete .10a
B   Easy Corner .8
C   Deep Blue .10c
D   Left Crack .9+
E   Right Crack .9
F   Left Variation .10b
G   Thin to Slim .12
H   Arch Nemesis .11b
I   Cruz .9

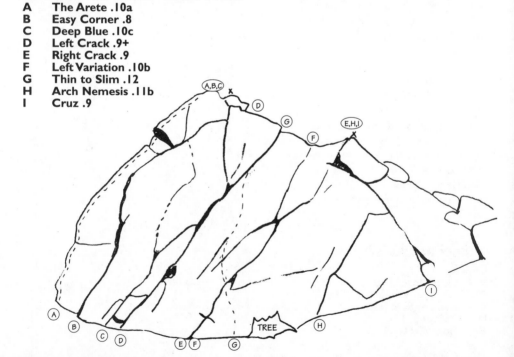

Ballbuster Rock—South Face (con't)

THE CHIMNEY .5

Climb the obvious chimney to the anchors of *Knob Job*.

INSIDE JOB .10B

Climb the inside wall of the previous route via a short finger crack. Belay at the anchors of *Knob Job*.

THE ARETE .10A

Climb the arete to the top.

SPOONER CRAG

Spooner Crag lies hidden in the trees above a frontage road just west of the junction of Nevada Highway 28 and U.S. Highway 50. This small formation of volcanic tuff has good edges and pockets. You can climb here throughout the year.

To find Spooner Crag, turn onto the road that links the west edge of NV 28 to US 50. Park in a pullout about halfway down the road. Hike uphill for several hundred yards to the crag.

Spooner Crag—Southwest Face

ANCIENT ROUTE .10A R (pro: to 2" and two bolts)

Not shown. Around the corner left of *Nightcrawler*.

HANGER-18 .11B (four bolts)

Not shown. Also, around the corner left of *Nightcrawler*.

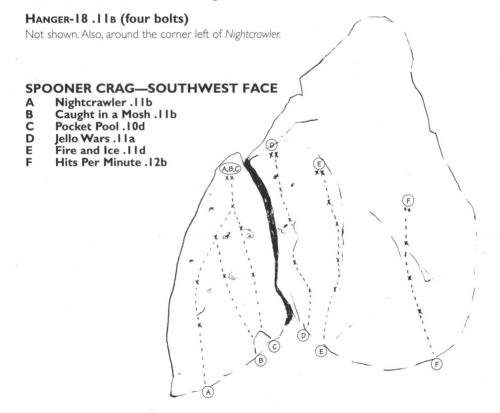

SPOONER CRAG—SOUTHWEST FACE
A   Nightcrawler .11b
B   Caught in a Mosh .11b
C   Pocket Pool .10d
D   Jello Wars .11a
E   Fire and Ice .11d
F   Hits Per Minute .12b

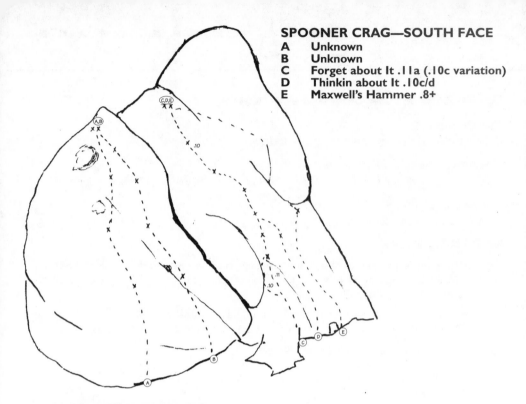

SPOONER CRAG—SOUTH FACE
A Unknown
B Unknown
C Forget about It .11a (.10c variation)
D Thinkin about It .10c/d
E Maxwell's Hammer .8+

SHAKESPEARE ROCK

This formidable andesite plug rises 400 feet above U.S. Highway 50 and Glenbrook. Its name was derived from the likeness of Shakespeare etched into the lichen. Because it faces north, Shakespeare is a good place to climb in the heat of summer. The rock is very fractured, creating blocks of all sizes, some of which are loose. Many of the routes lack well-developed crack systems and protection can be difficult to place. At least three routes have been done on the main face. Near the lower right side of Shakespeare, a roofless cave has several bolted lines; most of these require supplemental gear.

To reach the base of the face, follow the dirt road that cuts up from the highway below the rock. Drive up a short distance and park. Hike through the forest to the wall. There are some new bolted climbs on the far left side of Main Face.

Shakespeare Rock—Main Face (Not shown)

TEMPEST .6 (pro: to 3")
The first ascent of this line probably involved several shorter climbs done in succession. When completed to the summit, the climb was named *Monreau's Chute*. At some point the route became known as *Tempest*. Begin directly below the highest summit. Climb a fourth-class section to a large ledge. Follow a right-facing ramp/corner and belay at a block. Some face climbing up and left leads to a chimney and a belay. Ascend the chimney and the face above to the top.

HURRICANE .6 (pro: to 3")
This route begins inside the roofless cave, which is known as the Eye of the Hurricane. Climb the crack in the corner on the left side of the cave. The second pitch is fourth class, then third class along the ridge to the summit.

GALE .6 (pro: to 3")
This route also begins in the roofless cave. The first pitch ascends the corner on the right side of the cave. This climb then joins *Hurricane,* continuing up the third-class ridge to the top.

SHAKESPEARE ROCK—HEAVY METAL WALL (inside roofless cave)

A   OB's 5.10 .10c
B   View to a Thrill .10b
C   Rat Reach .11d
D   Bad Brains .11 R
E   Metallica .11b
F   Anthrax .11b

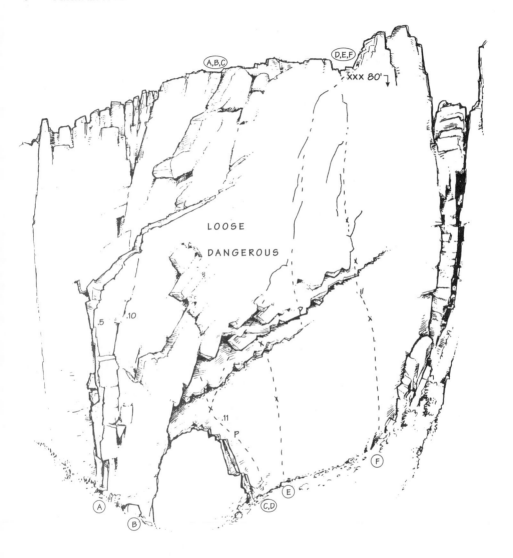

Shakespeare Rock—Face of Roofless Cave (Not shown)

On the face outside the roofless cave are four routes—three to the left of the opening and one to the right. These climbs are listed from left to right. Many of these routes require supplemental protection, especially RPs, TCUs, and Friends.

FELINE .11C/D (seven bolts, rap from anchors)

This route is outside the roofless cave to the left of the opening. Climb straight up just right of a small roof.

DEAF LEOPARD .11A R (four bolts, rap from two-bolt belay)

Begin just left of *The Mid-Evil.*

THE MID-EVIL .11B

Begin on the left edge of the cave's opening and climb past three bolts.

URANIUM ROOF .10D

Begin on the right side of the cave's opening and climb through a double corner and small roof to the top. Descend the other side into the cave room.

Shakespeare Rock—Heavy Metal Wall

The following routes are inside the roofless cave. Many of the climbs are loose and dangerous. Use extreme caution when climbing here.

POISON ARCH .11 X

This climb begins just left of *Rat Reach.* Ascend the right edge of the cave to its apex, then continue up.

CAVE ROCK

Cave Rock is simply stellar. It contains the highest concentration of difficult sport climbs in the Tahoe Basin. Due to the extreme overhanging nature of the climbing and the quality of the routes, the Cave has become a destination spot on the sport climbing circuit. Also, due to the eastern and sheltered exposure, you can often climb here throughout the winter.

Located just north of Zephyr Cove, the routes extend out the mouth of a large, shallow cave. Main Cave lies between the northbound and southbound lanes of U.S. Highway 50 at a point labeled "Cave Rock" on the road map. Lower Cave, more of an overhanging wall, is located below the highway at the edge of the lake.

The formation is a metamorphosed andesite plug through which US 50 passes. The rock has been shattered into blocks of every dimension, many of which are loose. The holds tend to be big edges and buckets, often sloping.

Although the walls of the caves are a grid of bolts, some runouts do occur here. Several bad injuries have resulted from climbers slamming back into the wall at the end of a fall, or pulling loose blocks onto spectators and belayers below. No one should stand beneath climbers, and extra precaution must be taken on routes near the highway. Due to rock fall and traffic, please do not climb left of *Bone Crusher* or right of *Asylum.*

Cave Rock is a historical state park, and climbers need to adhere to the attendant rules and regulations. Do not park on the median between the lanes of the highway. The best place to park is at the boat ramp, which costs a few dollars. A small pullout 0.25 mile south of Cave Rock also can be used for parking.

MAIN CAVE

LOWER CAVE

Cave Rock

To reach the Lower Cave, traverse along the edge of the lake by the boat ramp from the south. A third-class traverse beneath Lower Cave leads up to the Kona Wall, a short face 35 yards to the north. Kona Wall also can be approached from the north.

The following statement has been included as a request of concerned climbers and the Forest Service. Please be mindful of the request, as adherence is the only way to reduce the risk of closure to climbing.

Closure order 36 CFR 261.53 (c) was issued December 30, 1997 which prohibits any activity, including the installation of rock climbing bolts, that damages or defaces the surface of Cave Rock. The Forest Service is developing a management plan for Cave Rock. Because this guidebook predates the management plan, contacting the Forest Service information facility at (530) 573-2600 is suggested to receive the most current information.

Local climbers have learned a great deal about the Washoe Tribe and their history in the Tahoe Basin. Cave Rock is the Washoe's most spiritual site and climbers should treat the area with the utmost respect. We ask the following of all climbers:

- Use the restroom facilities at the boat ramp or pack it out. No other option exists!
- Climb and behave in a respectful manner. Cave Rock is an important spiritual site to the Washoe. Either treat it with respect and reverence or leave.
- In the rare occurrence that a Washoe tribe member asks climbers to leave so that they may be there undisturbed whilst seeking spiritual guidance, we ask climbers to honor this request.

Many local climbers have worked hard to keep Cave Rock open to climbing while also acknowledging the importance of the area to the Washoe. We hope that visitors and locals will honor these requests. Please show respect to each other and the Washoe.

Cave Rock—Main Cave

Many link ups and excellent variations have been done here.

METALLICA
Not shown. This excellent boulder problem traverses right from inside the main cave to the base of *Concave.*

TRASH DOG .11c/d
Not shown. Off-limits to climbing.

TON OF BRICKS .11c/d
Not shown. Off-limits to climbing.

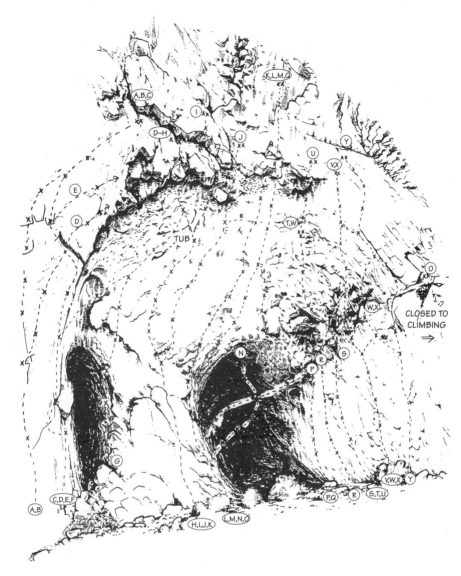

CAVE ROCK—MAIN CAVE

A	Bone Crusher .12c	M	Slayer .13d/14a
B	Coppertone .12a/b	N	Bat out of Hell .12b
C	Sea and Ski .12a/b	O	Pipeline .12b (traverse to right side
D	Tahiti .11d (finish at *Port of Entry*		of the main cave past *Asylum*)
	anchors)	P	Pigeon Hole .12b
E	Fiji .12b/c (finish at *Port of Entry*	Q	Super Monkey .14a
	anchors)	R	Underground .12a (bolts above
F	Port of Entry .12a		belay, project)
G	Fire in the Hole .12b	S	The Pit .11c
H	Cave Man .12a	T	Shut up and Climb .13a
I	Cave Man Direct .13a	U	Shut the Fuck up and Climb .13a
J	Psycho Monkey .13a	V	Messiah .13a/b
K	Psycho Lord .13b	W	Concave .12c/d
L	Phantom Lord .13c/d	X	Karncave .13a/b
		Y	Asylum .12a

Bill Sinoff high above Lake Tahoe on the Cave classic *Shut Up and Climb*, 5.13a. Photo by M. Carville.

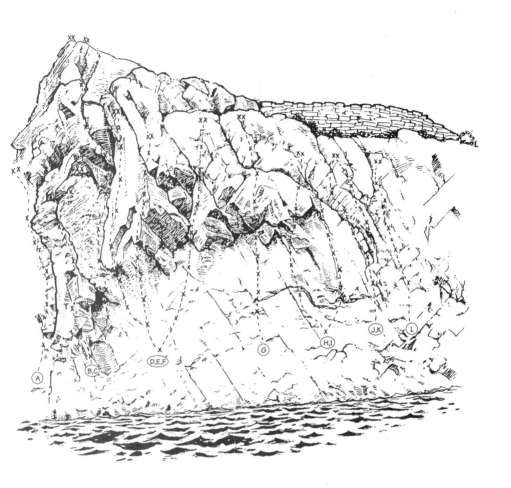

CAVE ROCK—LOWER CAVE

A   Banny's Buttress .10c/d
B   Club Med .11b
C   Project
D   Project
E   Project
F   Maco .11d AO
G   Project
H   Rip Curl .12a
I   Impact Zone .12a
J   Over the Falls Direct .11a
K   Over the Falls .11a
L   Green Room .11b

Sally Bartunek on *Over the Falls*, 5.11a, at Lower
Cave Rock. Photo by Jim Thornberg

CAVE ROCK—KONA WALL

A   **Bora-Bora .11a**
B   **Kona Crack .11a**
C   **Maui Zowie .11d**
D   **Moleki .12a TR**

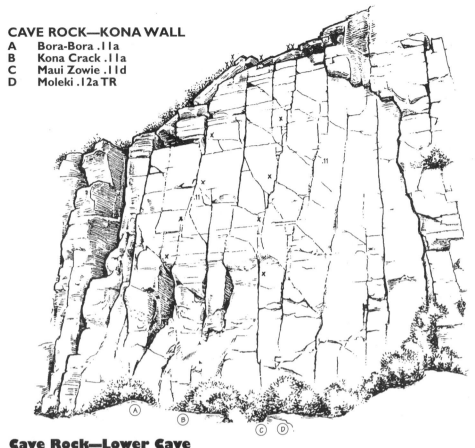

Cave Rock—Lower Cave

THE TAHOE MONSTER .10D (pro: to 4" and two bolts)

Not shown. Locate this climb up and left of *Banny's Buttress*. It is the route on the left.

THE REEF .10C (pro: to 2.5" and three bolts)

Not shown. The route to the right of *The Tahoe Monster.*

CASTLE ROCK (Not shown)

This tri-summited formation of poor-quality rock is on the hillside north of Kingsbury Grade (Nevada Highway 207). The rock is coarse and knobby, and many of the holds are friable. Two known routes climb the south face; both are about 200 feet long. Descend the north side.

To reach Castle Rock from U.S. Highway 50, drive about 2.5 miles up Kingsbury Grade, then turn left onto North Benjamin Drive and follow it to Andria Drive. Continue on Andria to the end of the pavement. Turn left on the dirt road, which leads to another dirt road rising west out of the canyon. The rock lies about 100 yards north of a grassy meadow.

CHIMNEY ROUTE .8

This route follows a chimney near the left side of the south face. A chockstone overhang is found on the first pitch.

OVERHANG ROUTE .8

This climb begins below the highest summit. From the largest boulder leaning against the wall, climb the face to a sloping belay ledge. Traverse 50 feet across a low-angle section, then climb a right-slanting crack through some small overhangs.

Pie Shop Overview

RECOMMENDED ROUTES

Face:

Short Cake .6 (slings for knobs)
Shelob's Face .9 TR
Dudley Doright .10 TR
Wind .10b
Battle Axe .11a
Buttons to Nuttin' .11b
The Last Dance .11b
Walk Like an Egyptian .11d
Bear Claw .12a
Space Invaders .12a
Jet Set .12b
Double Dragon .12d

Crack:

The Saw .5
Crepes Corner .7
Fluted Crust .7
Humble Pie .7
The Archer .8
Clean Corner .8
Hands Masseuse .8
BT Express .9
Deliverance .10
The Price Is Light .10 TR
Road House Blues .10b
True Grip .10b
Cake Walk .11b
Natural High .11c

SPACE DOMES

PIE SHOP

LUNCH ROCK

Boulders

Parking

To South Lake Tahoe

50

To Sacramento

Sawmill Road

Summit Drive

Lamor Court

Mount Canary

Twin Peaks

Echo View Estates

Boulders

N

Pie Shop

This popular crag, located about a mile south of South Lake Tahoe, was named after a roadside bake shop that sold pies below the formation. The approach is relatively short and leisurely, and the quality of the rock is good, although a bit coarse in places. Because of its sunny southern exposure, Pie Shop is one of the few areas in the Tahoe Basin where you can often climb during winter. The majority of the routes ascend knobby faces and convoluted cracks. You will also find one of the better bouldering sites around Tahoe here. There is camping, lodging, good food, and entertainment in South Lake Tahoe.

To reach Pie Shop from South Lake Tahoe, follow U.S. Highway 50 west (you are actually driving south) from the junction of US 50 and California Highway 89 (called the Y). A short distance past the airport, turn right onto Sawmill Road and continue for 0.25 mile. Park in a pullout on the left side of the road across from a couple houses. The approach trail begins to the right of the houses and heads uphill past a group of large boulders. Continue winding up a brushy slope to Lunch Rock, a large boulder with a flat top that lies near the left side of Pie Shop. From this point, the trail goes left or right, following along the base of the formation and leading to various routes.

To descend from Pie Shop, walk northwest along the top to a ravine that separates it from a similar formation. Head down the ravine, then swing right as soon as possible to reach the trail running along the base of the main face.

THE CREAM PUFF

The Cream Puff is a wild-looking, freestanding pinnacle located 100 yards uphill from *The Archer,* near the west end of Pie Shop. The following routes are on the south and west sides of this 70-foot-high formation. To descend the Cream Puff, rappel from a bolt or downclimb a scary and loose section to the east.

CREAM PUFF .7 (pro: to 3.5")
Climb a diagonal crack on the west side of the pinnacle, then move up the short face.

7-11 CRACKS .8/.10c/.10c (pro: thin)
There are three prominent cracks on the south side of the Cream Puff, below the overhanging summit block. The left crack is 5.8. The middle crack (5.10c) begins as a lie back and then widens to accept fist jams. The route continues up and right to a flake and a lunge, which gives way to larger holds and the summit block. The right-hand crack features awkward and tenuous moves (5.10c) with difficult-to-place protection. Pass through the overhang with a hand traverse and mantel. Easy face moves lead to the top.

Pie Shop: 1.Road House Blues, 2.Wind, 3. Crepes Corner, 4. Bear Claw, 5.True Grip, 6. The Slot, 7. Drop Out, 8. Hair Pie

PIE SHOP—LEFT

A   Project
B   Sugar Daddy .9
C   The Saw .5
D   Fear of Flying .9 R
E   Delicate Edge .10a TR
F   Battle Axe .11a
G   Road House Blues .10b
H   Zig-Zag Finish .10a
I   Cruise Control .8
J   Mad Wife .8 (off-width)
K   Shelob's Lair .9 R (pro: to 4")
L   Shelob's Face .9 TR
M   Cake Walk .11b (crack)
N   Jewel of the Nile .12a/b
O   Iotolla .12d
P   BT Express .9 (pro: to 2")
Q   Buttons to Nuttin' .11b
R   Unknown .9
S   The Price Is Light .10 TR
T   Wind .10b
U   Crawford's Face .10

V   Hurricane .11c TR
W   Knob Hill .7 (pro: slings)
X   Fluted Crust .7 (pro: to 2")
Y   Crepes Corner .7 (pro: to 2.5")
Z   Earn Your Wings .9 X (best to toprope)
1   Pie in the Sky .7 (pro: small)
2   Head Jammer .8 R (pro: slings)
3   Miller's Highlife .9 R
4   Teenage Wasteland .10b R
5   Pie Face Dihedral .9
6   Head East .9 R
7   Fluff Boys in Bondage .10
8   Bear Claw .12a
9   Head Up .11b
10 Deliverance .10 (pro: to 4")

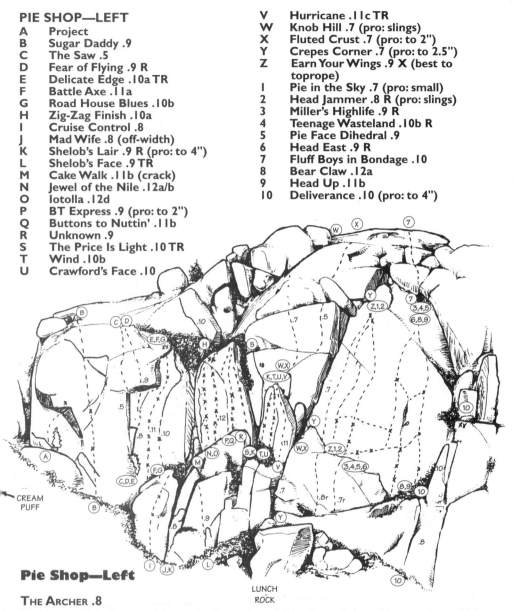

Pie Shop—Left

THE ARCHER .8

Not shown. Climb the same flake on the face as *Fear of Flying*. Then climb straight over the roof flake above, just right of *The Saw*.

CLEAN CORNER .8

Not shown. Climb the obvious clean corner to the right of *Road House Blues*.

WALK LIKE AN EGYPTIAN .11D

Not shown. Traverse from the crack to the second bolt of *Jewel of the Nile* and then continue to the top. This variation avoids the crux start of *Jewel*.

SHORT CAKE .6 (pro: slings)

Not shown. Climb the left-slanting corner beginning just left of *The Price Is Light*.

PIE SHOP—RIGHT

A	Deliverance .10 (pro: to 4")	N	The Slot .8 (pro: to 3")
B	Project	O	Humble Pie .7
C	Desiderata .10b (pro: to 1.5")	P	Hindsight .8
D	Hands Masseuse .8 (pro: to 3")	Q	Drop Out .10d (pro: to 2.5")
E	The Last Dance .11b	R	Marmot Cave .12c
F	New Blood .12a	S	Marmot Pie .8 A4 (new bolts—free
G	The Ancient Route .7		climb project?)
H	Herbert's .10c (crack)	T	Hair Pie .10c (pro: to 2")
I	Pinchin' the Lip .11b (crack to face)	U	The Walrus .8 A3 (pro: pins and
J	True Grip .10b (pro: to 2")		nuts to 2")
K	Poly Grip .11	V	Moss Pie .8 (pro: to 3")
L	Mincemeat Variation .9	W	Ambrosia .7 (pro: to 2.5")
M	Natural High .11c (traverse left	X	Altar .10d (pro: to 3")
	through a roof via a crack)	Y	Cake Walk .10 TR (arete)
		Z	Wipe Out .11a (pro: thin stoppers
			and slings)
		I	Dudley Doright .10 TR

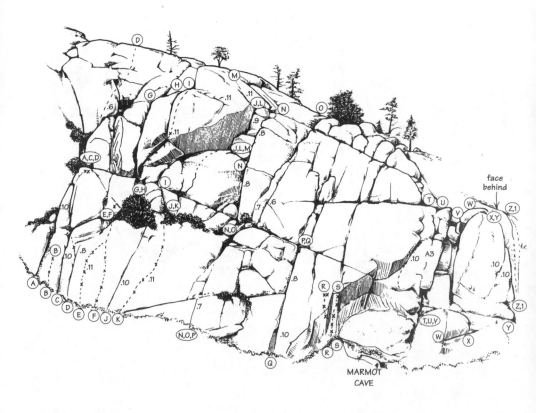

Pie Shop—Right

NO FUTURE .9 R
Not shown. Climb the crack to the face right of *Altar*.

J-WALK .7 (pro: to 2.5")
Not shown. Climb around right of *No Future*.

BURNT PIE .3 (pro: to 2")
Not shown. Climb a blunt arete to a squeeze chimney.

SIMPLE SIMON .2 (pro: to 2")
Not shown. This route follows the arch right of the pillar, which is right of *Burnt Pie*.

SPACE DOME AND SPACE INVADERS

Echo View Estates is about 2 miles down Sawmill Road from U.S. Highway 50. This area offers some outstanding bouldering. Space Dome and Space Invaders, two huge boulders, have spectacular and challenging routes. See the overview map for the exact location.

Space Dome

Space Dome is a sunny, south-facing crag with several good routes.

SPACE DOME
A   Meteor .12a
B   Jet Set .12b
C   Flight for Life .11c R
D   Fight for Life .11c R
E   Saturn III .11c R
F   Battle Star Galactica .12+ X (best to toprope)
G   The Jetsons .10 R

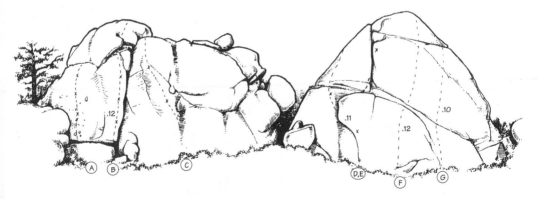

Jeff Merrifield on *Space Invaders*, 5.12a, at the Pie
Shop. Photo by Petch Peitrolungo

Space Invaders

Space Invaders is a huge, north-facing, overhanging boulder on a steep slope above a shallow gully. The climbing is thin and powerful. Medium to large cams and long slings are useful to construct anchors on top of the formation. Many variations have been climbed.

SPACE INVADERS
A America's Most Wanted .11d
B Project 5.13
C Project 5.13
D Double Dragon .12d
E Space Invaders .12a
F Sky Shark .12c
G Blaster Pals .12d
H Donkey Kong .11+ TR

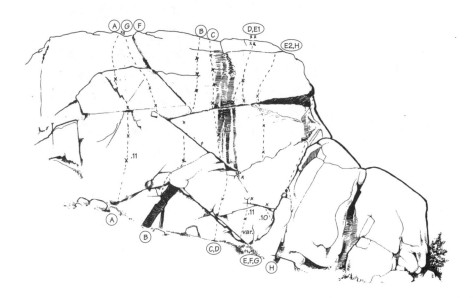

Christmas Tree Valley

Hidetaka's Hideout: 1. Deceptive Pillar, 2. Stir Fry, 3. Lady Dihedral

RECOMMENDED ROUTES

Moonshine .10c
Rockin' into the Night .10c
With Draws .11a
Loading Dose .11a/b
Deceptive Pillar .11b
Bar Fly .11b
Fallen Spirits .11c/d
Got Your Hammer Hangin' .11c/d
Seven & Seven .11c/d
Yards of Ale .11c/d

Christmas Tree Valley

There has been some outstanding new route activity in the Christmas Tree Valley. While Hidetaka's Hideout has been popular with locals for years, the Distillery Wall and Detox Wall are relatively new crags. These two walls are really the true prize of this area. Although the approach is long, the routes are fantastic and offer an escape from the more crowded areas.

HIDETAKA'S HIDEOUT

The Hideout, an obvious cluster of orange and brown granite pillars, lies on the east hillside above Christmas Tree Valley. Some excellent bouldering is under development, and you often can climb here during the winter. From U.S. Highway 50 in Meyers, drive south on California Highway 89 for 0.9 mile. Park and walk east on a dirt road that parallels the highway until you reach a faint trail. Follow it uphill to the Hideout. The approach takes about 25 minutes. Most of these routes require supplemental protection.

PLAQUE SMEAR .10c TR
Not shown. Climb the north face of a small pillar left of the main area known as the Golden Tooth.

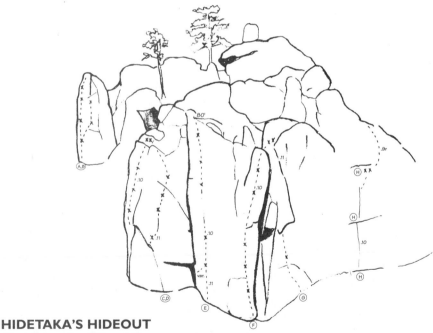

HIDETAKA'S HIDEOUT
A   **Deceptive Pillar** .11b
B   **Our Lady of Fatima** .11b
C   **Rockin' into the Night** .10c
D   **Stir Fry** .11c
E   **Larry's House** .11a (.10b variation)
F   **Ripper Arete** .10b
G   **Got Your Hammer Hangin'** .11c/d
H   **Lady Dihedral** .10a R

LUTHER ROCK AND THE SHIRE

Luther Rock, the site of recent new route activity, is part of a long formation of marginal rock above California Highway 89 about 3 miles southeast of Meyers. Although much of the rock is fragmented and poor quality, the following routes are very good. The Shire stands on the ridge up and to the right of Luther Rock. Because the majority of the rock is bad, little has been done here.

Drive south through Christmas Tree Valley. Park in the small pullout on the right about 0.9 mile past Portal Road. Cross the highway and follow an established trail east through the forest to a long talus field. Hike up the talus until even with Detox Wall. The approach takes about 45 minutes.

Distillery Wall

THE FOSSIL .11A
Not shown. Climb the left side of a steep prow, up and right of *Political Shots*.

GREYHOUND .10B (pro: mostly small)
Not shown. Climb the crack right of *Bar Fly*.

SKID ROW .9 (pro: to medium)
Not shown. Climb the obvious left-facing corner/ramp to the right of *Five Nine*.

BOTTOMS UP .9 (pro: to 3")
Not shown. Climb to the right of *Happy Hour*.

Luther Wall: 1. Seven & Seven .11c/d, 2. After Hour .12a, 4. Jonesin' .10a, 5. Loading Dose .11a/b

DISTILLERY WALL
A   Chip Shot .11b
B   Moonshine .10c
C   Seven & Seven .11c/d
      Variation: Yards of Ale .11c/d (fun link from route C to D, 20 bolts)
D   Bar Fly .11b
E   Five Nine .9+
F   After Hours .12a
G   Happy Hour .11b
H   Political Shots .11a

DETOX WALL
I   Jonesin' .10a
J   Methadone .10a
K   With Draws .11a
L   Loading Dose .11a/b
M   Fallen Spirits .11c/d
N   Straight Jacket .11d

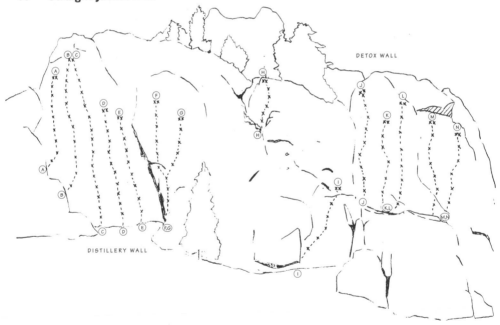

Detox Wall

This wall sits on a large ledge, which you can approach from the south (5.0) or from *Jonesin'*.

The next three routes begin on the left side of Luther Rock. The other two lines begin on the right side of the wall.

SUNSHINE SADNESS .8 (pro: mostly thin to 2")

Not shown. Begin in a short chimney about 30 feet left of two prominent right-facing dihedrals. About 15 feet up the chimney, move left onto a rounded buttress and continue up a thin crack to Sunshine Ledge, which is 50 feet above the ground. From the ledge, climb a widening crack system and overhang to a third-class area.

SUNSHINE MADNESS .10D (pro: to 2")
Not shown. Follow an overhanging crack just right of the start of *Sunshine Sadness* to Sunshine Ledge.

WARM DOWN .7 (pro: mostly thin to 2")
Not shown. Begin 30 feet right of the prominent right-facing dihedrals. To reach the base of the route, climb a fourth-class corner to a broken ledge with a fixed pin. Continue straight up some short cracks, knobs, and edges to a light-colored, right-facing corner that leads to the top.

PEARL PILLAR .10B R (pro: to 2")
Not shown. On the right side of the cliff, there are two steep pillars traversed by a 10-foot-wide band of quartz. This "loose death route" climbs the overhanging center face of the left pillar. Begin in a shallow, left-facing corner and climb 25 feet to the top of the corner, then step right and climb through the band of quartz on loose holds (with no pro) to another left-facing corner. Belay on a ledge to the right above the corner. Continue straight up the crack system and overhang to some steep cracks above.

GULLY WACKER .9 (pro: to 3")
Not shown. Climb a jam crack on the left side of the gully that separates the two previously mentioned pillars. For a 5.8 variation, climb about 100 feet up *Gully Wacker*, then follow an exposed traverse leading left to the belay ledge of *Pearl Pillar*.

Photo by Brian Biega.

Echo Lakes Overview

RECOMMENDED ROUTES

Slip 'n' Slide .7
Pay Day .7
Summer Breeze .8
The Ramp .8
Rawl Will .9
Metal Head .10a
Coin Toss .10a
Kangaroo .10b R
The Trooper .10b
Peon .10b
Gold Finger .10b
Hoser .10c
Show No Mercy .10c
Mangod .11a
Power Stance .11b
Flash the Blade .11b
Run 'n' Gun .11b
If I Had a Hammer .11b
The Crackler .11c TR
Freon .11c
Crack Babies .11c/d
Uncle Buck .11d
Gold Finger Arete .11+
Chore Boy .12a
Golden Shower .12a
A Good Day to Die .12a/b
Baby Jones .12b
Hair Trigger .12b
The Drill Press .12b
Aesop .12c R
Metallica .12d

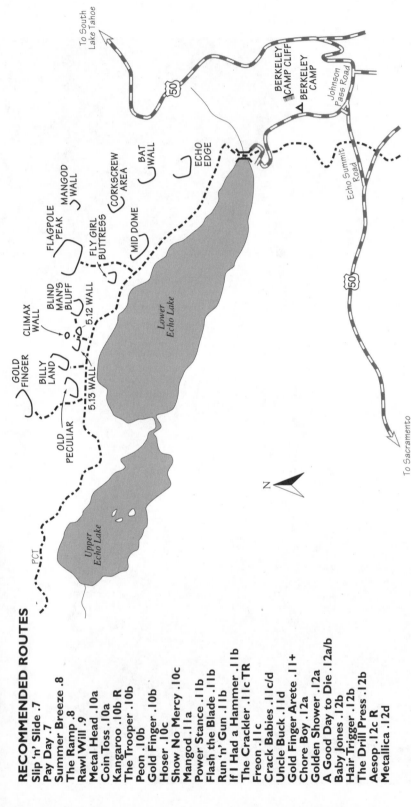

Echo Lakes

Echo Lakes rest in a granite basin northwest of U.S. Highway 50. A lodge and small marina sit at the east end of Lower Echo Lake. Rustic cabins dot the shoreline. Above the north side of the lower lake, you will find a scattered series of south-facing cliffs, small domes, and walls. The Pacific Crest Trail runs along the north edge of the lake, making the majority of the crags easily accessible. With the exception of Echo Edge and the Corkscrew Area, the rock is good, ranging from coarse-grained to clean, compact granite.

Exquisite panoramic views include Lake Tahoe and the surrounding landscape. The Desolation Wilderness lies to the south. Even with a good variety of quality routes clustered in an alpine setting, Echo Lakes does not receive a lot of traffic. The best routes require a half-hour hike from the lodge, and there are no designated camping facilities. This seems to have deterred many climbers from Echo. The area is a quiet place with good climbing and fantastic views.

To reach Echo Lakes, travel 2 miles west of Echo Summit on US 50 and turn north on Echo Summit Road. Follow this road for about 2 miles to Lower Echo Lake and park by the lodge and marina. If you are driving up from South Lake Tahoe, turn right just before Echo Summit onto Johnson Pass Road, which links up with Echo Summit Road.

To approach the climbing areas, pass over the lake's outlet and walk west along the PCT above the north shore of the lake. The first obvious cliff is Echo Edge. Flagpole Peak is the large face dominating the north skyline. The majority of formations lie in front and to either side of Flagpole Peak. See the overview map for more detailed information.

MANGOD WALL (Not shown)

Above the Meyers Grade, which climbs to Echo Summit on U.S. Highway 50, there is an obvious gray slab with a left-facing corner on its right side. This is Mangod Wall. Approach the slab by heading straight up from US 50 (parking by the gun platform beyond the first big curve), or by starting from Echo Lake and following the gap between Echo Edge and Flagpole Peak. Although the first four climbs have bolts, some additional gear may be needed. The routes are listed from left to right.

GREAT GOLDEN BEAVER .10B

MANGOD .11A

THE RIGHT HAND OF GOD .10B/C

SON OF GOD .10B/C

DIRTY DEEDS .10B
This high-country route ascends a diagonal crack splitting the center of a diamond-shaped face about 0.25 mile southeast of Echo Peak.

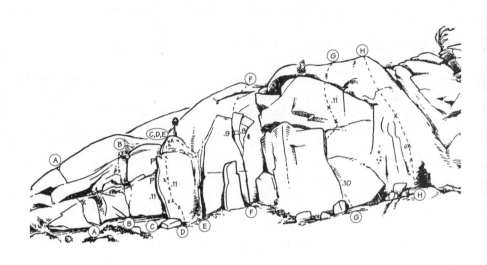

BERKELEY CAMP

A First Stage .9
B New Jersey Turnpike .11b
C Flu .11d
D Witch Doctor .12b
E Salt Water Flush .10c
F Nurse's Aid .9 A2
G Lelfie .12a (stick clip first bolt)

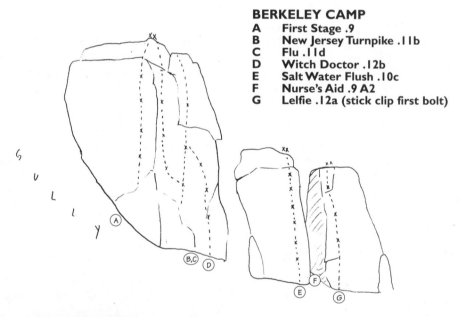

BERKELEY CAMP

This small granite crag is located on the hillside below Berkeley Camp, an old, run-down summer camp retreat. Turn off U.S. Highway 50 and drive north on Echo Summit Road for about 1 mile. To approach the crag, descend the gully east of the camp to the base of the first wall.

ECHO EDGE

A	Little Sir Echo .11+ (thin)	I	Rock-a-Bye .9 R
B	Rehumanize Yourself A3	J	Rough and Ready .8 (pro: to 2.5")
C	Bolt Race .11c	K	Bushfreak Corner .8 (pro: to 2")
D	We've Created a Monster .11b	L	Bushfreak Eliminate .9 (pro: to 2")
E	Dumbo .9 (chimney)	M	Squeeze and Wheeze .9 (pro: to 2")
F	Pitchfork .8/.9/.10	N	Metal Blade .12a
G	Mojo Hand .11	O	Blade Runner .12a R
H	EB's Wall .10b (pro: to 1.5")		

ECHO EDGE

This prominent wall is 400 yards from the lodge and just above the trail. The rock is exfoliated and rotten in many places; you will find better rock on the formations above. For the easiest descent, walk northwest to the left corner, then down third-class slabs.

BAT WALL (Not shown)

Bat Wall stands behind Echo Edge and about 100 yards down and to the right of the Corkscrew Area. This narrow buttress is traversed by a large ledge.

AFTERMATH .9 (pro: to 3.5")

Climb a flake to a wide crack above the right end of the ledge. Near the top of the crack, pass through a bulge and continue up some third-class terrain to the top.

HOLD ON LOOSELY .10c

Climb the thin crack right of *Aftermath*.

ANGRY INCH .11A

Climb right of *Hold on Loosely*.

GREEN ROOM .10B

This route is located on the backside of Bat Wall. Follow a bolted face to a thin crack.

NYE'S CORNER .9+

Also on the backside of Bat Wall. Climb to the right of *Green Room*.

CORKSCREW AREA (Not shown)

This big wall on Flagpole Peak's southeast ridge is located below the descent route. The rock is severely weathered and crumbly.

I DON'T CARE .10A R

This route is to the left of a right-facing corner right of *Leapin' Lizards.* Ascend the face past a couple knobs to a Y-shaped crack. Belay on the ledge.

LEAPIN' LIZARDS .9

This route begins on a knobby wall left of a solitary, windblown pine tree. From the left side of the wall, climb diagonally right to the largest knob on the wall. Clip a bolt and continue to the top.

SUMMER BREEZE .8 (pro: to 2")

Climb the left of three wide, parallel cracks that split the main wall. The first pitch uses the 2-inch crack inside the shallow chimney and climbs to a large ledge. Instead of continuing straight up, climb the zigzag crack on the left wall.

BOPPY'S CRACK .8 (pro: to 3")

This line takes the middle of the three parallel cracks. Jam twin cracks to a large ledge, then follow an easy corner to the top.

CORKSCREW .7 (pro: to 3")

Climb the right of the three parallel cracks. Follow the knobby chimney for about 100 feet. A left-facing corner capped by a roof leads to the top.

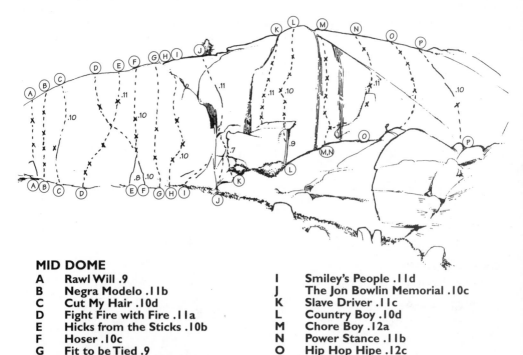

MID DOME

A	Rawl Will .9	I	Smiley's People .11d
B	Negra Modelo .11b	J	The Jon Bowlin Memorial .10c
C	Cut My Hair .10d	K	Slave Driver .11c
D	Fight Fire with Fire .11a	L	Country Boy .10d
E	Hicks from the Sticks .10b	M	Chore Boy .12a
F	Hoser .10c	N	Power Stance .11b
G	Fit to be Tied .9	O	Hip Hop Hipe .12c
H	Puppet Master .10a/b	P	Black Panther .10b

MID DOME

This low-profile dome of clean, compact granite is located above the PCT. Mid Dome has some of the finest face climbing in the Echo Lakes area. To descend, walk off the northwest side.

TOPROPE .9

Not shown. Climb the face to the right of *Black Panther.*

RIGHT PARALLEL CRACK .10A

Not shown. Climb the obvious right-slanting crack up and right of Mid Dome.

FLAGPOLE PEAK

This 8,363-foot-high peak, the massive formation on the north skyline, is located about 1 mile from the lodge. Flagpole Peak includes the largest cliff face in the Echo Lakes area. The quality of the rock improves with altitude.

To reach the base of the wall, hike along the PCT until you reach the main face (about 0.75 mile from the parking area). Hike up the hillside toward the peak. To descend, walk down the southeast ridge for several hundred feet (some third class), then scramble down boulders and slabs toward the lake.

SAMURAI PSYCHOLOGIST .10A

Not shown. This two-pitch route climbs the left skyline and out the right side of a roof.

SLIP 'N' SLIDE .7 (pro: to 1")

Not shown. Begin near the center of a 400-foot-high slab, high on the northeast face of Flagpole Peak. Climb a long, shallow, right-facing corner to a belay ledge. Move up and left to a right-slanting seam near the end of the pitch, then step left to a dihedral. The final pitch heads up and right around a corner to a fourth-class gully, which leads to the top.

5.12 WALL

This trailside wall is packed with quality routes on excellent rock. Although short, the routes represent some of the best crack climbs in the area. The hike takes 20 to 30 minutes.

UNNAMED .9

Not shown. Climb the crack right of *Corner Pocket.*

5.13 WALL (Not shown)

This superb face stands to the left of 5.12 Wall.

TEMPEST .11C

This line starts just right of center. Climb a corner straight up to a flake and Y-shaped crack.

CHEMICAL WARFARE .10B

Climb a left-facing flake past some face moves to another flake on the right side of the wall.

GERM WARFARE .11B TR

Follow a longer flake right of *Chemical Warfare,* then finish with some face climbing. Send it!

FLAGPOLE PEAK

A   If I Had a Hammer .11b
B   Downward Bound .8
C   Monkey Cam .11b (pro: thin to medium)
D   The Ramp .8 (pro: to 3")
E   Kangaroo .10b R (pro: to 4")
F   Jam Session .10a (pro: to 4")
G   Crystalline Dream .9+ (pro: to 4")
H   Grin and Bare It .10a (pro: to 4.5")

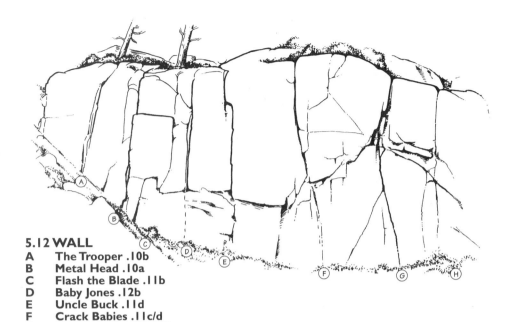

5.12 WALL
A   The Trooper .10b
B   Metal Head .10a
C   Flash the Blade .11b
D   Baby Jones .12b
E   Uncle Buck .11d
F   Crack Babies .11c/d
G   The Crackler .11c TR
H   Corner Pocket .11b TR

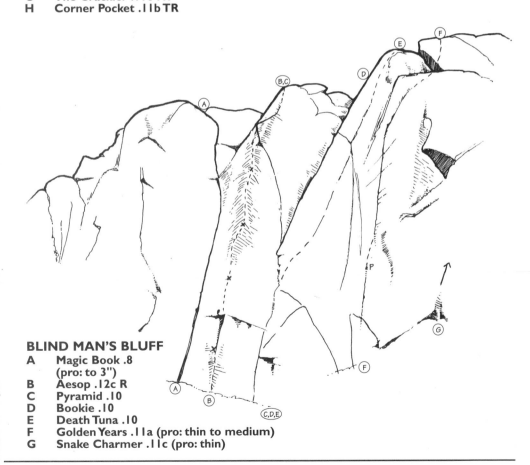

BLIND MAN'S BLUFF
A   Magic Book .8
     (pro: to 3")
B   Aesop .12c R
C   Pyramid .10
D   Bookie .10
E   Death Tuna .10
F   Golden Years .11a (pro: thin to medium)
G   Snake Charmer .11c (pro: thin)

BLIND MAN'S BLUFF

Follow the PCT past the west end of Flagpole Peak and the switchbacks to reach some large boulders and a cliff. Blind Man's Bluff is the small cliff high on the hillside with two striking corners on its face. The rock is good. To descend, hike down the north side to the trail.

SLITHERING SLIT .5
Not shown. This obvious chimney is left of Magic Book.

CLIMAX WALL (Not shown)

This crag lies uphill from 5.12 Wall. There are three good routes and the potential for many more.

SYMO .11B/C
Ascend a right-facing flake right of a corner, then past some fixed pins and a bolt to the top.

HAIR TRIGGER .12B
This route is just right of *Symo*. Climb a flake and face past two bolts, then up a crack protected by three bolts. The crux is at the top.

SANITARIUM .11B
This route is on a boulder to the far right. Climb up a corner to a splitting crack.

METALLICA .12D
This route is high on the hill above Climax Wall and east of Gold Finger. Run up an arete past four bolts on a concave boulder.

BILLY LAND

This dome lies just above the trail and past 5.13 Wall. The rock and the routes are good.

BILLY LAND

A 3-D .11b
B Run 'n' Gun .11b
C Hit and Run .7
D Coin Toss .10a
E Pay Day .7
F Easy Meat .6

Psycho Path .11a

Not shown. This route climbs by the obvious black streak up a right-curving crack followed by bolts. Begin on the slab left of 3-D.

OLD PECULIAR

This cliff, which sports a number of excellent routes, lies west of Billy Land and a couple hundred yards above the PCT. Old Peculiar is distinguished by a large cedar tree standing in front of the crag.

GOLD FINGER

This superb cliff is worth the hour hike. The granite is golden and compact, and the views from the top are spectacular. All of the routes are quality. To reach Gold Finger, follow a faint trail uphill past the left side of Old Peculiar, then third class past a section of slabs and brush to the base of the cliff. To descend, walk off to the west, then back toward Echo Lake.

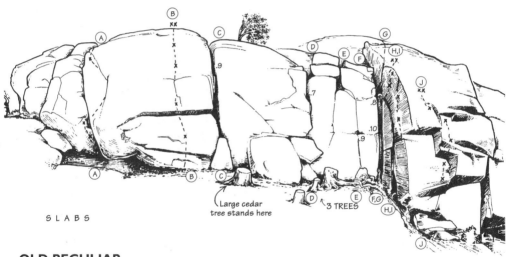

OLD PECULIAR
A Hanus Anus .11b
B Sun and Steel .11c
C Offwidth Their Heads .9 (pro: to 4")
D Sayonara .7 (pro: to 2")
E Yodeler .9 (pro: to 2")
F Old Peculiar .8 (pro: to 3.5")
G Knee On .10b (pro: to 5")
H Freon .11c
I Peon .10b
J The Drill Press .12b

Dave Hatchett on *Testament*, 5.11c, Gold Finger at Echo Lakes. Photo by M. Carville.

GOLD FINGER

A	Rage for Order	.11b
B	Testament	.11c
C	Show No Mercy	.10c
D	A Good Day to Die	.12a/b
E	Fool's Gold	.11a
F	Golden Shower	.12a
G	Gold Finger	.10b
H	Gold Finger Arete	.11+
I	Mind's Eye	.11a
J	Odd Job	.11d TR

Lover's Leap Overview

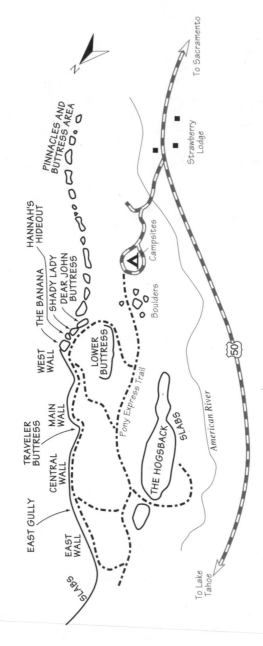

SLABS

EAST GULLY

TRAVELER BUTTRESS

MAIN WALL

CENTRAL WALL

EAST WALL

WEST WALL

THE BANANA

SHADY LADY

DEAR JOHN BUTTRESS

HANNAH'S HIDEOUT

PINNACLES AND BUTTRESS AREA

LOWER BUTTRESS

Pony Express Trail

THE HOGSBACK

SLABS

Boulders

Campsites

American River

50

Strawberry Lodge

To Sacramento

To Lake Tahoe

N

RECOMMENDED ROUTES

Deception .6
Pop Bottle .6
East Wall .6
Harvey's Wallbanger .6-.8
Bear's Reach .7
Corrugation Corner .7
Lady Bug .7
Haystack .8
Anesthesia .8 (first pitch)

East Crack .8
West Wall .8 (chimney)
April Fools .9 R
Fantasia .9 R
The Line .9
Eagle Buttress right .9
Traveler Buttress .9
Showtime .10a (first pitch)
Hospital Corner .10a

God of Thunder .10a (first pitch)
Showtime .11c
Main Line .11c
Anesthesia .11c
Stony God .11d/.12a
Fight the Power .12a
Unknown Soldier .12b
Stone Cold Crazy .12c
Silly Willy Crack .12c

146

Lover's Leap

From U.S. Highway 50, the sheer walls of Lover's Leap appear formidable and devoid of holds. This inspiring cliff is more than 0.5 mile wide and rises 350 feet on the east end and almost 600 feet near the west end. Lover's Leap is unique because the cliff is streaked with horizontal dikes that make the nearly impossible sections of rock climbable at relatively moderate grades. While dikes are not rare in the Sierra, the Leap has more than its fair share.

The dikes were formed long ago when molten rock was forced through horizontal fractures in the cliff face. The molten material solidified and, being rich in feldspar and quartz, eroded more slowly than the surrounding granite. The result? Generally positive edges (dikes) range from a fraction of an inch to over 8 inches in width. Please note that pieces break from the dikes occasionally and can cause dangerous falls. While the Leap includes climbs of all difficulties, the majority of routes settle in between 5.6 and 5.10.

Superb rock, easy access, short approaches, and free camping make Lover's Leap a popular and enjoyable place to climb. On summer weekends, expect the campground to be full and many of the classic routes to have waiting lines. However, the Leap is a big place, and solitude usually can be found on the less popular lines, many of which are classics in their own right.

Lover's Leap is located just off US 50 behind the community of Strawberry, about 18 miles southwest of Lake Tahoe and 40 miles east of Placerville. To find the campground and the trailhead for the approach, turn off US 50 at the Strawberry Lodge and continue slowly toward the cliff on the small road. At the fork, stay left; then continue until you reach the campground. Please abide by all campground rules and regulations and be sensitive to the rights of property owners. The Strawberry Lodge offers hearty meals and hot showers for a reasonable fee.

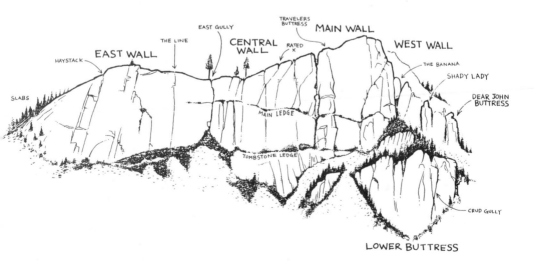

MAIN WALL

WEST WALL

DEAR JOHN
BUTTRESS

LOWER BUTTRESS

MAIN
LEDGE

CENTRAL WALL

EAST WALL

THE
HOGSBACK

Lover's Leap

To reach the base of Lover's Leap, follow the trail that begins at the northeast end of the campground and hike past several large boulders to an old road, which is a remnant of the Pony Express Trail. Several small trails exit the road and lead to different sections of the cliff. A trail also contours along the base of the wall. Please refer to the overview map for more detailed information.

Lover's Leap is divided into four main areas: East Wall, Central Wall, Main Wall, and West Wall. The Lower Buttress is the obvious but separate cliff below West Wall. The Leap also includes several smaller formations.

Main Ledge bisects Central and Main Walls and accesses routes on the upper wall. Main Ledge runs from near the west end of the cliff to the right-hand corner of Eagle Buttress. From here, a scary and loose 5.9 traverse connects the final portion of Main Ledge, which extends past the *Bookmark*. Main Ledge can be reached by scrambling up the talus slope and following the trail below Main Wall or by climbing any of the routes that begin at the base of West Wall.

To descend from the routes on top of the Leap, follow a trail winding eastward through the forest. Be sure to stay on this trail, not the trail leading south from the top of West Wall. Near the east end of the descent trail, you will reach a small spring. Below the spring, the trail veers left down a series of switchbacks to a long slabby section of rock. At the bottom of the slabs, the trail continues through the trees back to Pony Express Road.

The American River runs alongside Lover's Leap. There are many peaceful spots to swim, relax, and take in the sun. Just up US 50 near Twin Bridges, Pyramid Creek Trail enters the Desolation Wilderness, one of the most spectacular alpine environments in California. A local store and gas station offer limited groceries and supplies. South Lake Tahoe is a large town, a half hour east up US 50.

Don't miss the opportunity to climb at Lover's Leap. The tremendous beauty of the area, the outrageous nature of the climbing, and the wide range of difficulty levels make the Leap one of the most unique and popular areas in California.

EAST WALL

Several of the notable routes on the East Wall deserve more extensive descriptions.

POP BOTTLE .6 (pro: to 2.5")

This route begins on the far left side of East Wall at a 30-foot-high flake that vaguely resembles a "pop bottle." Climb the right edge of the pop bottle and belay on a narrow ledge. Move left and up a shallow right-facing corner, past a white scar and through a break in some ceilings, to a large ledge. The final pitch ascends the arete edge of *East Corner* past a bolt and up the slabs above. Descend third class to the left.

HAYSTACK CRACK .8 (pro: to 2")

This classic route follows a long, intermittent right-facing dihedral with a prominent 4-foot-wide roof about halfway up. Climb a long pitch that begins in a corner and finishes as a crack leading to a good belay ledge. Then continue straight up and over a roof—the crux—staying in the corner system to the top. A third-class traverse pitch offers an escape left from the end of the third pitch.

FANTASIA .9 R (pro: to 2.5" and slings for knobs)

This is an exceptionally beautiful line, thought by many to be one of the finest climbs at the Leap. It is committing, with several long, runout sections and minimal protection in places. Climb the face below a prominent arch to a corner beneath a roof, then move left via a hand traverse until you can continue up. Pull the right side of a small lip and climb the face above on gray knobs to a horizontal flake with a bolt and a pin. Belay from here. The next pitch ascends a concave headwall on dikes and knobs to a belay ledge high above. Step left past the overlapping corners to a small overhang. At the first opportunity, mantel the overhang and continue up. From the belay, escape left or move up the slabs over a small roof and then diagonal right to a pale wall. Step left and climb to the top.

EAST CRACK .8 (pro: to 2.5")

This route merges with several other lines on Bushy Ledge, a small ledge about 300 feet above the ground. There are no bushes on this ledge. Follow two prominent parallel cracks past a couple of small roofs to a ledge on the left. Continue up the cracks over some bulges and ceilings until you reach Bushy Ledge. Climb straight up or traverse right to obvious lie-back flakes. Both options lead to a ledge just left of the lie-back flakes. From this point, head up and right on the dike to a ramp and the top.

BEAR'S REACH .7 (pro: to 2.5")

This is another classic of the area. The climb begins slightly right of Bushy Ledge. Ascend a right-facing flake to another flake—these are linked by a couple of face moves on sloping dikes. Climb a long flake system to a good belay ledge. Climb a crack to some balance moves on fragile flakes. Then it's on to a ceiling (the "bear's reach" move) and up a fantastic flake-and-corner system to Bushy Ledge. Proceed to the top from Bushy Ledge via the description given under *East Crack*.

EAST WALL .6 (pro: to 2.5")

This enjoyable and popular route offers some of the finest dike-hiking imaginable. Begin in a large, right-facing dihedral near the center of the East Wall. Belay from the top of the dihedral on a great ledge. Then climb a large flake and follow the crack above a short ways until you can easily traverse left to a small belay stance with a horn. Make a wild and exposed traverse farther left on dikes to Bushy Ledge. Continue to the top via the description under *East Crack*.

THE LINE .9 (pro: to 2.5")

This route is one of the finest crack climbs of its grade anywhere. Ascend the obvious plumb-line crack that drops from the summit overhangs just right of center on East Wall. The first pitch involves some face moves to reach the crack, then demands continuous lie-backing and jamming. From a small belay stance, climb a mix of flakes, cracks, and small corners to a poor belay ledge below the summit overhangs. The exit moves through the overhangs are exciting and exposed—a fitting end to a spectacular climb.

East Wall—Left

MDA .9 R (pro: to 2")

Not shown. This route traverses through all the first belay stances on East Wall from left to right.

HIGH TOUR .9 (pro: to 2")

Not shown. This route traverses through all the second belay stances on East Wall from left to right.

HAY FEVER .11B

Not shown. This line runs up a series of roofs between the last pitches of *Haystack* and *Fear No Evil*.

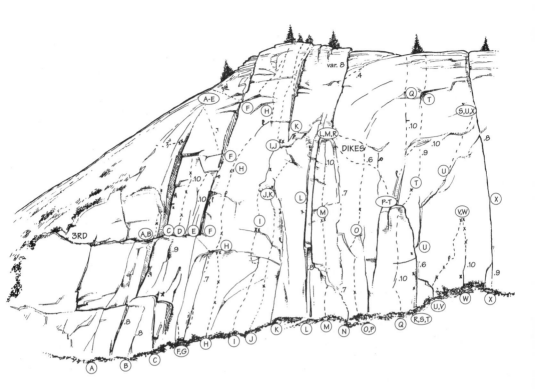

EAST WALL—LEFT

A	Pop Bottle .6 (pro: to 2.5") See previous description of notable routes.	*5/12/02 L*
B	Far East .9 R (pro: to 1")	
C	East Corner .9 (pro: to 2") The crack in side wall on second pitch is 5.10d.	
D	Out to Lunge .10d R (pro: tiny to 0.5")	
E	Rednecks .9+ (pro: to 1.5")	
F	Haystack .8 (pro: to 2")	
G	Preparation H (pro: to 2")	
H	Fear No Evil .9 R (pro: to 2")	
I	Fantasia .9 R (pro: to 2.5" and slings)	
J	The Last Sandwich .10b R (pro: to 2")	
K	Scimitar .9 R (pro: to 2")	
L	East Crack .8 (pro: to 2.5") See previous description of notable routes.	
M	Between the Lines .10a	
N	Bear's Reach .7 (pro: to 2.5") See previous description of notable routes.	*2001 with Ben*
O	Ham Sandwich .9 R	
P	Horn Blower .8 (pro: to 2.5")	
Q	Pigs on the Wing .10a X (pro: to 1.5" and slings)	
R	East Wall .6 (pro: to 2.5") See previous description of notable routes.	
S	Flying Circus .10a R (pro: to 3")	
T	Fireworks .9 R (pro: to 2.5")	
U	Bad Moon Rising .10c R (pro: to 2", Friends)	
V	Easier Said Than Done .10d (pro: to 2", Friends)	
W	End of the Line .10c	
X	The Line .9 (pro: to 2.5") See previous description of notable routes.	

N - lead with Vince 8/7/02

East Wall: 1. Haystack, 2. Fantasia, 3. East Crack, 4. Bear's Reach, 5. East Wall, 6. The Line, 7. Psychedelic, 8. Bookmark

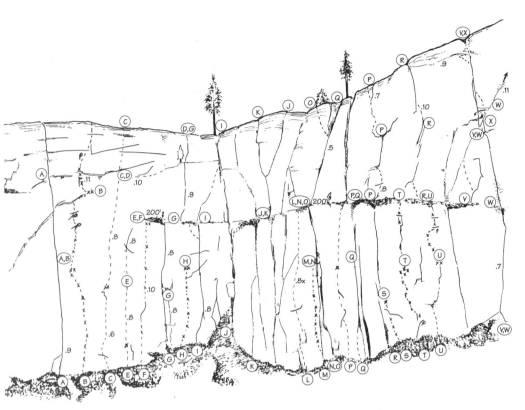

EAST WALL—RIGHT

A   The Line .9 (pro: to 2.5")

B   Showtime .11c (first pitch, *Labor of Love* .10a.; last pitch, serious)

C   A Few Dollars More .10 R (pro: to 2")

D   Deviate .10 R (pro: to 2")

E   Mystery Route .8R

F   Psychedelic Direct .10a R (pro: to 3")

G   Psychedelic Tree .9 (pro: to 2.5")

H   Unknown

I   Fandango .9 (pro: to 2")

J   East Gully .6 (pro: to 3") Begin where Main Wall meets East Wall. A long, muggy pitch leads to Main Ledge. Move to a ramp with a crack in the corner. The final pitch requires the negotiation of a chockstone ceiling.

K   Paramour .9 (pro: to 3") This route is a bushwhack. Climb the first crack right of *East Gully*, making 5.9 moves to avoid the bushy sections. Belay on a ledge atop a left-facing corner. Follow the gully to Main Ledge. Climb a 3-inch crack to a left-facing book that terminates at the rim.

L   Sky Rocket .8 (pro: to 2")

M   D.O.A. .11b (pro: thin and bolts)

N   Bastard Child .8 (pro: to 2.5")

O   Lover's Chimney .5 (pro: to 3")

P   Sudden Death .8 R (pro: to 2")

Q   Bookmark .7 (pro: to 3")

R   Incubus .10b X (pro: to 2")

S   Unknown

T   Glaze Her Face .11a A0 (pro: to 2")

U   Unknown Soldier .12b

V   Rated X Direct .11b R

W   Rated X .11a

X   Tic-Tic-Tic .11a

CENTRAL WALL

A	Unknown
B	Eagle's Highway .8 R (pro: to 0.5" and slings)
C	Roofer Madness .10c (pro: to 2")
D	Eagle Buttress Left .8 (pro: to 3")
E	Eagle Buttress Right .9 (pro: to 3")
F	More Madness .11b
G	Carpal Tunnel Syndrome .10b (pro: to 2.5")
H	Flying High .10c (pro: to 3")
I	Excelsior .10a (pro: to 3")
J	East of Eeyore .8
K	Dirty Dihedral .12a TR
L	AZ Route
M	The Hourglass .11a (pro: to 3") A variation exists that is loose and scary. After the first pitch, climb the left side crack, then traverse across the face when possible to the upper pitch of *East of Eeyore*.
N	Hourglass Wall .11c A0 (pro: to 3")
O	Unknown .11c
P	Approach Pitch .7
Q	Eeyore's Ecstasy .7 (pro: to 3") Ascend the deep and prominent chimney system between *The Hourglass* and *Traveler Buttress*.

MAIN WALL

R	Eeyore's Enigma .10a (pro: to 4" and larger) This scary route ascends the large corner via a squeeze chimney on the outside edge.
S	Under the Big Top .10d (pro: to 4" plus many wireds and Friends) Traverse right for two pitches under a large roof.
T	Out the Big Top A3
U	Epitaph .10c (pro: to 2")
V	Freak Show .11c/d
W	R.I.P. .11d
X	Tombstone Terror .10c (pro: to 2.5")
Y	Boothill .11a
Z	Traveler Buttress .9 (pro: to 3.5 inches) See following description of notable routes.
1	Dead Pool .11c (pro: thin)
2	Silly Willy Crack .12c (crack on the side wall)
3	Purple Haze .10d (pro: to 2.5")
	Variation: Cross Town Traffic .11a (roof crack)
4	Corrugation Corner .7 (pro: to 2.5")
5	Power Lust .11a
6	Up from the Skies .10d R (pro: to 2.5")
7	North Face .11 (pro: to 2.5")
8	Batman's Nightmare .12a
9	Wall Flower .10a (.10c variation; pro: to 3")
10	Stem Mister .10a (pro: thin to medium)
11	Yankee Dog .11 (pro: to 1")
12	Dragon Back .10b
13	Cheap Shot .10a
14	North Country .10 (pro: to 3")
15	The Slash .9
16	Bombs Away .10b R (pro: small wireds to 4")
17	Arrowroot .10c (pro: to 3.5")
18	Arctic Breeze .10a
19	Unknown .10d
20	Youthful Exuberance .10c (pro: to 2")
21	Main Line .11c (pro: to 2.5")
22	Magnum Force .10b (pro: to 1.5")
23	Project

MAIN WALL

CENTRAL WALL

WEST WALL

MAIN LEDGE

1. Bookmark, 2. Rated X, 3. Eagle Buttress Right, 4. The Hourglass, 5. Tombstone Terror, 6. Traveler Buttress, 7. The Slash, 8. Main Line, 9. Hospital Corner

MAIN WALL (CORRUGATION CORNER AREA)

Several of the notable routes at the Main Wall deserve more extensive descriptions.

TRAVELER BUTTRESS .9 (pro: full range)

This famous route, featured in the book *Fifty Classic Climbs of North America,* takes the longest line at the Leap. The route begins on Tombstone Ledge. Climb the leftmost of two parallel flake/cracks to some ceilings that may be turned to the right or to the left. Continue to Main Ledge. This pitch may be climbed as a single long one, or a belay is possible beneath the ceilings. From the ledge, climb a strenuous 5.9 chimney/jam crack. Move right from the top of the crack and belay at the base of a ramp. Proceed up a face and turn an exposed arete, moving up and left to a ledge near a rib on the right. From here, two more pitches of splendid dike climbing lead to the top.

CORRUGATION CORNER .7 (pro: to 2.5"; .8/.9 variation)

This popular route ascends the beautiful corner that forms the right side of Traveler Buttress. From Main Ledge, head up the large corner, move left past a ceiling, and then slant right to a small belay ledge in the main corner. Climb in the corner for a short ways, then slant left to some cracks. Follow these to a sloping ledge at the base of a chimney. Climb the chimney until it narrows, then traverse right across the wall on a dike to the main corner. Climb the corner to its end, then up to a dike belay. A steep but easy pitch leads to the top.

MAIN WALL
(CORRUGATION CORNER AREA)

A   **Under the Big Top .10d (pro: to 4" plus many wireds and Friends)**
B   **Traveler Buttress .9 (pro: to 3.5") See previous description of notable routes.**
C   **Purple Haze .10d (pro: to 2.5") The roof crack is a variation of *Cross Town Traffic*.**
D   **Crash Landing .10a**
E   **Big Thunder .12a**
F   **Corrugation Corner .7 (pro: to 2.5") See previous description of notable routes.**
G   **Power Lust .11a**
H   **Up from the Skies .10d (pro: to 2.5")**
I   **Batman's Nightmare .12a**
J   **Wall Flower .10a (.10c variation; pro: to 3")**
K   **North Face .11 (pro: to 2.5")**
L   **Stem Mister .10a (pro: thin to medium)**
M   **Yankee Dog .11d (pro: to 1")**

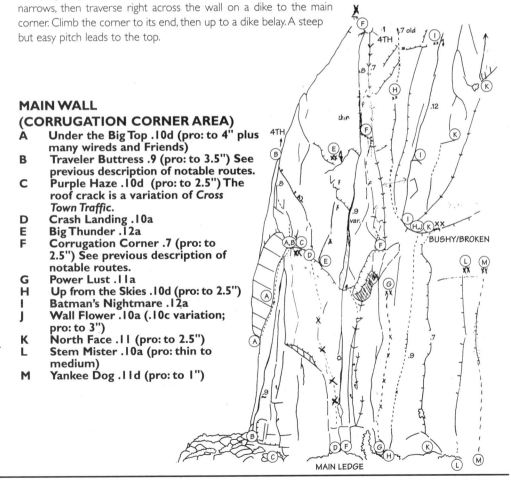

MAIN LEDGE

WEST WALL

THE BOWL FOURTH CLASS
Not shown. Wander through mostly fourth class and end at the slash formation.

DEAR JOHN BUTTRESS

Dear John Buttress lies between West Wall and Lower Buttress. A high concentration of difficult climbs are located on its east face, which is concealed by trees. To descend, walk north off the summit.

The following four routes are located to the left of *Hushed Passage* and are listed from left to right.

SINBAD TAKES A TAXI .10c (pro: to 2")
Not shown. Climb the hand crack and traverse left under a roof. Continue to a two-bolt anchor.

SKISM .11c
Not shown. Face and arete climb past five bolts (tricky) to the two-bolt anchor on the previous route.

GODS OF PLUNDER .8 (pro: to 3.5")
Not shown. Just right of the arete, climb the face past a bolt to a crack that leads to the top.

BROTHER JOHN .8 (pro: to 3")
Not shown. Climb the face past a bolt and follow the wide crack to the top.

SHADY LADY

This small formation is located above Dear John Buttress. The best approach is from the trail that runs along the base of West Wall. Descend via the easy gully on the left or continue uphill from Dear John Buttress.

SHADY LADY .8
This obvious curvy crack splits the face.

DIRTY HARRY .9 (pro: to 2")
Ascend the crack in the corner on the left side of the buttress.

THE SICKLE .8 (pro: to 3")
Follow the sickle-shaped crack on the buttress.

HANNAH'S HIDEOUT
Hannah's lies uphill and right of Shady Lady.

PINNACLES AND BUTTRESS AREA

The Pinnacles and Buttress Area is located about 0.25 mile west of Lover's Leap. As you pass over the bridge in Strawberry, you can see this area straight ahead and up the hill.

The Box

To reach this obscure buttress, diagonal across from the campground, but be careful not to cut across private property.

MANZANITA EXIT .8
Climb straight up the crack on the lower side of the buttress.

4TH

SLASH

.10r

.10
fist

120'

BOWL

.9

.10

.8

.8

.8r

.10

MULTI
STARTS

.10

.11

WEST WALL

A   Main Line .11c (pro: to 2.5")
B   Magnum Force .10b (pro: to 1.5")
C   The Slash .9
D   Bombs Away .10b R (pro: small wireds to 4")
E   Arrowroot .10c (pro: to 3.5")
F   Al Tahoe .9 R
G   Arctic Breeze .10a
H   Unknown .10d A bolted arete with two short pitches and two-bolt anchors.
I   Youthful Exuberance .10c (pro: to 2")
J   West Wall .8 (pro: to 4") Ascend the 5.8 crack to a chimney with a roof on the left side of a giant dihedral. Another pitch leads to the slash.
K   Crazy Daze .9 (pro: to 3") This variation ascends the other chimney past a ceiling, then rejoins West Wall after the first pitch.
L   Hospital Corner .10a (pro: to 1.5") Ascend the dihedral for two pitches.
M   The Gamoke .9 (pro: to 2")
N   The Last Laugh .10 (pro: to 2") Follows crack system.
O   Anesthesia .11c (pro: to 2")
P   April Fools .9 R (pro: to 3")
Q   Dead Tree Direct .7 (pro: to 3") Best exit pitch to reach the top.
R   Craven Image .7 (pro: to 3")
S   Lady Bug .7 (pro: to 3")
T   The Clonedike .9 Cracks lead to some face climbing to a two-bolt anchor.
U   Captain Coconuts .10a (pro: thin wireds for first pitch.) Face climb left of the obvious corner/crack to the same two-bolt anchor as The Clonedike.
V   Vanishing Point .10c (pro: to 4") Climb the wide right-facing corner/crack and belay at the first bolt. Continue up past a wide overhang and belay near the top of the crack above. It is possible to escape the wide overhang by traversing left to the bolted anchors on Captain Coconuts.
W   Ozzie .10a (pro: thin wireds) Climb the face right of Vanishing Point.
X   Third Stone from the Sun .10c (pro: to 4") A right-facing corner. Traverse left out of the main corner (5.9) just below the top of the pitch.
Y   Here We Go Again .10c (pro: thin and bolts) Climb cracks to the obvious face climb.
Z   The Banana .8 (pro: to 3") Route on the left side of a giant block.
1   Sinbad .10a R (pro: thin to 2")
2   Shorts Only .8 (pro: to 3") Route on the right side of a giant block.

DEAR JOHN BUTTRESS

A   Hushed Passage .10 (arete)
B   God of Thunder .11b/c (pro: to 5"; .9 and .10 starts)
C   Fight the Power .12a (pro: to 2")
D   Stone Cold Crazy .12c (pro: thin)
E   Drug Crazed .11c
F   Stony End .11c
G   Stony Highway .11c
H   Stony God .11d/12a Climb the first pitch of route **A** and the second half of route **C**.

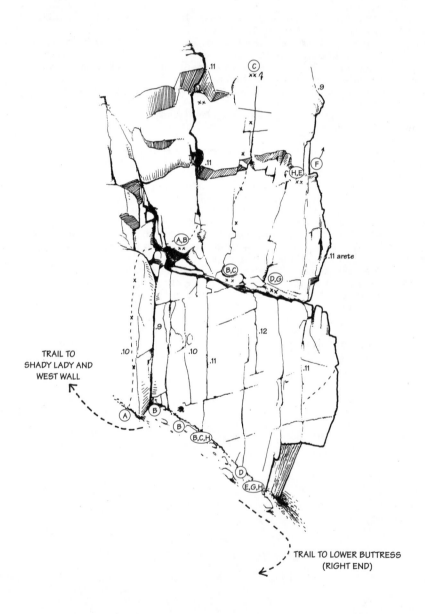

The Box (con't)

HANDS ACROSS THE WATER .8
This two-pitch route is on the right side of the buttress. Climb a roof to a ledge that lies a full pitch up. Next, ascend the obvious flake leaning against the face.

ENDLESS PLIGHT .11A
Begin on the ledge that splits the lower and upper buttress. To the right and around the corner, climb a shallow groove that requires balance moves and difficult-to-place protection. Beautiful roof moves lead to a crack that finishes with a hand traverse.

HANNAH'S HIDEOUT
A   **Lisa's Wire .3**
B   **Jim's Wire .7 (pro: to 3")**
C   **Hannah's Hideout .10a**
      (pro: to 0.5", bolts)
D   **White Scar .12b**
E   **Code Name Daisy .11a**
      (pro: to 1", bolts)

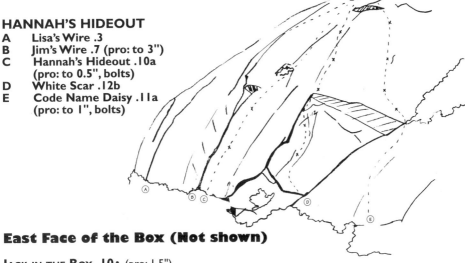

East Face of the Box (Not shown)

JACK IN THE BOX .10A (pro: 1.5")
Climb the diagonal crack on the east face of the Box.

Lower East Face of the Box (at the toe of the buttress) (Not shown)

SPECIAL K .7 (pro: four bolts to a two-bolt belay)

FRUIT LOOPS .7 (pro: to 1")
Left of *Special K.*

SNAP, CRACKLE, POP .5
Exact location unknown. Look for an obvious line.

COCO ROOS .5
Exact location unknown. Look for an obvious line.

West Face of the Box (Not shown)

SINBAD'S HIGH SEA SIMULATOR A2+ (pro: rurps, blades, and small angles)
Around arete and left of *Big Drive.*

BIG DRIVE .10A (pro: to 1" and a fixed pin)
Climb the crack on the west face.

THE BOX

A   Schnauzer .11a (bolts) Arete direct to *Optimator*.
B   Optimator .11a (pro: 0.5", bolts)
C   Endless Plight .11a (pro: 1.5")
D   Dog Party .12a (pro: thin to 2" and many TCUs)
E   Power Box .12b
F   Box Boy .8 (pro: thin to 3", bolts)
G   Box Envy .11b (pro: thin to 3", bolts)
H   Magic Box .11d (pro: thin and bolts)

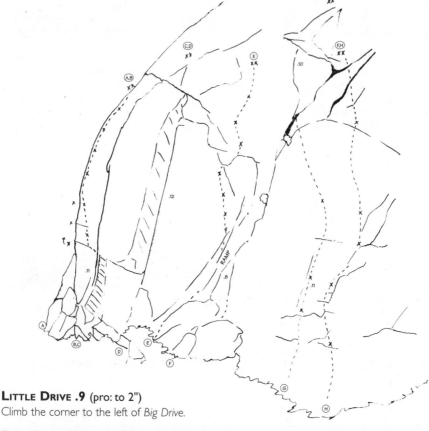

LITTLE DRIVE .9 (pro: to 2")

Climb the corner to the left of *Big Drive*.

DEEP SPACE PROJECT .10B (pro: to 3"; two pitches)

From the northeast toe of the buttress, climb left up a hand crack on the side wall. Continue up a shallow dihedral left of the arete. Two pitches.

Mountain Surf Wall (Not shown)

This formation is farther west of the Box. Currently, two quality routes ascend the obvious overhanging face.

GIDGET TAKES OFF .12B (pro: thin to 0.5" and bolts).

Climb the flake through the overhang.

MOUNTAIN SURF

This is currently a project. When completed, climb from the first bolt on *Gidget*, traverse right into an arching crack, and then continue up the overhanging face above.

Petch Pietrolungo on an early ascent of *Endless Plight*, 5.11a, The Box at Lover's Leap. Photo by Steve Strosheim.

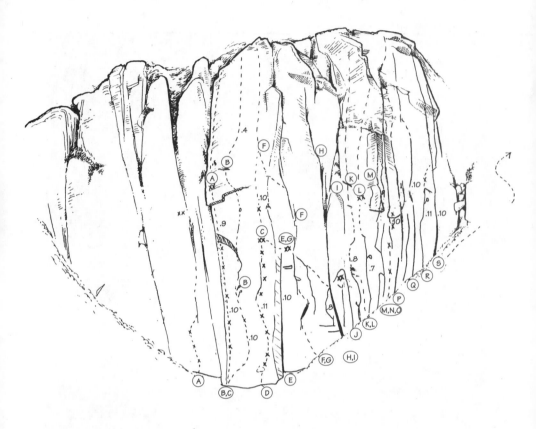

LOWER BUTTRESS

A   Unknown
B   Sinbad's Arete .10d
C   Piece of Mind .11d R (pro: tiny to 1")
D   Pillar of Society .12a This broken dike may be more difficult.
E   Surrealistic Pillar Direct .10a (pro: to 3"; .10c variation)
F   Surrealistic Pillar .7 (pro: to 3")
G   Jail Break .8 (pro: to 1.5") A popular variation start to *Surrealistic Pillar.*
H   For Real Crack .7 (pro: to 3") Scramble up Crud Gully to a two-pitch, crack-and-chimney system that ends on a sloping ledge. Move up and left on a slab to reach a gully that leads to the top.
I   Bearhug .9 (pro: to 2.5") Wander past *For Real Crack* to the base of a corner capped by a roof. Climb up to a large, downward-pointing horn that must be bearhugged. Just before the roof, step right into a long crack. Belay just above the roof. Climb the slab above, passing a large overhang near its left side.
J   Short Step .10a TR
K   Wild Turkey .8 R
L   The Groove .7
M   The Farce .4
N   Novitiate's Nightmare .9
O   Hemorrhoids in Flight .10c
P   Black Pyre .11a
Q   Black Opal .10c
R   Black Magic .11c
S   Blue Wind .10a

LOWER BUTTRESS

Lower Buttress is a tri-pillared formation below West Wall. The 300-foot-high north face is covered with dikes and knobs, and the rock is excellent. To approach Lower Buttress, cut right off Pony Express Trail just beyond the large boulders and follow a small path that leads to the base of the wall. Crud Gully (5.8) ascends the dirty gully between the middle and west pillars, just right of Surrealistic Pillar. Descend from the top of Lower Buttress by walking west on ramps through bushes (third class). After 50 yards, it is easy to cut back and contour down along to the base of the rock.

Several of the notable routes on the Lower Buttress deserve more extensive descriptions.

SURREALISTIC PILLAR .7 (pro: to 3")

This route ascends the prominent flakelike crack on the main pillar. Begin just left of Crud Gully and traverse up and left to a crack. From the top of the crack, move left again to the prominent crack system, then up to a belay. Climb up 20 feet, then traverse left to a horn below a ledge. Step left around the corner and continue to a giant staircase. Belay from a small ledge with a large knob. A short and easy face pitch leads to the top.

BEER CAN ALLEY .10c R (pro: to 1")

Not shown. This line lies just left of the gully that separates the east and west pillars. Climb past three bolts, traverse right and up to a poor bolt and past a bush, then fade left and belay on a flake with a bolt. Climb straight up a dirty face with some 5.9 runout moves near the top.

FLAKY FLAKES .10B (serious)

Not shown. Begin this route 100 feet up and left of Beer Can Alley on a lie-back flake. Ascend the middle of the face using loose holds for placing marginal protection.

CRAWDADDYS IN FLIGHT .10c

Not shown. This route climbs a 10-foot roof on the upper right side of a small outcrop above Lower Buttress.

THE HOGSBACK

The Hogsback is a long, slabby hump of granite about 400 hundred feet high located just north of Lover's Leap on the opposite side of Pony Express Trail. The north face looks down on the American River and U.S. Highway 50. The climbing is good, although not as spectacular as other areas at the Leap. Most of the routes follow multipitch crack systems; however, some hard face climbs have been done. The south side is a great, sunny vantage point for viewing routes on Lover's Leap.

To reach the base of the north face, follow Pony Express Trail for 150 yards past the big boulders until you reach a notch up and to the left. A small trail leads through the brush to the notch. From here, hike down and left on broken slabs until you can follow the base of the face to the routes. For another option, take a faint trail that leaves the campground and parallels the river, swerving up to several sections of the face.

Several of the notable routes on the Hogsback deserve more extensive descriptions.

RED'S DELIGHT .9 (pro: to 1")

Begin by climbing right of Deception for 80 feet, then move up and left to a belay stance on top of two blocks. Climb up and left for 40 feet to a bolt. Continue straight up to another bolt about 30 feet higher. Move up to a right-facing corner, then to a belay in a left-leaning corner. The final pitch runs straight to the top.

CRAZY LACE .9 (pro: to 2")

Not shown. This is a good girdle traverse. Begin midway up on the north face above *Wave Rider* and follow a dike and thin crack toward the middle of the face to a bolt. Climb past an overhang and slant left to the second belay of *Wave Rider*. From here, move down and left under an overhang to a dihedral. Continue left on a 5.9 face to reach a belay bolt. Climb straight left for 50 feet to a bolt, then up another 50 feet to a good belay stance. The last pitch is easy fifth class and links up with the top part of *Deception*.

Most of the following routes are on the west end of the Hogsback. This face receives early morning sun and is a good place to climb when it is too windy or cold elsewhere.

JEFF'S FOLLY .7

Not shown. This climb runs up the slabs right of the broken area on the north face.

THE NUMBER .7

Not shown. This is a three-pitch route that follows an indistinct line to the right of *Jeff's Folly*.

PEANUT BRITTLE .7 (pro: to 2.5")

Not shown. This route begins below a windblown tree on the steepest section of rock on the south face. Climb up and left on a small, upward-sloping ledge to reach a crack that goes up the left side of a white slab. Continue up to a windblown tree. A fourth-class scramble leads to the top. (For a 5.8 variation, start at the top of the white slab and undercling an overhang to the right to reach a leaning, right-facing arch system.)

SINBAD AND THE DEVIL .8 (pro: to 1" and three bolts)

Not shown. Begin climbing up the glassy slab and arete about 15 feet right of *Peanut Brittle*. The route ends at the windblown tree.

SMOOTH SUNSHINE .8 (pro: to 1.5" and two fixed pins)

Not shown. Climb the corner right of *Sinbad and the Devil*. The route ends at the windblown tree.

RASPBERRY BYPASS .10B (pro: to 1.5")

Not shown. Just left of *Peanut Brittle*, climb the steep face past a bolt to a left-slanting ramp. Stay left of *Peanut Brittle* all the way.

STRAWBERRY OVERPASS .10B

Not shown. This good face climb is just to the left of *Raspberry Bypass*. A bolt 20 feet up leads to easier ground and the top.

ACCESSORY DOGS .9 (pro: to 0.25", bolts)

Not shown. Begin on the westernmost part of the north face of the Hogsback. Climb for 85 feet past bolts to a two-bolt belay.

THE HOGSBACK

A   Knapsack Crack .3 (pro: to 3")   *5/12/02 with Harry*
B   Red's Delight .9
C   Deception .6 (pro: to 2.5")
D   Deception Direct .8
E   Dancin' Feet .10d (pro: thin)
F   Settle Down .9 (pro: to 2")
G   Harvey's Wallbanger Left .6
H   Harvey's Wallbanger Center .8
I   Pip's Pillar .8
J   Harvey's Wallbanger Right .8
K   Carly Ann's Butterflies .8 R (pro: to 2.5")
L   Manic Depressive .8
M   Wave Rider .8 (pro: to 1.5")

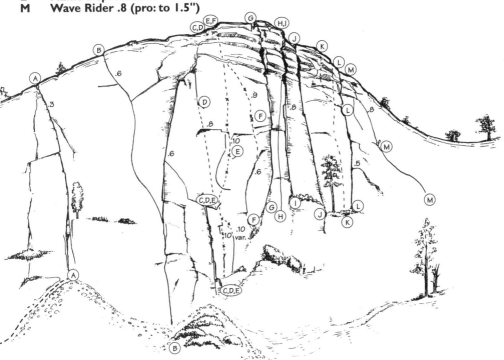

PYRAMID CREEK CANYON (Not shown)

This canyon lies above Twin Bridges and U.S. Highway 50, just a couple miles north of Lover's Leap. This beautiful place has great hiking and some good climbing. The following climbs are located on Little Sentinel, a large and obvious steep slab on the west (right) side of the canyon near the entrance. The approach is longer than it looks and requires some intense bushwhacking.

THE ARENA .12A (five bolts and a pin/bolt belay)
This 70-foot-long route climbs up the center of the face on thin edges and difficult smears. The crux moves are said to be temperature dependent.

MIRACLE MAN .10A
This 160-foot-long route begins 25 feet right of *The Arena*. Face moves lead to a classic lie-back flake.

Phantom Spires Overview

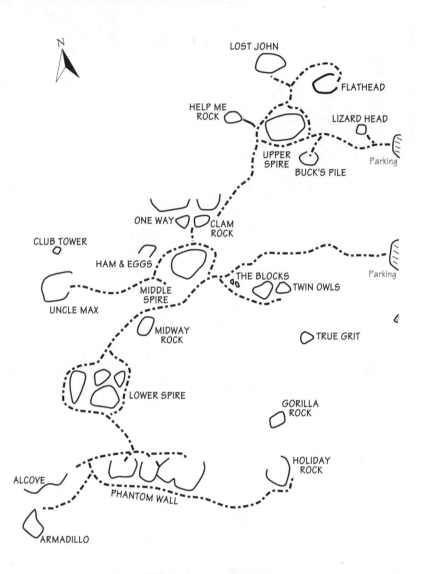

N

LOST JOHN

FLATHEAD

HELP ME
ROCK

LIZARD HEAD

UPPER
SPIRE

Parking

BUCK'S PILE

ONE WAY

CLAM
ROCK

CLUB TOWER

HAM & EGGS

THE BLOCKS

TWIN OWLS

Parking

MIDDLE
SPIRE

UNCLE MAX

MIDWAY
ROCK

TRUE GRIT

LOWER SPIRE

GORILLA
ROCK

HOLIDAY
ROCK

ALCOVE

PHANTOM WALL

ARMADILLO

RECOMMENDED ROUTES

Tyro's Test Piece .5
Ginger Bread .7
Over Easy .7
The Clown .8
Up for Grabs .8
Cornflakes .9
Jack Corner .9
Crispy Critters .10a
Desperado Roof Variation .10b
Phantom of the Opera .10b

Candyland .10c
Burnt Offerings .10d
Steppin' Stone .11a
Sizzler .11b
Wraith .11c
Nahoul Wall .11c
Electra .11c
Sour Puss .11d
The Siren .11d
Dewlap .11d

Phantom Spires

A hauntingly beautiful group of spires stands high on the north side of the American River Canyon among the burnt remains of a pine forest. The three largest and most distinct formations—Upper Spire, Middle Spire, and Lower Spire—are surrounded by a multitude of smaller pinnacles and boulders. The quality of the rock is excellent and often knobby with good cracks.

Due to their location on an unsheltered south-facing slope, the spires are bathed in sun and buffeted by wind. It's usually too hot to climb by midsummer; however, during the fall, winter, and spring, the temperature is nearly perfect. If the access road is covered in snow, you can approach the spires from the highway below.

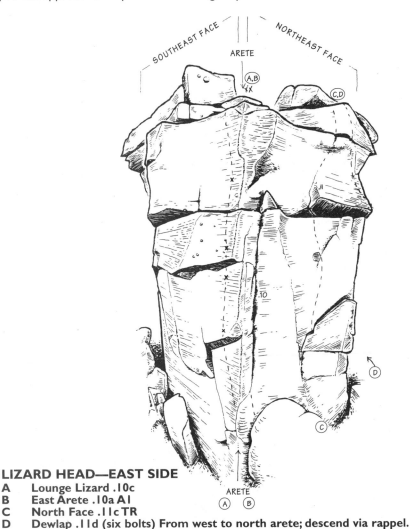

LIZARD HEAD—EAST SIDE
A Lounge Lizard .10c
B East Arete .10a A1
C North Face .11c TR
D Dewlap .11d (six bolts) From west to north arete; descend via rappel.

Phantom Spires: 1. Lower Spire, 2. Phantom Wall, 3. Middle Spire, 4. Upper Spire

To reach Phantom Spires, drive 4.9 miles east on U.S. Highway 50 from the community of Kyburz. Turn north onto Wrights Lake Road. After a mile, you will see the spires. Continue up the road, then cut left on a logging road heading west toward Middle Spire. Two-wheel-drive vehicles with medium or high clearance can handle this road if it is dry. For the majority of crags, the best approach is from the middle parking area across from Middle Spire. Camping is not regulated, so please be careful with fire and pack out all trash. A small spring intersects the logging road, but usually dries up by summer, so bring water. To locate the individual formations, see the overview map for Phantom Spires.

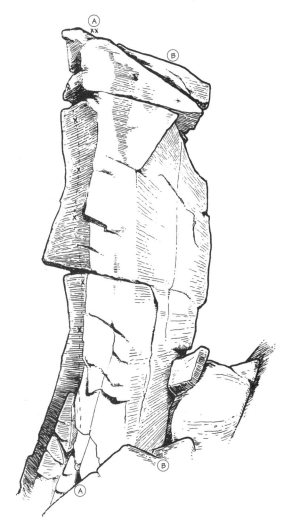

LIZARD HEAD—WEST SIDE
A   **Dewlap .11d (six bolts) From west to north arete.**
B   **South Face A3 Horizontal cracks and vertical seams on southwest side; descend via rappel.**

FLATHEAD (Not shown)

CHOCKSTONE .6
Climb an awkward chimney past a chockstone on the east side.

NO PROBLEM .9
Climb a short roof and thin crack on the west side.

LOST JOHN

WHOLE SLOT OF TROUBLE .11C/D
Not shown. Climb a left-facing crack near the center of the buttress. Two bolts and slung knobs protect the section above.

TURNING POINT .10B
Not shown. Climb the cracks on the steep south face.

LOST JOHN
A   Lost John .10b
B   Unknown .12b
C   Unknown .12a

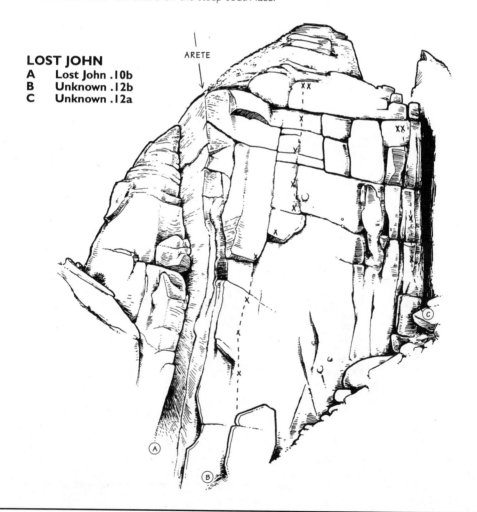

UPPER SPIRE

For the routes on the Upper Spire, descend from the summit by rappelling 40 feet to a large ledge. From here, make an 80-foot rappel over the west side.

UPPER SPIRE—NORTHEAST SIDE
A Burnt Offerings .10d (pro: RPs, wireds, and Friends)
B Steppin' Stone .11a (pro: to 3")
C East Face Route .9 (pro: to 3")
D Desperado Roof .9 (.10b variation; pro: to 3")
E Dot to Dot .10b
F North Ridge .6 (pro: to 3")

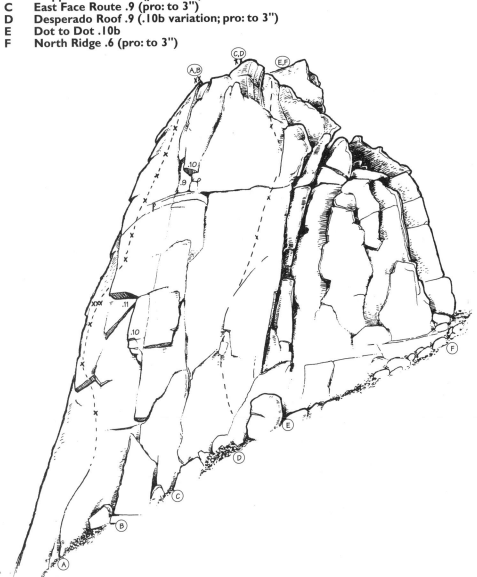

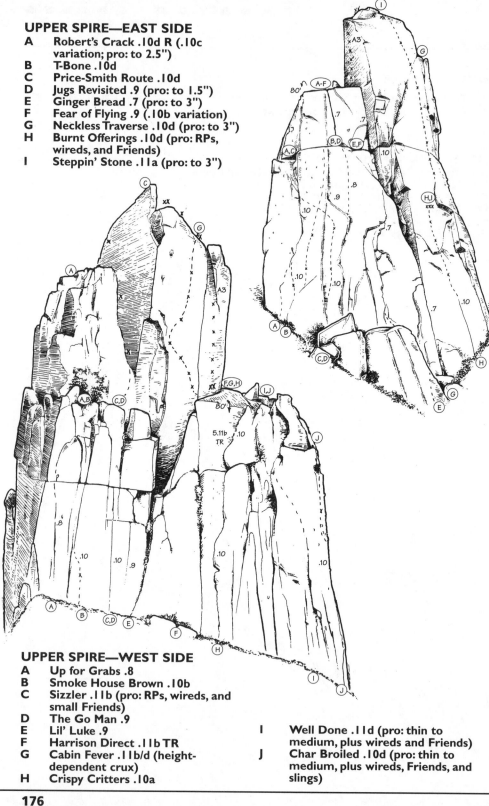

UPPER SPIRE—EAST SIDE

A Robert's Crack .10d R (.10c variation; pro: to 2.5")
B T-Bone .10d
C Price-Smith Route .10d
D Jugs Revisited .9 (pro: to 1.5")
E Ginger Bread .7 (pro: to 3")
F Fear of Flying .9 (.10b variation)
G Neckless Traverse .10d (pro: to 3")
H Burnt Offerings .10d (pro: RPs, wireds, and Friends)
I Steppin' Stone .11a (pro: to 3")

UPPER SPIRE—WEST SIDE

A Up for Grabs .8
B Smoke House Brown .10b
C Sizzler .11b (pro: RPs, wireds, and small Friends)
D The Go Man .9
E Lil' Luke .9
F Harrison Direct .11b TR
G Cabin Fever .11b/d (height-dependent crux)
H Crispy Critters .10a
I Well Done .11d (pro: thin to medium, plus wireds and Friends)
J Char Broiled .10d (pro: thin to medium, plus wireds, Friends, and slings)

BUCK'S PILE (Not shown)

CHEAP SHOT .10D TR (crux is midway up; two-bolt anchor)

CLAM ROCK AND MIDWAY ROCK (Not shown)

A couple short, bolted face climbs are located on the south face of each of these two boulders. There are bolt anchors on top.

The Blocks

Several short, bolted routes ascend the south side of these boulders, which lie between Middle Spire and Twin Owls. Long slings and some gear are necessary to supplement the bolt anchors on top. The routes are listed from left to right.

THE BOWLING BALL .10B (overhang with large knobs on left)

BLUE NOTE .10A/B (face)

FRENCH LETTER .10C (face)

MY FAVORITE THING .10D (right arete)

MIDDLE SPIRE

Not shown. Descend the east side via rappel.

Middle Spire—East Side

COCKABOOTY 5.7
Not shown. The cracks to right of *Chainsaw Willie.*

HAM AND EGGS (Not shown)

This small buttress, which lies to the southwest of Middle Spire, can be identified by the large roof on its west side.

HAM AND EGGS .9 A1

Climb a ramp to a ledge just beneath a roof. A few moves of aid lead over the roof to a finger crack and the top.

HARDING'S OTHER CHIMNEY .6

Follow the prominent cleft on the west side of the buttress.

CLUB TOWER (Not shown)

This small crag is up and left of Uncle Max.

SOUR PUSS .11D (pro: thin to medium)

Two bolts lead to the crux moves; then climb up a crack and over a roof, clip a bolt, move past a small flake to another bolt, and continue to the top.

MIDDLE SPIRE—NORTH AND WEST SIDES

A   Over Easy .7 (pro: to 2.5")
B   Hard Up .9 (pro: to 2.5")
C   Slow Dancer .9
D   The Prow .10a/b
E   Leaner and Meaner .11 (pro: anywhere you can get it)
F   Lean and Mean .9 (pro: 2.5")
G   Cornflakes .9 (plus a .9 variation)
H   Fancy Dancin' .10
I   Candy Ass .10d
J   Candyland .10c (pro: thin and slings)

MIDDLE SPIRE—EAST SIDE

A   The Clam .8 **X**
B   Anal Sex .8 **X**
C   Regular Route .8 (pro: to 2.5")
D   Rain Song .7 R
E   Tyro's Test Piece .5 (pro: to 2")
F   Chainsaw Willie .8 R
G   The Prow .10a/b

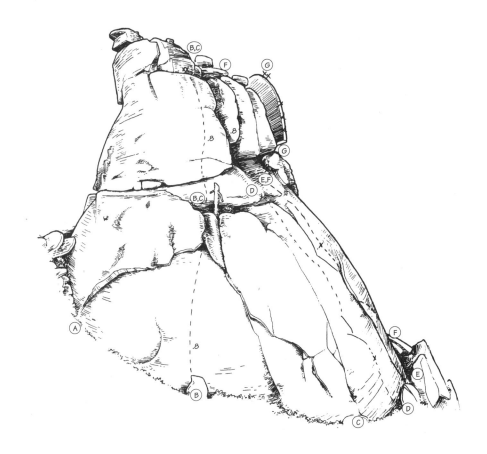

UNCLE MAX (SOUTHWEST SIDE)
A   **Love Knobs .10a R** (pro: thin to medium and one bolt)
B   **Lemon Head .12a**
C   **Aunt Clara .11c**
D   **The Clown .8**
E   **Mean Moe .10c** (pro: mostly thin to medium)
F   **Corquett .8**

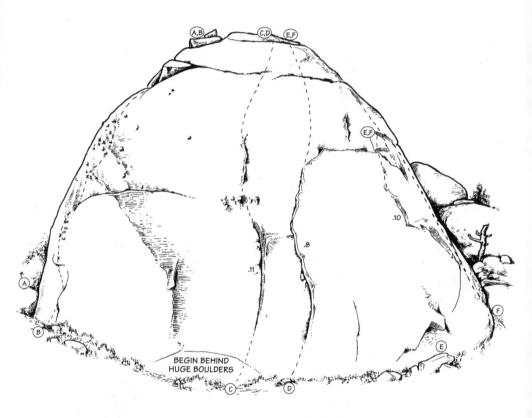

BEGIN BEHIND
HUGE BOULDERS

Lower Spire—Northwest Side

Descend via rappel, 70 feet down the northwest face.

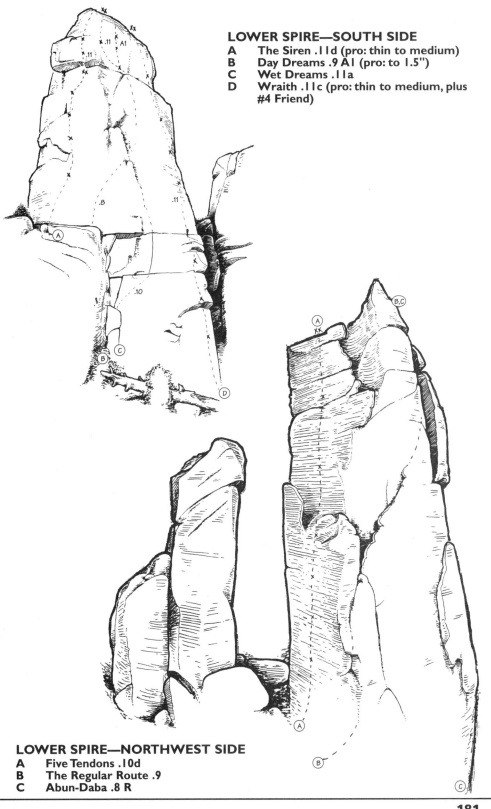

LOWER SPIRE—SOUTH SIDE
A   The Siren .11d (pro: thin to medium)
B   Day Dreams .9 A1 (pro: to 1.5")
C   Wet Dreams .11a
D   Wraith .11c (pro: thin to medium, plus #4 Friend)

LOWER SPIRE—NORTHWEST SIDE
A   Five Tendons .10d
B   The Regular Route .9
C   Abun-Daba .8 R

181

LOWER SPIRE—EAST SIDE

A K.E. Cracks .11 (pro: thin to medium) Begin in a gully and climb the cracks past some pins and a bolt.
B Stage Fright .9 (pro: serious, rurps to 3")
C Last Lock-up .11a
D Jack Corner .9 (pro: to 2.5")
E Fire Fly .5

PHANTOM WALL

Phantom Wall—Left

To descend, walk off the back side.

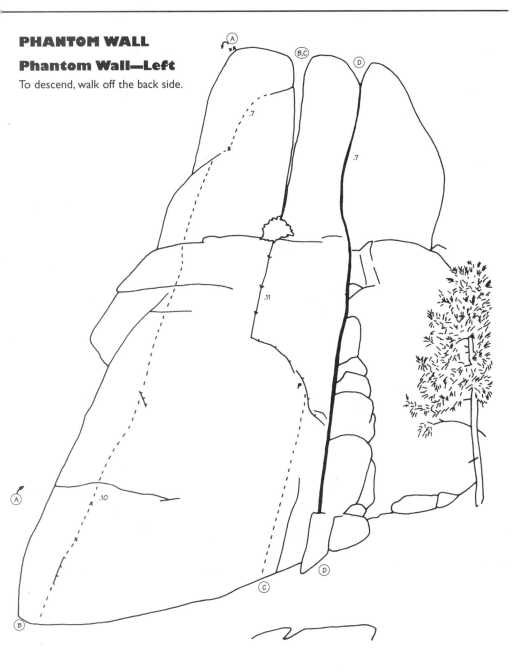

PHANTOM WALL—LEFT

A **Wally Gator .11c** Climb a huge flake, then up the face past five bolts to a two-bolt belay.

B **Oktober Fest .10c**

C **Quick Pullout .11a (pro: mostly thin to medium)**

D **Burrowing Owl .7 (pro: wide)**

PHANTOM WALL—RIGHT (A-C)
A   Platitude .8 R
B   Nahoul Wall .11c
C   Zoo Tramp .9

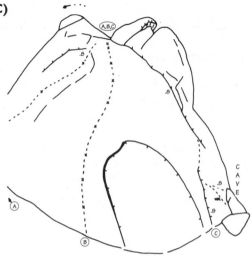

PHANTOM WALL—RIGHT (D-I)
D   La Chute .10a R Follow a flake up and left around the corner, then climb up the face past a bolt.
E   Oedipus Rex .7 Climb the tree to the crack.
F   Electra .11c Follow an arch to the crack.
G   Dr. Jeckel and Mr. Hyde .11a Climb the face to the crack.
H   Finders Keepers .11 (face climbing)
I   Eraser Head .10b

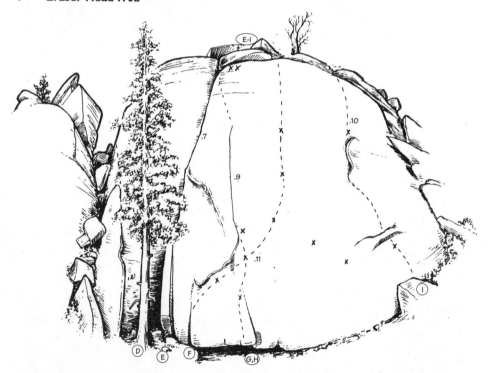

Phantom Wall—Right (D-I)

The following routes are located on a wall 50 yards to the right of *Zoo Tramp*.

ROADSIDE INJECTION .11A

Not shown. This climb lies on the east face of a boulder, downhill and slightly right of Phantom Wall. Just right of the block, face climb past a bolt to a flake, then continue face climbing past three more bolts to a bolted belay. There appears to be an unfinished bolted line to the right of this route.

ARMADILLO (Not shown)

This fantastic fin of granite stands below Phantom Wall.

PHANTOM OF THE OPERA .10B (eight bolts)

Climb the stunning southwest arete.

GORILLA ROCK (EAST SIDE)

Descend via a rappel off a horn.

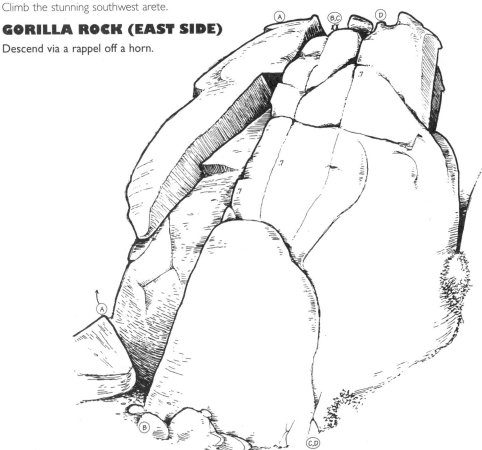

GORILLA ROCK (EAST SIDE)

A   Joe Young .8 A2 Begin on the right side of the west face. Follow a seam past a pin to a thin crack, then over a roof to a finger crack. From here, face climb (5.8) past two bolts that lead to the top.

B   Ko-Ko Box .7
C   Ant Crack Left .7
D   Ant Crack Right .7

HOLIDAY ROCK (NORTH SIDE)

July .8
Not shown. Begin in a chimney on the right side of the east face and climb to a ledge on the north side. Continue to the top.

101 Dalmatians .10c (pro: slings)
Not shown. Start left of *July* and climb the knobby wall above using bolts and dicey tied-off knobs for protection.

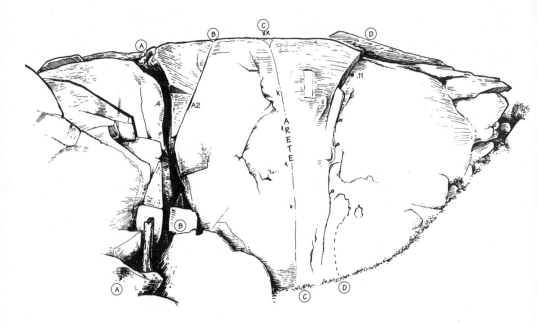

HOLIDAY ROCK (NORTH SIDE)
A   Soot .4 (chimney)
B   Blue Tango A2
C   Unknown .12c?
D   Singe City .11b (pro: RPs, wireds, and Friends to #1.5)

EUREKA CLIFF AND HIDDEN SPIRE

This climbing area lies below and west of Phantom Spires. On U.S. Highway 50, drive 3.6 miles east of Kyburz or 1.3 miles west of the turnoff for Wrights Lake. Pull into the paved pullout and look for the short road that leads to a dirt parking area 100 yards above the north side of the highway. Hike east a couple hundred yards along the trail to Treasure Rock, a long thin slab. Continue about 200 yards farther to Hidden Spire, which sits 200 feet above the trail. Teaser Rock lies below the highway and next to the river by the Mile-34 housing tract.

Eureka Cliff

Cedar Crack is located near the center of this 70-foot-high slab. The thin crack has a baby cedar growing out of it. The other three routes are clustered about 100 feet to the left.

Hidden Spire

The best approach to this cliff is from U.S. Highway 50.

Teaser Rock

This 65-foot-high boulder, a short distance west of Eureka Cliff, stands below the highway next to the American River. Turn south off U.S. Highway 50 at the Mile-34 housing tract and continue to the end of the road at the north edge of the river. You will see the boulder just ahead.

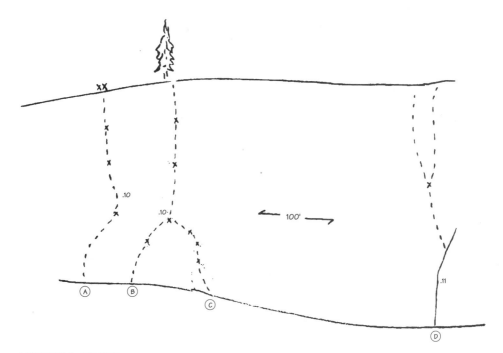

EUREKA CLIFF
A   Panned Out .10a (three bolts)
B   Twist and Shout .10b (four bolts)
C   The Slider .11d (five bolts)
D   Cedar Crack .11b (pro: thin to 1.5" and bolts)

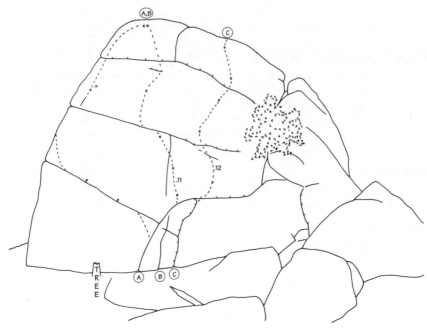

HIDDEN SPIRE
A   All Right .11c (pro: Friends to 3")
B   Hide and Seek .11c (pro: Friends to 3.5")
C   Mediator .12a (pro: medium)

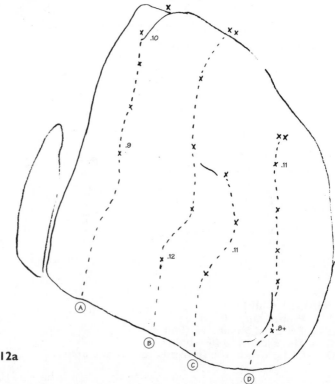

TEASER ROCK
A   Quickie .10c
B   Trojan .11d
C   Seduction .12a
D   Fear of Rejection .12a

Photo by Jim Thornburg

Sugarloaf Overview

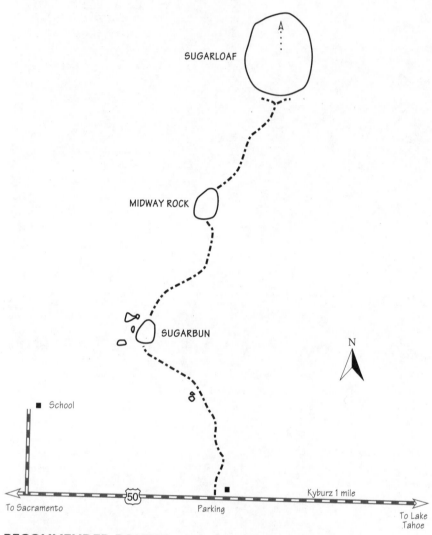

SUGARLOAF

MIDWAY ROCK

SUGARBUN

N

School

To Sacramento — [50] — Parking — Kyburz 1 mile — To Lake Tahoe

RECOMMENDED ROUTES

Face:

Blue Velvet .10c (first pitch)
Bolee Gold .10c
The Man Who Fell to Earth .11b
Only the Young Die Brave .11c
Bird Man .11d
Beast of Burden .11d
The Ghost in the Machine .12a

Crack:

Scheister .7
Harding's Chimney .7
East Chimney .7
West Chimney .8
TM's Deviation .9
Pony Express .9
Farley .9
The Fang .9
Dominion .10a
The Fracture .10d
Taurus .11b
Captain Fingers .12c
The Grand Illusion .13b/c

Sugarloaf

This 400-foot-high granite spire rises above the forest on a steep hill north of Kyburz, a small roadside community 30 miles west of South Lake Tahoe. The climbing is reminiscent of Yosemite with well-formed crack and chimney systems and sustained face climbs. The relatively low elevation (4,900 feet) and sunny exposure allow for year-round climbing.

To approach Sugarloaf, park along the south shoulder of U.S. Highway 50 east of Silverfork School and right across from the telephone company service building. Kyburz lies about 1 mile to the east. Please do not park at Silver Fork School or cut across private property to access the crag. From behind the service building, follow the trail that winds uphill. You will notice many large boulders on the way up; and although several of these have been climbed, only Sugarbun and Midway Rock see regular ascents. The hike is steep and takes 20 to 30 minutes.

Sugarloaf has three distinct summits, and the south summit is detached from the other two. To descend the south summit, rappel into the notch and continue down Harding's Chimney or climb the "summit pitch," which leads from the south notch to the central summit. For the central and the north summits, descend by walking north to a tree, then scrambling down a series of third-class gullies.

Free camping is available at Phantom Spires, which is located a few miles east up US 50. A cool swim in the South Fork of the American River, which flows down the canyon, is a refreshing way to end a day of great cragging.

SUGARLOAF

Several of the notable routes at Sugarloaf deserve more extensive descriptions.

PONY EXPRESS .9 (pro: to 3.5")
From behind a stately oak tree, climb a serrated flake past a short bit of 5.8, then go up some left-facing books to a broken area and belay. Move up and left into a wide crack in a gully (5.9), then follow third-class ledges along a ramp that leads to the north notch.

TM's DEVIATION .9 (pro: to 3.5")
Climb the first pitch and 70 feet of the second pitch on *West Chimney*, then move right to the base of an overhanging chimney (5.8). A full pitch of sustained chimneying and jamming ends at the belay atop the corner (5.9). A short pitch leads to the central summit.

HARDING's CHIMNEY .7 (pro: to 3")
This classic route ascends the long chimney/crack system to the south summit. Climb up an easy ramp and steep blocky rock (5.3) on the right side of *The Fang* to an alcove beneath a ceiling at the base of a chimney. Move up the chimney to a broken area above and belay (5.7). Head up and left to another chimney behind the south summit, which ends on a large ledge in the south notch. A Bolt Ladder .10 or A1. This bolt ladder variation leads to the south summit. From the north end of the notch, climb an arching dihedral around a corner and along a trough that leads to a cave just below the top. From here, several fourth- and easy fifth-class lines reach the central summit. (Instead of moving left after the third pitch, climb a 5.8 variation straight up a clean, right-facing corner.)

Sugarloaf: East Face

SCHEISTER .7 (pro: to 3")
Begin in the gully to the right of *Harding's Chimney.* Climb up some blocks and a chimney/dihedral (5.7). Next, climb a lie-back crack to a ledge (5.7). A left-facing book (5.4) and a traverse left lead to a large ledge above the south notch. Continue up *Harding's Chimney* to the top.

FARLEY .9 (pro: to 3", mostly large)
A sustained lie-back flake leads to a belay in a chimney. Continue up the corner above to a belay ledge. The exposed and poorly protected "knobby wall" pitch lies above. After this, a short pitch leads to the top.

EAST CHIMNEY .7 (pro: to 3")
This obvious line ascends a trough into a short chimney and then to a belay beneath the huge and spectacular east ceiling (5.5). Traverse up and right past some small roofs, then continue straight up to the north notch (5.7).

SUGARLOAF—WEST FACE
A   **Hyperspace .10b (pro: mostly thin to 1.5")**
       Trumpled under Foot .10 TR (a variation)
B   **Twist and Shout .10a R**
C   **Back in Black .11d R**
D   **The Man Who Fell to Earth .11b (pro: thin to medium) The direct start follows**
       a thin right-diagonal crack to the face past a bolt (5.11).
E   **Only the Young Die Brave .11c**
F   **The Podium .9 (pro: to 3.5")**
G   **Under the Spreading Atrophy .11b (pro: medium)**
H   **Pony Express .9 (pro: to 3.5") See previous description of notable routes.**
I   **Cry Uncle .12a R**
J   **Expresso .11a**
K   **West Chimney .8 (pro: to 3") See previous description of notable routes.**
L   **TM's Deviation .9 (pro: 3.5") See previous description of notable routes.**
M   **Hard Right .10c (pro: to 2")**
N   **Pan Dulce .10d–**
O   **Grand Delusion .12+**
P   **Fat Merchant Crack**
       .10b X
Q   **Blind Faith .9**
       (traverse)
R   **The Ghost in**
       the Machine
       .12a

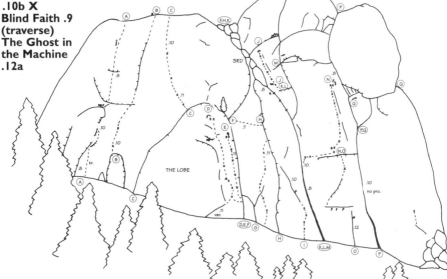

SUGARLOAF—SOUTH FACE

A   Fat Merchant Crack .10b **X**
B   Blind Faith .9 (traverse)
C   The Ghost in the Machine .12a (pro: small to medium, plus slings for knobs)
D   Harder Than It Used to Be .12? (knob broke, no known second ascent)
E   Bolee Gold .10c (pro: to 3")
F   Hooker's Haven .12a
G   The Fang .9 (pro: to 2")
H   Bird Man .11d (pro: #2.5 Friend; difficult bolt clip)
I   Talking Heads .11a
J   The Stone .10a **R** (pro: to 2")
K   Harding's Chimney .7 (pro: to 3") See previous description of notable routes.
L   The Gallows Pole .11b **R**

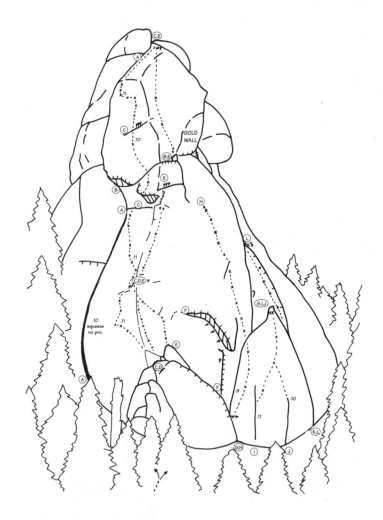

Hidetaka Suzuki on the *Grand Illusion*, 5.13b/c, at
Sugarloaf. Photo by Greg Epperson.

SUGARLOAF—EAST FACE

A   Hooker's Haven .12a
B   Bird Man .11d (pro: #2.5 Friend, difficult bolt clip)
C   The Fang .9 (pro: to 2")
D   Harding's Chimney .7 (pro: to 3") See previous description of notable routes.
E   Beast of Burden .11d
F   Over the Edge .8 R
G   Scheister .7 (pro: to 3") See previous description of notable routes.
H   Blue Velvet .10c
I   Tapestry .10b X (pro: slings for knobs)
J   Farley .9 (pro: to 3", mostly large) See previous description of notable routes.
K   Opus 7 .11d R
L   Taurus .11b (pro: to 2")
M   Lady Luck .10a R
N   The Fracture .10d (pro: mostly thin to 1.5")
O   The Grand Illusion .13b/c (pro: thin to medium)
P   Telesis .11a R
Q   Dominion .10a (pro: to 3")
R   Captain Fingers .12c (pro: thin to 1.5")
S   East Chimney .7 (pro: to 3") See previous description of notable routes.
T   Lurch .8 (pro: to 2" and slings for knobs)
U   Hanging Jugs .8 R (pro: to 3")

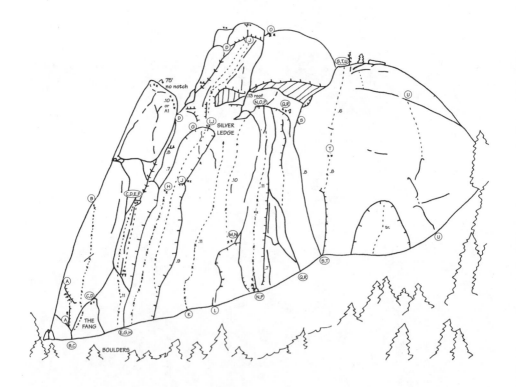

Sugarloaf—East Face

ETHICS .10B (three bolts)

Not shown. Climb out of the notch between the south and central summits.

LOST IN THE FOG .9 A2 (pro: small to medium nuts, Friends, blades, and hooks)

Not shown. Ascend the blank wall left of *Taurus* past some bolts. Climb a 5.9 face beyond the third bolt to a ledge up and right. Follow cracks and chimneys to Silver Ledge. Finish via *Farley.*

SCORPIO .7 (pro: to 2.5")

Not shown. This route begins uphill from *Hanging Jugs* and follows a left-facing arch past some face moves to a crack.

EAST FACE .11A (pro: to medium)

Not shown. Walk up a ramp to a flat ledge with a tree. Follow the chimney between a boulder and the wall. Climb the face past four bolts and a crack to the top.

SUGARBUN

Sugarbun is a popular, house-sized boulder with many fine routes. The approach takes about five minutes. See the overview map for Sugarloaf. There is no easy way up Sugarbun. Descend via a rappel off the north side from bolts and a tree.

SUGARBUN

A   **Make That Move Now, Baby .11 (pro: ten bolts) From atop a boulder, climb thin face moves to the crux, which surmounts a small roof and continues up the arete to the top.**

B   **The Hatchett .11a (pro: two bolts) Unfinished.**

C   **Fingerlock .10b (pro: thin to 2") This excellent finger crack runs alongside an oak tree growing against the face. Use the tree to bypass the initial bulge.**

D   **The Southwest Corner .12a TR This good route was damaged when someone smashed all the bolt hangers with a hammer.**

E   **Wintergreen .10d (pro: three bolts) Climb a clean face along the edge.**

F   **Dirty Dog .10c (pro: three bolts) This somewhat dirty route starts next to *Wintergreen* and fades left.**

G   **Dog Fight .11c (pro: thin to 1" and three bolts) Begin just right of *Flytrap* and climb the face to the crack of *Mad Dog.* Continue to the top.**

H   **Flytrap .7 (pro: to 2") A wide flake hides a chimney on the north face. From the top of the flake, clip a bolt and wander right to a small tree.**

I   **Mad Dog .10c (pro: to 1") This route follows a diagonal crack from the top of the chimney on *Flytrap.***

J   **Rug Doctor .11c (pro: three bolts) Climb a brushy face left of *Flytrap.* Presently, this route does not reach the top. Climb to the last bolt and lower off.**

K   **East Corner .9 (pro: to 4") Jam and lie back a sustained corner on the east face to reach the top of a flake. Continue past the bolt up Flytrap to the top.**

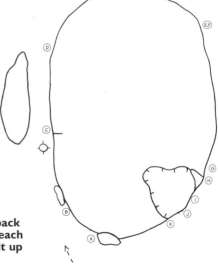

MIDWAY ROCK

This huge boulder lies between Sugarbun and Sugarloaf. Many routes have been done on the boulders around this area. Descend by walking off the north side.

TROPHY HUNTER .10B (three bolts)
Not shown. This route is on a flat wall above Midway Rock.

SUGAR PLUM .11A (four bolts, two-bolt belay)
Not shown. This route is on the east face of a large boulder below Midway Rock.

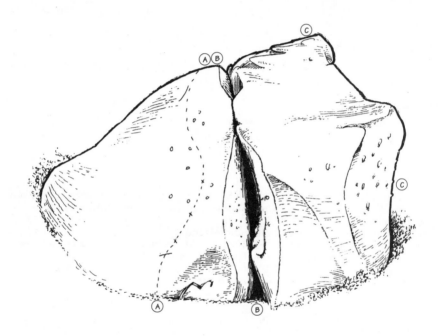

MIDWAY ROCK
A   **Flight Deck .11b/c R**
B   **Self Abuse .10b**
C   **The Diagonal .9/Undercling .8 (cracks up and right)**

Photo by Jim Thornburg

Reno and Carson Valley Area

RECOMMENDED ROUTES
Evolution of Man .7
On Safari .7
UNR Crack .7
Spring Break .8
Skull and Crossbones .9
Deadman's Rappel .9
Tom's Traverse .10
The Left Seam .10a
Karl's Crack .10a
Africa Flake .10a
Plant Food .11b/c
Crank Call .11d
Ultimate Violence .11d
Son of a Dentist .12a/b
Blade Runner .12b
Ton-Ton .13a

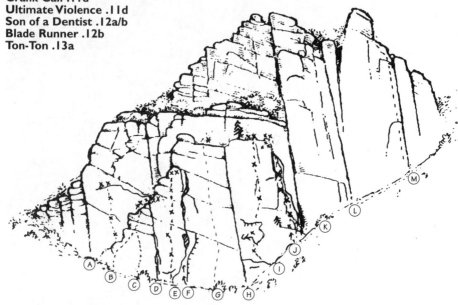

RIVER ROCK
A   Drunken Sporto's .10d
B   Just to Watch Him Die .10d
C   Improbable .10b
D   UNR Crack .7
E   Total Recall .11b
F   Spring Break .8 (pro: to 3")
G   Deliverance on the Truckee A2+
H   Karl's Crack .10a
I   Africa Flake .10a
J   On Safari .7
K   Project
L   Project
M   The Old TR .8

Reno and Carson Valley Area Crags

In the high desert, outside Reno, Carson City, and Gardenville, there are several fine crags. Although these are not major climbing areas, each has its own charm and personality. The climbing surface is varied, including tuff, granite, and basalt. Temperatures are usually just right for climbing in early spring and late fall. You can often climb during the winter; the snowpack is usually minimal to nonexistent.

RIVER ROCK

River Rock is a granite formation with moderate climbs on the south side of the Truckee River between Truckee and Reno. Plenty of sun and low elevation make this area a great place to climb during the winter when other crags in the Tahoe Basin are unfavorable. This crag is very accessible to climbers in the Reno area.

River Rock is about 2.5 miles east of the Farad exit off Interstate 80. Park in the wide pullout with a gate at the west end. The approach takes about 20 minutes. From the gate, walk the road past some small rock outcroppings, then walk downhill and cross the railroad tracks. From this point, walk downstream on the road that parallels the railroad tracks and crosses the suspension bridge. Once across the bridge, stay on the left side of the levee until you can cross the channel and hike directly to the rock.

PIG ROCK

Pig Rock is a small, steep outcrop of volcanic rock in the Nevada desert northeast of Reno. The rock is fragile and resembles dried mud. Note that when it rains, water is absorbed into the slightly porous rock and weakens the holds. To avoid route damage, climbers should allow the wall to dry before climbing at Pig Rock.

Pig requires good finger strength to cling to the small edges and pockets that cover its face. With challenging movements, well-bolted lines, and conveniently placed anchors, Pig is an excellent training area for local climbers who are willing to make the hour and forty-five minute drive from North Lake Tahoe. The climbing season begins in the fall and continues, depending on weather, through winter and into early spring; then it becomes too hot to climb here.

Finding Pig Rock for the first time is complicated. From Interstate 80, exit onto Nevada Highway 445 (Pyramid Way) in Sparks. Continue north along NV 445 until it intersects with McCarren Boulevard. Set your odometer and continue north on NV 445 for 25.6 miles, then turn left onto a dirt road just past a low culvert bridge (two-wheel-drive is usually OK). Every few years, floods damage the access road and this approach information may change slightly.

Follow the dirt road for 0.7 mile and stay left at the fork. After a total of 1.7 miles, branch left to stay on the main road. Several smaller roads intersect or diverge from the main road. Keep the Wolf's Tooth, a large pointed spire on the horizon, to your right and continue on the main road. After a short distance, enter a small canyon, and as the odometer trips a total of 2.6 miles, a small steep wall about 60 feet high will appear on the left.

PIG ROCK

A   Rage in Eden .12b/c
B   Ultimate Violence .11d
C   Splatomatic .11c/d
D   Bingo's Revenge .11c
E   Elastique .11+/12 (rating is to chains; .12b over the top)
F   Plant Food .11b/c (rating is to chains; .11+/.12- over the top)
G   Son Be a Dentist .12a/b
H   American Graffiti .13c
I   Ton-Ton .13a
J   Blade Runner .12b (arete)
K   Le Beouf .11b/c

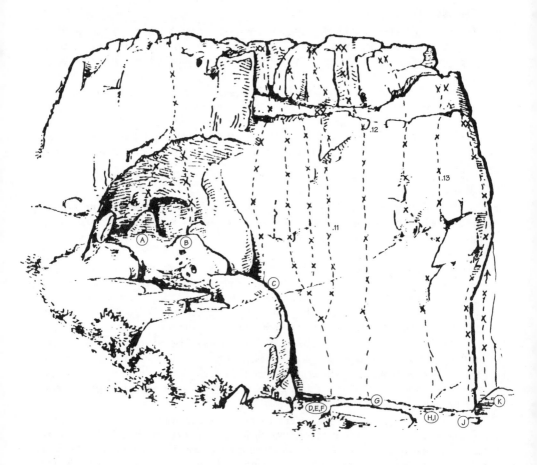

LAKE VIEW SLAB AND THE EGG

A   Lake View .9R
B   The Cleft .8
C   Quartz Crack .9
D   Slab Cracks .6 and .7
E   Struttin' .9

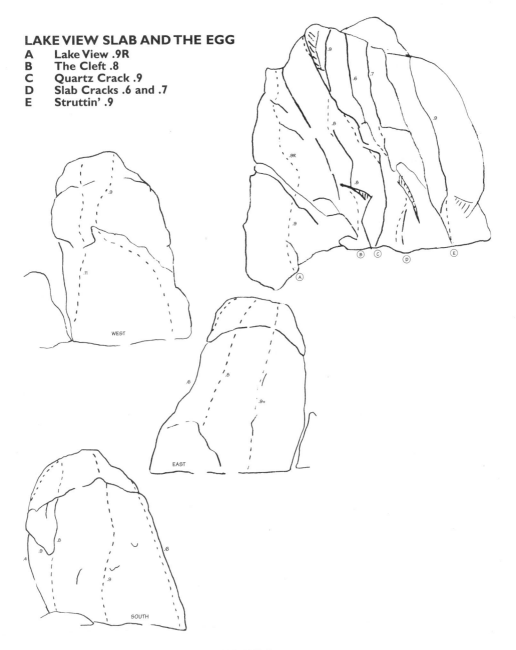

LAKE VIEW SLAB AND THE EGG

Lake View has been climbed since the early 1960s. The quality of the rock is excellent and you often can climb here during the winter. The Egg is an 18-foot-high boulder that lies about 200 yards west of Lake View Slab. Descend from the Egg via the 5.6 route on the south face. Please note that the small cluster of boulders in the subdivision is off-limits to climbing. Do not climb on these boulders because it could affect access to Lake View and the Egg.

Lake View Slab lies on the hill above the west side of U.S. Highway 395 north of Carson City. Exit US 395 at Lake View Estates. Drive west and take the first left. Continue until you are below the obvious slab. The approach takes about 5 minutes.

DINOSAUR ROCK

A   Sauron's Nest .5
B   Evolution of Man .7
C   P.A. Corner .10a (pro: to 1")
D   Big Bang .11b
E   Edge of Doom .11c Climb the left arete past three bolts.
F   Lizard King .11b Climb the right side of the pillar on the arete using both the face and inside wall of the chimney.
G   End of Time .6
H   The Left Seam .10a
I   Green Hell .11b/c
J   Color Me Gone .9
K   Tom's Traverse .10
L   Afternoon Corner .6
M   Quadzilla .4
N   The Gash .7
O   Deadman's Rappel .9
P   Bloodshot .10a (pro: to 1.25")

DINOSAUR ROCK

Dinosaur is a 140-foot-high crag on the north-facing side of a small canyon south of Carson City. Although the rock is slightly decomposed in places, the climbing is generally fun. The water in the creek is contaminated with *giardia*. Dinosaur is sunny in the morning and shady the remainder of the day. Because of its northern exposure, Dinosaur is generally too cold for climbing in the winter.

Turn right (west) on Clear Creek Road from U.S. Highway 395, just south of the U.S. Highway 50 intersection. Drive about 1.5 miles. Park in the small pullout on the left below Dinosaur Rock. To approach Dinosaur, cross the creek to the right of the crag.

NOSE BLEED .10D TR

Not shown. Climb the pillar around the corner from the previous route. Stay on the middle of the pillar until 20 feet from the ledge. From here, lie back the left edge of the arete to a two-bolt anchor.

FLYING LIZARD .8 (pro: to 3")

Not shown. Climb the chimney with the large chockstone to the right of *Nose Bleed*. The crux is near the top where the chimney narrows to an off-width.

THE BOOK OF RED

The Book of Red offers some fun toproping on a clean, 40-foot-high basalt wall. Some of the cracks have been led. The area was developed by Dan Osman, Bill Griffen, and other Gardnerville climbers.

From Gardnerville, head south on U.S. Highway 395 past the River View Adult Mobile Home Park. At the base of the first substantial grade on the highway, turn right onto a paved road. Drive past the house and turn left onto a dirt road before the river (two-wheel-drive is OK). Continue uphill. The first fork in the road leads to Dam Wall, which offers great swimming and 30 feet of bouldering above the East Fork of the Carson River. Water levels vary, so beware of submerged objects.

To reach the crag, stay on the main road until it ends at a gravel parking area. From here, hike for about 150 yards to the entrance of a small canyon. The Book of Red is the rock that forms the right side of the canyon.

THE BOOK OF RED

A	Fingers to Hands .10b
B	Overhanging Hands .11a
C	Crank Call .11d
D	Thin Arete .11c
E	Thin Face .11c/d
F	Hand to Fist .7
G	Skull and Crossbones .9
H	River Run .11+

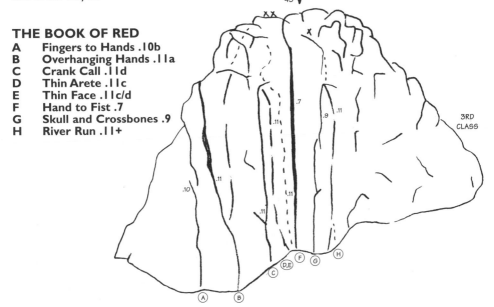

A climber enjoying one of the finest aretes at Split Rock. Photo by Brian Biega.

Bouldering and Toproping

For the boulderer, the possibilities in the Tahoe area are limitless. The potential for great bouldering circuits has hardly been explored. A casual day hike near any area of exposed rock most likely will yield the discovery of a new site. Several places do experience a regular flow of bouldering activity, and a compilation of the more popular and accessible areas is listed below.

DONNER SUMMIT AND TRUCKEE

The most accessible areas at Donner Summit are School Rock and Grouse Slab. Donner Peak is excellent and worth the hike. In Truckee, Split Rock and the Truckee Boulder are the best places to go.

Good bouldering exists along a series of steps on the east ridge of School Rock. There are a few small cliff bands left of Sun Wall that also are fun. Below the west face of Grouse Slab. there is a group of large boulders with many fine problems.

For those who don't mind the 45-minute hike, some of the best bouldering traverses in the Tahoe Basin are found atop Donner Peak. To reach the peak, just walk up the slabs and talus slopes above Snowshed Wall to the summit. The best bouldering is on the west side of the peak.

Split Rock is the most popular bouldering spot in the Truckee area. It is located near the east end of Donner Lake behind the Forest Service campground. The problems are excellent and varied with good landings. Many other boulders lie scattered throughout the forest.

To find Split Rock, turn off Donner Pass Road at an intersection between two gas stations and the Cold Stream Stables, about 0.3 mile east of Donner Lake. Follow this road a short distance to the head of Cold Stream Canyon and park at the end of the pavement just before a small reservoir. Walk west through the trees between the reservoir and the south boundary of the campground. After a few minutes, you will reach the boulders visible.

The 20-foot-high Truckee Boulder has an off-width crack splitting its west face. This boulder lies behind the large shopping area between the railroad tracks and Deer Field Drive, off California Highway 89.

CRYSTAL BAY, LAKE TAHOE

Speedboat is a great place to lie in the sun and swim—and boulder. Most of the problems are on short, slabby boulders. This area is near Kings Beach, 0.5 mile west of the California-Nevada state line. To get there, turn off California Highway 28 onto Speedboat Avenue. Park near the end of the street and walk down to the lake. The best boulders are off the first road to the right.

The 40-foot-high Crystal Bay Boulder has two good crack climbs on its face. To the left, *Crystal Crack* (5.10a) ascends a flaring corner to a Y-shaped crack. On the right, *Crystal Bay Off-Width* (5.10c) follows the left-slanting crack, then cuts back right. This boulder is located on the east side of Brockway Hill between Kings Beach and Incline. Turn off CA 28 onto Amagosa Street, then turn right on Warsaw Road. Drive to the end of the road; the rock is visible 50 yards up the hill overlooking the lake.

Crystal Tower is the obvious 80-foot-high cliff up and left of Crystal Bay Boulder. *Crystal Tower Direct* (5.11d) takes the left line up a seam to knobs. On the right, *Crystal Eyes* (5.10a) climbs past a roof to the double cracks.

The Crystal Cracks are an excellent group of short cracks below Crystal Bay Boulder. On the left, *Hand of Doom* (5.10b) climbs the corner, then traverses left onto the face near the top. *Master of Reality* (5.11c) is to the right. *Snowblind* (5.11c) runs up a crack on the left side of the next formation. *Crystal Meth* (5.10c) is a thin hand crack to the right. An unnamed 5.10a route lies between these two climbs.

The Lycra Eliminator is an excellent overhanging face located above the ski area in Incline Village. The rock is on the north side of Tyrol Drive, a short ways after the sharp left curve. There are five routes from 5.11c to 5.12a, all of which can be conveniently toproped from the anchor bolts on top.

Sand Harbor State Park is located off CA 28, 4 miles south of Incline and 8 miles north of Spooner Summit. The boulders are scattered along the water's edge, and the best ones are at the east end of the park. Most of the problems tend to involve thin moves up slabby boulders with dangerous or wet landings. The cove and beach areas are incredibly beautiful. There is a charge to park and use the area.

WEST SHORE

D. L. Bliss State Park, one of the finer bouldering sites in the Tahoe Basin, has an abundance of excellent problems. The park is located off California Highway 89, a few miles north of Emerald Bay. You will find some good problems in the camping area, but the best bouldering lies on the north edge of the park. Park off CA 89 in one of the two pullouts about 1 mile north of the park's entrance. From either parking area, you can access the majority of the best boulders, which are scattered throughout the forest. There is also good bouldering 0.5 mile south of the park, above and below the highway.

SOUTH SHORE

The best bouldering in Emerald Bay lies below U.S. Highway 50, just north of Eagle Falls. The south faces of several low granite formations are visible from the falls. The Bay Cliffs and God Wall also are in this area. An obscure trail north of the falls leads to the formations.

Many boulders lie along Kingsbury Grade and its connecting streets. The finest collection begins 1.5 miles above US 50 and extends for several miles over the summit grade and down the backside. The best side street bouldering is on North and South Benjamin Ways and on Tramway Drive. Some of the boulders are as tall as 40 feet and should be toproped.

Pie Shop is surrounded by excellent bouldering, particularly near the beginning of the approach trail off Sawmill Road (see the section on Pie Shop in the main text). The Echo View Boulders are to the west of Pie Shop and Space Invaders. You will find many good problems here. To reach this area, turn off Sawmill Road onto Echo View Estates and follow it to Mount Canary Road. Park at the end of Mount Canary and hike straight off the pavement, slanting up through the forest. The boulders are just a few minutes away.

The Boulders, several huge blocks of granite, are located at Lover's Leap. There are several problems, from steep face climbs to off-widths. A couple short roofs and the Royal Robbins aid ladder (old bolts) can be toproped. The Boulders stand alongside Pony Express Trail, a few minutes east of the campground.

The hillsides surrounding Phantom Spires offer superb bouldering. A bit of exploration is necessary because the area is so vast. Many formations are suitable for toproping.

Pack Saddle Pass is a great area with huge potential. Of the 30 or so boulders, 12 have been worked, revealing over 60 problems ranging from 5.7 to 5.12. The rocks range from 10 to 40 feet high, and the majority of the landings are on soft pine duff. To find this area, take Mile-42 Tract Road off US 50, 1 mile west of Strawberry. Make a right turn after crossing the bridge that spans the American River. Drive approximately 5 miles up this poorly paved road and be sure not to turn onto the many dirt roads intersecting it. At the summit marker for Pack Saddle Pass, there are three roads. The left one is Silver Fork Road (paved). The middle road is not paved or marked, but is known as Middle Fork Road. Proceed down Middle Fork Road for about 1 mile, then make a right turn. This road leads to five rocks called the Entrance Boulders, which have several fine problems. Continue for 0.3 mile to a pullout on the left side of the road. Many large boulders exist here.

Jason Schultz bouldering at D. L. Bliss State Park.
Photo by Brian Biega.

Ice Climbing Areas Overview

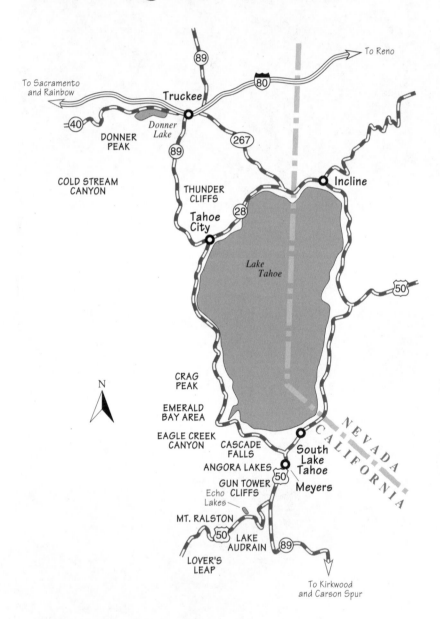

To Reno

89

80

To Sacramento
and Rainbow

Truckee

40

Donner
Lake

267

DONNER
PEAK

89

COLD STREAM
CANYON

THUNDER
CLIFFS

28

Incline

Tahoe
City

Lake
Tahoe

50

N

CRAG
PEAK

EMERALD
BAY AREA

EAGLE CREEK
CANYON

CASCADE
FALLS

South
Lake
Tahoe

NEVADA

CALIFORNIA

ANGORA LAKES

50

GUN TOWER
Echo   CLIFFS
Lakes

Meyers

MT. RALSTON

50

LAKE
AUDRAIN

89

LOVER'S
LEAP

To Kirkwood
and Carson Spur

Ice Climbing

It has been said that a California ice climber's most important piece of gear is a fast car. The formation of ice in California is inconsistent. Ice conditions can be excellent one morning, and, a few days later, poor or nonexistent.

Some flows form regularly; however, their challenges will vary with the temperature, quality of ice, and specific line you choose to ascend. These ever-changing factors are part of the adventure of ice climbing around Lake Tahoe.

Most of the areas described in this guide form between early December and March, although an occasional cold snap will result in superb ice climbing in November, before the deep snows cover portions of the routes. Tahoe ice is never considered "out of condition;" rather, it becomes more difficult and dangerous until it is gone.

A WORD ABOUT RATINGS

The rating of ice climbs is more subjective than the rating of rock climbs. This is due in part to the fact that ice is ever changing and the formation is highly dependent on precipitation and temperature. It is also important to take into account that secure protection placements depend on the quality of the ice. The variability of these factors is not directly reflected in the rating of ice climbs.

The ice climbing rating system used in this guide is definitive of a route's technical grade and is listed as WI 1 through WI 7. This system does not take into account factors such as difficulty of the approach, winter hazards, avalanches, the sustained nature and length of the route, and the difficulty of the descent.

A technical rating takes into account the difficulty of the moves and the sustained nature of those difficulties. It also covers specific conditions such as ice thickness, chandlers, bugles, mushrooms, and overall pitch. The lengths of these climbs are given in meters.

WI (water ice) Grading System

WI 1 Walking with crampons.

WI 2 Climbing up to 65-degree ice with good anchors and belays.

WI 3 Sustained sections on 65- to 80-degree ice, generally thick and solid with good rests, anchors, and belays.

WI 4 Sustained climbing on 75- to 85-degree ice with short vertical sections, occasional resting places, and satisfactory protection.

WI 5 Sustained and very strenuous climbing on 85- to 90-degree ice. Generally good quality with technical factors such as chandlers and mushrooms. Protection is good to fair.

WI 6 Very sustained and strenuous climbing with few or no rests on 85- to 90-degree ice. Long pitches with difficult and poorly protected sections requiring a high level of technical proficiency.

WI 7 Extremely sustained and difficult ice from 85 to 90+ degrees. Ice tends to be poor and thin, with doubtful adhesion to the rock in places. Protection is difficult to nonexistent; the highest level of technical expertise and boldness is required.

RAINBOW

This fine roadside climb forms most years and offers enjoyable climbing. The difficulty varies with thickness of the ice, but usually ranges from WI 3–4, 40 meters. Rainbow is a summer rock climbing area located off Interstate 80, about 17 miles west of Truckee, reached via the exit at Big Bend-Rainbow. The formation is located on the right side of a granite cul-de-sac (next to the rock climb *Light Special*) and is visible from the road. The hike in takes about 15 minutes. Please consult the section on Rainbow in the main text for approach information.

COLD STREAM CANYON

Some of the most impressive ice formations in the Tahoe area are found on two steep cliffs at the head of Cold Stream Canyon. A long backcountry ski approach with no guarantees may keep this a seldom-visited area. At least six independent lines have been led, ranging from 50 to 70 meters and WI 3–5.

The lower cliff is divided by a steep buttress. On the left side, there are two lines: *Code Red* (WI 4+, 60 m) is on the far left and *Candle Spooge* (WI 5, 60 m) is on the right. Four lines usually form to the right of the buttress. Listed from left to right, they are *Coldstream* (WI 4, 50 m), *Coldscream* (WI 4, 60 m), *Code Blue* (WI 4, 60 m), and *Walk on the Wild Side* (WI 3+, 60 m).

The upper cliff has some shorter climbs and good ice bouldering. Two ropes are necessary to toprope the main routes. Ski skins are recommended for the approach.

Use the USGS 7.5-minute Norden topo map to locate this area. It lies at the 7,000-foot contour, 0.25 inch down and right from the red number 34 in the center of quadrant 34, and 3.25 inches above Anderson Peak. To avoid fines and trespassing violations, do not cut across Sugar Bowl Ski Area.

Begin the approach from the Alpine Skills Hut at the top of Donner Pass Road. Ski south toward Mount Judah, then make a long traverse along its west slope to the saddle between Mount Judah and Mount Lincoln. Traverse across the backside of Mount Lincoln and gain the prominent ridge that leads south toward Anderson Peak. Follow the ridge for about 1 mile, climbing to "Point 8,043" printed on the topo map. From that point, ski due east down forested slopes for 0.5 mile to reach the top of the cliffs. Three to four hours should be allotted for the ski back out following the same route. Route finding can be difficult and avalanche hazards exist.

DONNER PEAK

Several hundred feet of ice and snow lie on the north face of Donner Peak, humorously referred to as the "Donner Norwand," which is above the snowsheds that cover the railroad tracks. This route has an alpine feeling and difficulties vary from WI 3 to WI 4. To reach the ice, ski down the road just west of the Alpine Skill Hut atop Donner Pass Road to the base of Donner Peak's north side. Traverse eastward above the railroad tracks until beneath the summit of the peak. The ice is directly above.

THUNDER CLIFFS

The volcanic cliffs on the east side of California Highway 89 between Tahoe City and Alpine Meadows Road seem an unlikely place for ice. Yet, for a short time almost every year, a solitary drip forms an impressive pillar called *Here Today, Gone in Twenty Seconds* (WI 4–5, 15 m). As the name implies, the route doesn't last for long.

From the Alpine Meadows Road, drive south on CA 89 toward Tahoe City for about 1 mile until you reach the first private bridge crossing the Truckee River. Park in the turnout alongside the highway. From the middle of the turnout, look straight up across the highway to a prominent cliff. If there is a black streak, you're out of luck. If ice has formed, grab your tools and hurry.

CRAG PEAK

Crag Peak is a backcountry route; and, under good conditions, it is one of the longest ice climbs in the Tahoe area. About 200 meters long, this mixed climb forms in the main gully/chimney system on the north face of the peak. Expect steep and technical pitches on both rock and ice. Be sure your rack includes ice and rock protection.

Crag Peak is located near the east boundary of the Desolation Wilderness, southwest of Rubicon Peak. Several approach options exist, but the most direct is to ski up Rubicon Peak and descend toward Stony Ridge Lake. From here, ski to the base of Crag Peak. Refer to the USGS Fallen Leaf topo map for more detail. It is probably best to spend the night; otherwise be prepared for a long day.

EMERALD BAY AREA

Some of the most reliable ice is in and around the Emerald Bay area above the south end of Lake Tahoe. California Highway 89 enters this area, but sometimes it is closed in winter, so plan accordingly by checking with the California Highway Patrol or Caltrans for road conditions.

EAGLE CREEK CANYON

There are many small formations in this canyon and on the cliffs above Eagle Lake. Sometimes the large waterfall below the highway freezes. Locate the parking lot at Eagle Lake off California Highway 89 in Emerald Bay, then head south up Eagle Creek Canyon. Most of the formations are hidden in the trees or up gullies on the north side of the canyon.

Mayhem Cove, a black and gray cliff, is located on the right side of the canyon near the entrance. Under favorable winter conditions, this summer climbing crag produces a delicate curtain of icicles called *The Devil's Coat Tails* (WI 4–5, 20 m).

The convoluted north side of Maggies Peak, above Eagle Lake, offers some of the most demanding ice climbs in the area. These lines are seldom climbed because they form infrequently. Be prepared for mixed climbing on thin ice. Hike or ski up Eagle Lake Trail toward Velma Lakes until you are beneath Maggies Peak. Work up the steep slopes to the base of some ice gullies. These gullies are about 200 meters long and rate WI 3–4 with steep sections of ice and rock.

To reach Eagle Lake, hike south from the parking area at Emerald Bay, then up the canyon for about 1.5 miles. Several distinct lines form on the cliffs immediately south of the lake (WI 3–4, 20 to 40 m). More ice lies upstream from the lake's inlet. A thrash through the alders about 1 mile above the lake leads to a wide ice fall that is sunny in the morning, called *The Sunny Falls*. Several 20-meter-long lines can be climbed at WI 3–4. Occasionally some excellent routes form on the north-facing cliffs between the lake and *The Sunny Falls* (WI 3–4, 20 m).

Just south of the parking lot at Eagle Creek on CA 89, there are several steep slabs of ice. A couple hundred yards south of the parking area and up the hill, some 50 yards through the forest, there is an overhang of rock that harbors a 20-meter-high pillar of ice called *The Inertia Tube* (WI 4+).

CASCADE FALLS

The waterfall at the head of Cascade Lake usually forms a thick low-angle flow. It is a great place to learn to ice climb. The main falls are about 50 meters wide and 70 meters long, with moderate sections of stepped ice (WI 2). The cliffs on either side of the main falls are steeper, with sections of thin ice (WI 3, 30 m).

To reach the falls, begin behind Bay View Campground at the south end of Emerald Bay. Walk or ski south, contouring across the slope above Cascade Lake. About 0.5 mile from the campground, the approach trail cuts across a creek, which you follow downhill to the top of the waterfall. To arrive at the base of the falls, rappel from the rim or climb down some tricky terrain 30 yards right of the falls. The approach takes anywhere from 20 minutes to an hour.

Jay Smith on the Carson Spur near Kirkwood.
Photo by Richard Leversee.

CARSON SPUR

Several good ice climbs form in the steep erosion gullies above California Highway 89 along the Carson Spur, and on the prominent Red Cliff above the Nordic area in Kirkwood Meadows. The climbing is characterized by short steep sections separated by sloping terraces. Most of the flows are WI 3, 20 meters. During a cold spell, these short sections can be linked into long intricate routes. Please note that climbing above the highway is illegal and the area is highly prone to avalanche.

Park inside the Kirkwood entrance road or at the other end of the cliff in a large plowed turnout on the north side of the highway. (Parking and walking along the highway is illegal.) Ski well to the side of the road in order to reach the base of the cliff. Do not approach this area if the snowpack appears to be unstable; you could release an avalanche onto the road.

GUN TOWER CLIFFS

This band of cliffs and slabs offers excellent ice bouldering and climbing. It is located northwest of U.S. Highway 50 about 1.5 miles south of the agricultural station in Meyers. It is illegal to ski into the cliffs from above the highway because the potential exists to set loose an avalanche onto the road. Park just before the big left curve leading up to Echo Summit and by the Caltrans gun tower (used to mount a howitzer cannon for avalanche control). The cliffs are located about 70 yards to the north. Although the majority of the climbing is low angle (WI 2–3, 15 to 20 m), the ice often is thin, which makes it a good place to refine thin ice technique.

LAKE AUDRIAN

This area is located at 7,300 feet near the top of Echo Summit. The ice forms on a regular basis in and around several slabs, gullies, and steep faces. Some winters, thick pillars of vertical ice yield WI 4; however, most of the ice is WI 2–3, 20–30 meters.

Park 0.5 mile west of Echo Summit in a turnout on the south side of U.S. Highway 50, several hundred feet above Little Norway Resort. Begin skiing south across a bridge and up a low ridge. You will see the ice on the far side of Lake Audrain. Contour along the north and east shore of the lake to the base of the cliffs. To descend, head west and then down the snow slopes.

MOUNT RALSTON

Sometimes, ice can be found in the couloir on the northeast face of this peak. Mount Ralston lies just to the southwest of Echo Lakes. Ski from the Echo Lakes Lodge along the south shore of the lake until you are beneath the face.

ANGORA LAKES

This climb lies in a rocky cirque above Angora Lakes in the north bowl of Echo Peak. The long approach is said to be worth the effort for this quality climb.

Ski up Angora Ridge Road to Angora Lakes Resort. The route ascends a wide gully near the eastern end of the cliff band above the upper lake. To descend, walk north and down to the lake. Use extreme caution; high avalanche hazard exists in this area.

LOVER'S LEAP

The main attraction at Lover's Leap is the somewhat mythic *Eeyore's Fantasy* (WI 4–5, 150 m). In the summer, the route is known as *Eeyore's Ecstasy*. The ice appears to form rarely below the chimney, giving the impression that the route is out of condition. Ironically, the bulk of the route usually is fine, but it is hard to recognize this until you reach the end of Main Ledge. Even under the best conditions, be prepared for tricky route finding, mixed sections, and thin ice.

Ascend ice and rock via a third-class gully to Main Ledge. Traverse about 100 yards to the wide chimney of *Eeyore's Ecstasy*. The first pitch is a full rope length to a block with rappel slings. The next pitch wanders up and into a cave, continuing up a wide slot past a chockstone to the base of an overhanging chimney. The third pitch ascends an ice smear (hopefully formed) on the left wall. A good selection of rock protection and long slings, in addition to ice gear, is necessary. Other challenging ice climbs at the Leap include *Lover's Chimney* and the *East Gully*. For approach and descent information, refer to the section on Lover's Leap in the main text.

Alpenglow Sports in Tahoe City and Sierra Mountaineer in Truckee and Reno regularly post ice climbing and backcountry skiing conditions and are knowledgeable sources of ice and rock climbing information.

FIRST ASCENTS

. . . .

First ascents are listed by section in the order they appear in the book.

THE EMERALDS

Ambushed in the Night: M. Carville, May 1989
Apathy: Dave Nettle, Jim Quirk, M. Carville, June 1989
Apathy: Dave Nettle, Jim Quirk, M. Carville, June 1989
Aqua: M. Carville, April 1990
Arid Oasis: M. Carville, July 1989
Atlantis: Jim Quirk, M. Carville, July 1989
Big Foot: Bill Sinoff, May 1990
Big Green: M. Carville, June 1991
Bustin' Rhymes: M. Carville, May 1990
Buzz Saw: Brian Mason, Dave Hatchett, Curtis Sykes, September 1990
Chasing the Dragon: M. Carville, June 1990
Chicks Dig It: Bill Sinoff, and Kari Paul, 1992
Chronic Fatigue Syndrome: Ray Munoz, Dave Hatchett, Brian Mason, September 1990
Cloud Factory: M. Carville, June 1990
Dam It: M. Carville, Jori Richnak, April 1989
Duppy Conqueror: M. Carville, August 1989
Dynamic Panic: M. Carville, W. Chen, Dave Rubine, July 1989
Electric Chair (project): M. Carville
Emerald Staircase (project): M. Carville
Fact or Friction: Gene Drake, M. Carville, September 1989
Fireball: Dave Hatchett, R. Munoz, C. Sykes, September 1990
Fish Face: J. Quirk, K. Burns, M. Carville, July 1989
Flake Bake: D. Hatchett, C. Sykes, April 1990
Green Ice: M. Carville, May 1989
Gypsy Moth: Sue McKim, M. Carville, June 1995
High and Dry: Jori Richnak, M. Carville, April 1989
Hundredth Monkey: M. Carville, June 1990 (to the top); variation: Don Welsh, Jim Zellers, June 1990
Indigo: Hanneli Francis, M. Carville, June 1990
Jail Break: Jori Richnak, M. Carville, July 1989
Jaws: M. Carville, May 1990
Juluka: M. Carville, June 1988
Kudos: M. Carville, June 1989
Lower Main Wall project: Bill Sinoff, M. Carville
Maniac: Hanneli Francis, M. Carville, June 1990
Mono Dioght: M. Carville, May 1989
Mosquito Coast: Will Chen, Herb Leager, July 1989
Narcada (project): M. Carville
Overflow: Jori Richnak, M. Carville, April 1989

Pimp the Ho: M. Carville, August 1989
Radio Static: M. Carville, July 1989
Second Time Around: Dan Day, Jim Zellers, Bonnie Leary, M. Jenserik, June 1989
Shadows on the Earth: M. Carville, August 1988
Solar Wind: M. Carville, Jenny Carville, May 1989
Steel Monkey: M. Carville, May 1988
Still Life: M. Carville, July 1989
Stone Fish: M. Carville, solo, May 1989
Stress Fracture: Jenny Carville, M. Carville, May 1989
Sub-Zero: D. Hatchett, R. Munoz, C. Sykes, September 1990
Sun Burn: Kia Burns, Dan Day, May 1989
The Cure: Dan Day, M. Carville, June 1988
The Dream Affair: Jeremy Werlin, M. Carville, June 1988
The E-Ticket Ride: Don Welsh, M. Carville, June 1988
The Fly: M. Carville, July 1989
The Invisible Man: T. Worsfold, July 1990
The Perils of Babylon: M. Carville, May 1989
Three Minute Hero: Kia Burns, M. Carville, May 1989
Three Minute Hero: Kim Burns, M. Carville, May 1989
Toprope Wall: Jeremy Werlin, Joel Richnak, M. Carville, June 1988
Ultraviolet: D. Hatchett, R. Lovelace, September 1990
Unnamed (project): Todd Worsfold
Voodoo Bliss: M. Carville, April 1990
White Riot: Dan Day, M. Carville, May 1988
Yellow Jacket: Inno Nagara, Troy Carliss, June 1990

BOWMAN LAKE

Routes by Doug Mishler, Steve Glotfelty, and Jim Neff.

INDIAN SPRINGS

Captain Cheese Dog: Rocco Spina and friends, 1990
Firestone: Rocco Spina and friends, 1990
Most FAs by Rocco Spina
Old Sea Hag: Rocco Spina and friends, 1990
Out of the Blue: Rocco Spina and friends, 1990
Pappy Smear: Rocco Spina and friends, 1990
Rocco's Corner: Rocco Spina and friends, 1990
Slick Dog: Rocco Spina and friends, 1990
Zephyr: Rocco Spina and friends, 1990

RAINBOW

38 Special: Victor Marcus, John Hoffman, 1982
Aja: Malcolm Jolly, 1977

Amazing Grace: Victor Marcus, John Hoffman, 1984

Black and Blue (project): Doug Mishler

Cheap Thrills: John Hoffman, Dick Richardson, 1987

Colors: M. Carville, 1990

Dark Special: Gene Drake, Victor Marcus, 1978

Dirty Deed: Unknown

Drain Pipe: Bill Clark, 1977

Gasoline Alley: Gary Allen, 1979

J.O.'s: Jim Orey, 1978

Jack the Ripper: John Hoffman, Victor Marcus, 1984

Jousting with the Jackal: M. Carville, 1989

Jumping Jack Flash: John Hoffman, Victor Marcus, 1984

Light Special: Jim Orey, Victor Marcus, 1978

Lockbuster: John Hoffman, Gene Drake, Karl Hammer, 1979

Malcolm's Route: Malcolm Jolly, Dick Richardson, 1978

Monkey Business: Hidetaka Suzuki, 1989

Over the Rainbow: Gary Allen, 1979

Peyote Pump: Gary Allen, Victor Marcus, 1978

Rainbow Bridge: Unknown

Rainbow Project: Doug Mishler

Scarecrow: John Hoffman, 1978

Skin Flick: John Hoffman, Gary Allen, Victor Marcus, Gene Drake, 1979

Sleeper:

The Force (project): Gene Drake

Walk and Don't Look Back: Mike Creel, Chris Craig, 1987

DONNER SUMMIT

2-25: Chris Bouman, 1990

A Steep Climb Named Desire: Scott Frye, 1990

Aerial: Unknown

Ajax: Todd Worsfold, 1988

Alien Sex: Victor Marcus, 1994

Alvin's Toprope: Alvin McClain

Animal Logic: Mark Diederichsen, 1990

Animal Magnetism: Ken Ariza, Kurt Smith

Ape Fire: Chris Bauman, 1992

Aqualung: Gary Allen, Max Jones, 1977

Assault and Battery: Rocco Spina, 1990

Baby Bear: Unknown, 1980

Bark Like a Shark: Steve Glotfelty, 1990

Bearclaw: Rocco Spina, 1990

Bell Bottom Blues: Kurt Smith, Steve Schnieder, 1984

Big Shot: Victor Marcus, Dan Patitucci, 1995

Bimbo Roof: Harrison Dekker

Bird Brain: Brian Biega

Birdy: Hans Standteiner, Dale Kim, 1987

Black September: Eric Beck, et al., 1973

Bliss Direct: Doug Mishler, 1987

Bliss: Max Jones, Victor Marcus, Gary Allen, 1979

Bluff: Unknown

Bolt Run: Karl Hammer, John Hoffman, 1974

Bottomless Topless: Unknown

Bourbon Street: Gary Allen, John Hoffman, Malcolm Jolly, 1977

Brain Child: Christian Griffith, 1980

Break It Out: Unknown

Break Out: Unknown

Bronco: Hidataka Suzuki, 1988

Bypass: Max Jones, et al., 1979

Caffeine Club: Don Welsh, 1990

Caifura: Rocco Spina, 1990

Cannibals: Scott Frye, 1988

Catch the Sky: Lori Sorensen, 1990

Change Up: Gene Drake, Jim Silfrast, 1977

Composure: Unknown

Cookie Mix: Scott Frye 1996

Cottontail Crack: Robert Chalfant, Mick Keane, 1995

Crack A No Go: Unknown

Crack of the Eighties: Alan Watts, 1987

Cream Puff: John Hoffman, 1983

Cucumber Slumber: Gary Allen, Max Jones

Dark Crystal: Mark Rogers, 1990

Death Tongue: Doug Mishler, 1989

Desire: Kevin Heckathorne

Devaluation: Unknown

Diamond in the Rough: Hank Ni, 1989

Diamond in the Ruff: Hank Ni, 1989

Disciples of the New Wave: Steve Glotfelty

Don't Try This at Home: Richard Leversee, Greg Smith, Bob Harrington, 1987

Donner Delight: Gary Allen, 1977

Easy Street: Dan Patitucci, Victor Marcus, 1997

Eleventh Grade Corner: Unknown

Empty Overgo: Unknown

Empty Sky: Max Jones, Geoff Smith, 1977

Escargot: Paul Scanell

Europa: Bela and Mimi Vadez

Exocette: Mark Diederichsen, 1990

Eyes of Silver: Dick Richardson, Malcolm Jolly, 1977

Far Side: Don Welsh, 1995

Farewell to Arms: Karl Hammer, John Hoffman, 1976

Fascination: Gary Allen, Max Jones, 1977

Father's Day: Tom Herbert, 1997

Finger Graffiti: aided in the 1960s

Pump Lust: Harrison Decker, 1987

Puppet on a String: Scott Frye, 1988; direct start Scott Frye 1988

Purple Toupee: Victor Marcus, 1990

Quarter Hit: John Hoffman

Rambo Crack: Hidetaka Suzuki, 1987

Rapid Transit: Unknown

Rat's Tooth: Unknown

Rhinestone Desperado: John Hoffman, Eric Perlman, 1990

Rhythm Killer: M. Carville, 1988

Roadkill: Rocco Spina, 1990

Rocco's Demise: Rocco Spina, 1990

Roccocator: Rocco Spina, 1990

Rolling Thunder: Hidataka Suzuki 1993

Sanitation Crack: Max Jones, 1977

Seams to Me: D. Grossman, R. Van Horn, 1980

Senior Prom: Unknown

Shoot Out: Unknown

Short Cake: John Hoffman, 1983

Short Subject: Mic Deiro

Side Winder: John Hoffman, Eric Perlman

Silver Book: Max Jones, 1976

Sky Pilot: Max Jones, Mark Hudon, 1977

Skywalker: Bill Anderson, Gene Drake, 1981

Slim Pickens: Scott Frye 1996

Slipstream: Max Jones, Gary Allen, 1976

Slowhand: Eric Barrett and friends, 1981

Space Invaders: Gene Drake, Rocko Rampino, 1981

Space Modulator: Pete Chasse, 1996

Spaceman: Steve Glotfelty, 1990

Split Pea: Unknown

Squeal Like a Seal: Steve Glotfelty, 1993

Star Wars Crack: Alan Watts, 1986

Suck Face: Unknown

Summer Breeze: Brian Biega, 1995

Super Slab: Max Jones, Gary Allen, 1977

Survival of the Fattest: Bill Sinoff

Taste the Pain: Don Welsh, 1990

Teacher's Pet: John Hoffman, 1975

The Drifter: Unknown

The Dropouts: (left) Max Jones, 1977; (right) Karl Hammer, 1976; (far right) Louise Sheppard, 1981

The Fuse: Max Jones, Gary Allen, 1978

The Hook: Unknown

The Texas Two-Step: Unknown

The Texorcist: Robert Chalfant, Mick Keane, 1995

The Thing: Max Jones, 1978

There Goes the Neighborhood: Gene Drake

Thunder Bolt Roof: Greg Smith

Tilt: Gary Allen, Max Jones, 1977

Tip Bitter Blues: Greg Smith, 1988

Torture Chamber: Gene Drake, 1988

Totem Pile: Jonny Woodword

Touch and Go: Kim Schmitz, Norm Simmons, 1971

Transmoggnifier: Steve Glotfelty, 1988

Two Fingers Gold: Mark Hudon, Max Jones

Varmint: Unknown

Voyeur: Gary Allen, Max Jones, 1977

Walk Away: Max Jones, Mark Hudon

Warp Factor: Scott Frye, 1988

Welcome to My Nightmare: Max Jones, John Hoffman, 1979

Wolf Crack: Unknown

Yellow Jacket: Rocco Spina, 1990

TRUCKEE RIVER CANYON

A Fine Line: J. Howle, Art Sable, 1989

All Guns Blazing: Dave Hatchett, Mike Hatchett, 1992

Arete: J. Howle, 1989

As You Like It: D. Hatchett, M. Hatchett, R. Lovelace, August 1990

Bat Ejector: T. Worsfold, Jeff Johnson, June 1990

Big Chief Arete: D. Hatchett, Jeff McKitterick, 1992

Bun in the Oven: D. Hatchett, M. Hatchett, 1993

By Fair Means: Paul Teare, J. Howle, 1990

Camel Hug: T. Worsfold, 1990

Chris Toe: Chris Walker, 1990

Clear the Bridge: Dave and Mike Hatchett, Rick Lovelace, 1990

Climb against Nature: D. Hatchett, Dave Griffith, 1992

Club Toe: John Collins, Dave Hatchett, M. Hatchett, 1990

Copper Feather: Todd Worsfold, April 1990

Cornered: Unknown

Countdown: William Jones, 1992

Dangerous Dan: Dan Betwainer, 1989

Don't Be Afraid of the Dark: Jay Smith and friends

Don't Skate Mate: Randy Ostenhuber, J. Howle, 1989

Donkey Show: D. Hatchett, Jeff McKitterick, 1993

Drill Drop: D. Hatchett, Brian Mason, October 1990

Early Bird: Unknown

Earth Girls Are Easy: J. Howle, Gerald Rockwell, 1990

Eat the Worm: D. Hatchett, Jeff McKitterick, 1991

Eye of the Beholder: Rick Lovelace, Dave Hatchett, June 1990

Farmboy: Dave and Mike Hatchett, Rick Lovelace, 1990

Festus: Brian Mason, D. Hatchett, October 1990

Sweat Hog: D. Hatchett, 1998

Tahoe Bolt Murder: J. Howle, Dave Nettle, 1989

The Accused: Dave Hatchet, Sean Sullivan, 1993

The Chief: Rick Sylvester, Wayne Wallace, July 1984

The Dagger: Unknown

The Dihedral: Dave Nettle, J. Howle, 1989

The Ghost: Unknown

The Scalper: D. Hatchett, R. Lovelace, M. Hatchett, June 1990

The Variant: Dave Hatchett, June 1990

Thrash under Pressure: M. Hatchett, D. Hatchett, Jeff McKitterick, 1993

Throne of Gold: M. Carville, 1989

Toilet Earth: D. Hatchett, Jeff McKitterick, 1993

Tommy Knockers: Dave and Mike Hatchett, Rick Lovelace, 1990

Too Light to Wait: D. Hatchett, Jeff McKitterick, 1993

Totally Board: Dave and Mike Hatchett, Rick Lovelace, 1990

Totally Chawsome: Dimitri Barton, D. Hatchett, Mike Hatchett, July 1990

Travail Buttress: Todd Worsfold, Kathy Bennet, June 1990

Tremors: Dave and Mike Hatchett, Rick Lovelace, 1990

Twin Fags: A. Sable, J. Howle, 1989

Uncle Sam's a Dirty Man: M. Carville, 1989

Undercooked: D. Hatchett, M. Hatchett, 1993

Unknown: Unknown

Vulgar Display of Power: Dave Hatchett, Mike Hatchett, 1992

Wampum: Unknown

War Paint: Unknown

War Path: Dave and Mike Hatchett, July 1990

Wicked Quickie: Dave Hatchett, Mike Hatchett, 1992

Wild Bull Rider: M. Carville, 1989

Witch Doctor: M. Hatchett, D. Hatchett, R. Lovelace, August 1990

EAGLE CREEK CANYON

A Line: Rick Sumner, J. Taylor, 1974; (var.) Greg Dexter, Bill Todd, 1976

Al Crack: P. Arthur, Barry Dow, Bob Dow, P. Sullivan, 1969

Alias Emil Bart: Unknown

All American Finger Crack: R. Sumner, Bill Todd, 1975

Atomic Punk: Jay Smith, Paul Crawford, 1982

Bachar's Line: John Bachar, et al.

Barney Rubble: A. Doehring, Mike Corbett, 1980

Bastille: Unknown

Black Abyss: P. Arthur, D. Person, 1966

Black Rain: Mike Ledlinski, Tom Gilje, 1990

Buster Brown: Rick Cashner, Mike Corbett, 1979

Cajun Hell: combination of first and second pitch, D. Osman, 1990; first pitch (Huntin' Gator) to hanging belay, D. Osman, P. Crawford, 1989; second pitch (Drinkin' White LIghtning) from hanging belay, D. Osman 1989

Casual Observer: Unknown

Changeling: Paul Tear, K. Haddock, 1982

Coma Sutra: P. Crawford, 1990

Coney Corner: Paul Arthur, Juris Krisjansen, 1966

Cracula: Rick Cashner and Bill Serniuk, 1979

Dave's Run: Unknown

Delbert's Diagonal: A. Doehring, B. and C. Serniuk, 1979

Delbert's Direct: A. Doehring, 1979

Der Fuhrer: Jay Smith, Paul Crawford, P. Obanheim, 1985

Distant Early Warning: R. Lovelace

Disturbing the Priest: D. Osman, 1990

Diversions: J. Altenburg and friends, 1975

Doolagoga Dihedral: C. Bryan, B. Crawford, 1972

Eagle Route: Dave Beck, Norm Wilson, 1963

East Ridge Route: Rick Sumner, Bill Todd, solo, 1974

Fallout: Unknown

Fatal Attraction: P. Crawford, T. Worsfold, 1989

Gator Bait: Gram Saunders, 1996

Gold Mettle: Paul Crawford, 1983

Gumby Goes to Hollywood: R. Lovelace, D. Hatchett

Hail Mary: P. Crawford

High Velocity: Jay Smith, Paul Crawford, May 1989

Holdless Horror: Unknown

Holy Moses: P. Crawford, D. Osman

I'm a Gumby Dammit: Morgan Kent, Dvorack

Ice Nine: Unknown

India Ink: P. Crawford, 1989

Indian Head: C. Bryan, P. Crawford, M. Shreve, 1976

Indirect Route: M. Shreve, R. Sumner, K. Wentworth, 1973

Ivory Book: D. Person, D. Tompkins, N. Wilson, 1963

Light Years: Paul Crawford, Fossonberger, May 1988

Lightning Bolt: Unknown

Lizard Man: Ken Ariza, 1989

Lost in Space: Unknown

Master of Disaster: Paul Obanheim, J. Mitchell, 1985

Master Race: Jay Smith, Paul Crawford, Paul Obanheim, 1985

Monkey Business: Rick Sumner, Bill Todd, 1974

Moonraker: Rick Cashner, Angie Morales, 1979

Mountaineer's Route: Unknown

Never Ending Story: Unknown

Off the Wall: D. Rennick, K. Volz, 1973; FFA Unknown

One More for the Road: Unknown

Orange Marmalade: J. Smith, J. Taylore, 1977

Orange Sunshine: K. Nelson, Bill Todd, 1974

Pigs in a Blender: D. Hatchett, R. Lovelace, 1990

Polar Circus: Unknown

Polecat: Bill Todd, 1976

Poopout Pinnacle: Dave Broan, Paul Holleb, Ken Volz 1973

Psycho: D. Osman, P. Crawford, 1990

Quest for Power: Dale Frixbee and friends, 1983

Race with the Devil: Paul Obanheim, Paul Crawford

Regular Route: Unknown

Relativity: Unknown

Rentier: Unknown

Riddler: T. Worsfold, 1990

Ripoff: Unknown

Sandbagged: Unknown

Seams to Me: D. Grossman, R. Van Horn, 1980

Section 20: Doug Tompkins and partner, 1963; upper Section: Paul Arthur and partner, 1967

Separated Reality: R. Clegg, K. Volz, 1973

Shuman the Human: Unknown

Slander: Todd Worsfold, 1992

Space Truckin': Rick Cashner, Angie Morales, 1979

Space Walk: Kevin Nelson, Bill Todd, 1973; FFA: Rick Cashner, Rick Sumner, 1979

Spontaneous Combustion: D. Hatchett, 1990

Stomach Ache: J. Attenburg, R. Sumner, J. Taylor, 1975

Strontium 90: Unknown

Tar Babies: T. Worsfold, 1992

The Buzzard: Jay Smith, Paul Crawford, P. Obanheim, 1985

The Criterion: Jay Smith, Paul Obanheim, J. Mitchell, 1981

The Diamond: Art Sable, Dave Nettle, Jim Howle, 1990

The Emerald Beyond: Bill and Charlene Serniuk, 1979

The Guillotine Direct: Todd Worsfold, 1987

The Jack Crack: Paul Crawford, solo, 1986

The Jester: Unknown

The Manny: Paul Crawford, 1986

The Mo Crack: Paul Crawford, 1986

The Nagual: Bill Todd, 1976; FFA: Rick Cashner, Angie Morales, 1979

The Plectrum East Face: Unknown

The Plectrum West Face: Mike Haskins, John Holkko, Ken Volz, 1972

The Vulture: Jay Smith, Paul Crawford, Paul Obanheim, 1985

Thin Fingers: Unknown

Thrust Is a Must: D. Grossman, Rick Van Horn, 1980

Ti-si-ack: Unknown

Venturi: J. Smith, Jo Bentley, May 1989

Verbal Abuse: Paul Crawford, D. Osman, 1990

Vintage 85: Unknown

White Lightning: B. Todd, 1976

White Walls: Unknown

Wild at Heart: T. Worsfold, M. Carville, August 1990

Wind Tree: Kevin Nelson, Bill Todd, 1974

EAST SHORE CRAGS

Acapulco: Jay Smith, Sue Gerberdine, 1988 (Off limits to climbing)

Ancient Route: Brad Clayton, 1972

Anthrax: Jay Smith, June 1988

Asylum a.k.a. The Sanitarium: Jay Smith, 1990

Bad Brains: Dan Osman, Paul Crawford, June 1988

Bone Crusher: Dimitri Barton, Dave Hatchett, Mike Hatchett, 1991

Bora-Bora: Jay Smith, Craig Reason, April 1987

Caught in a Mosh: Ray Munoz, Dave Hatchett, 1990

Cave Man Direct: Rolland Arsons, 1990

Cave Man: Dave Hatchett, Rick Lovelace, 1990

Club Med: Jay Smith, Paul Obanheim, April 1987

Concave: Paul Crawford, 1990

Coppertone: Paul Crawford, 1991

Crimper Overdose: Antu Cerretti, William Jones

Deaf Leopard: Paul Crawford, Jay Smith, September 1987

Feline: Paul Crawford, 1989

Fiji: Paul Crawford, 1991

Fire and Ice: Ray Munoz, Dve Hatchett, Todd Worsfold, 1990

Fire in the Hole: Dan Osman, 1991

First Dose: Ryan Wolfe, William Jones

Forget about It: Max Jonoes, Mark Kaminsky, 1991

Friction Route: Roger Moreau, Jim Jonas, July 1956

Gale: L Brown, C. Saal, J. Williamson, 1974

Great Ledge: Roger Moreau, Jim Jonas, Rich Jonas, July 1956

Hanger-18: Dave Hatchett, Brian Mason, 1990

Hits Per Minute: Todd Worsfold, 1990

Hurricane: Louis Brown, ChrisSaal, John Williamson, 1974

Impact Zone: Mike and Dave Hatchett, Rick Lovelace, 1990

Jello Wars: Todd Worsfold, Dave Hatchett, 1990

Karncave: Jim Karn, 1991

Kona Crack: J. Smith, April 1987

Leisure Suit: Oliver Datwyler, William Jones

Maco: Jay Smith, Robert Finnlay, 1989

Maui Zowie: J. Smith, April 1987

Maxwells Hammer: Max Jonoes, Mark Kaminsky, 1991

Messiah: Dan Osman, 1991

Metallica: Jay Smith, August 1987

Molokai: J. Smith, April 1987

Nightcrawler: Dave Hatchett, 1990

OB's: Paul Obanheim, Sue Sweet, September 1987

One Man Ledge: Roger Moreau, Jim Jonas, Rich Jonas, July 1956

Over the Falls: Dave and Mike Hatchett

Phantom Lord: Dan Osman, 1990

Pigeon Hole: John Goodman, Dave Griffith, 1989

Pipeline: Jay Smith, 1989

Pocket Pool: Dave Hatchett, Ray Munoz, 1990

Poison Arch: Dan Osman, solo

Pootang: Oliver Datwyler, William Jones

Port of Entry: Paul Crawford, Dan Osman, Dimitri Barton, 1990

Psycho Monkey: Dan Osman, 1990

Rat Reach: Dan Osman, Chris Bauer, September 1988

Rip Curl: Jay Smith, 1989

Roto Arete: Antu Cerretti, William Jones

Sea and Ski: Paul Crawford, 1991

Shut the Fuck up and Climb: Dimitri Barton, 1990

Shut up and Climb: Dave Griffith, 1990

Slayer: Dan Osman 1992

Super Monkey: Jason Campbell, 1996

Tahiti: Jay Smith, 1990

Tahoe Monster: Paul Crawford, Jay Smith, April 1987

Tempest: (aka: Great Traverse and Moreau's Chute): Roger Moreau, Jerry Steenblock, Gene Angus, August 1956

The Mid-Evil: Paul Crawford, 1990

The Pedestal: Roger Moreau, Jim Jonas, Rich Jonas, July 1956

The Pit: Dave Hatchett, Mike Hatchett

The Reef: Paul Crawford, Jay Smith, April 1987

Thinkin' about It: Max Jonoes, Mark Kaminsky, 1991

Thought about It: Max Jonoes, Mark Kaminsky, 1991

Ton of Bricks: Jay Smith, 1990

Trash Dog: Paul Crawford, 1991

Tweedle Dee: Unknown

Tweedle Doo: Unknown

Underground: Paul Crawford, 1989

Uranium Roof: Paul Teare, Jay Smith, June 1988

View to a Thrill: Jay Smith, Paul Crawford, September 1987

PIE SHOP

7-11 Cracks: Alan Swanson, Ken Black, Mark Bauer, 1985

Altar: Paul Crawford, John Rosholt, Rick Van Horn, 1977

Ambrosia: Unknown

America's Most Wanted: Dave and Mike Hatchett

Ancient Route: Unknown

Archer: Unknown

Battle Axe: Ron Volkmar and friends

Battle Star Galactica: Dan Osman

Bear Claw: Al Swanson

Blaster Pals: Graham Sanders

BT Express: Rick Sumner, Bill Todd, 1974

Burnt Pie: Unknown

Buttons to Nuttin': Al Swanson, Dan Osman

Cake Walk: Al Swanson

Clean Corner: Steve Miller, Jay Smith, 1980

Crawford's Face: Paul Crawford

Cream Puff: Unknown

Crepes Corner: Unknown

Cruise Control: D. Nidever, Kevin Nelson, 1981

Delicate Edge: Ron Volkmar and friends

Deliverance: Unknown

Desiderata: Bill Todd, 1976

Donkey Kong: Paul Crawford

Double Dragon: Tom Herbert

Dropout: Unknown; FFA: Richard Harrison, Jay Smith, 1977

Dudley Doright: Ron Volkmar

Earn Your Wings: B. Crawford, C. Crawford, 1979

Fear of Flying: B. Crawford, P. Crawford, 1978

Fight for Life: P. Crawford

Flight for Life: P. Crawford

Fluff Boys in Bondage: Bill Serniuk, Al Swanson

Fluted Crust: Unknown

Hair Pie: Unknown

Hands Masseuse: Paul Crawford, Mike Shreve, 1976

Head East: Unknown

Head Up: Kurt Rassmussen

Headjammer: Greg Dexter, Steve Miller, 1976

Hindsight: Unknown

Humble Pie: Unknown

Hurricane: Unknown

Iotolla: Tom Herbert

J-Walk: Tom Condon, R. Jamieson, 1971

Jewel of the Nile: Troy Mayr

Knob Hill: Unknown

Mad Wife: D. Nidever, K. Nelson, 1981

Marmot Cave: Dan Osman

Marmot Pie: Cactus Joe Bryan, Jeff Lowe, 1971

Miller High Life: Steve Miller, solo, 1976

Mincemeat Variation: Unknown

Moss Pie: Bill Crawford, D. Dvorak, 1972

Natural High: D. Waters, 1973; FFA: Paul Crawford, Rick Van Horn, 1980

New Blood: Al Swanson

No Future: S. Bushy, Paul Crawford, Eric Alexander, 1977

Pie Face Dihedral: Steve Miller, Jay Smith, 1978

Pie in the Sky: Cactus Bryan, Paul Crawford, 1971

Pinchin' the Lip: Dan Osman

Poly Grip: Paul Crawford, Rick Van Horn, 1980

Project: Dan Osman

Road House Blues: Dave Hatch, Rick Lovelace

Saturn: P. Crawford

Shelob's Lair: Bill Todd, 1976

Short Cake: Steve Miller, Jay Smith, 1978

Simple Simon: Unknown

Sky Shark: P. Crawford, Tom Herbert

Space Invaders: Unknown

Teenage Wasteland: Paul Crawford, Eric Alexander, 1979

The Jetsons: Unknown

The Last Dance: Rick Van Horn, 1980

The Price Is Light: Alan Swanson, Bill Price, 1985

The Saw: Bill Crawford, M. Franceschini, Dan Dvorak, Rick Jamieson, 1973

The Slot: Unknown

The Walrus: Bill Todd, 1976

True Grip: Paul Crawford, P. Steiner, 1975

Unknown: Dave LaWinter

Walk Like an Egyptian: Al Swanson and Paul Crawford

Wind: Paul Crawford, 1978

Wipeout: Bill Todd, 1976

Zig Zag Finish: Paul Crawford, 1978

CHRISTMAS TREE VALLEY

After Hours: Jeff Mayfield, Jay Sell, Brock Berry, 1997

Bar Fly: Jeff Mayfield, Jay Sell, 1997

Bottoms Up: Steven Briggs, Blake Berry, 1997

Chip Shot: Jay Sell, Brock Berry, 1996

Deceptive Pillar: Jay Sell, Chuck Brown, 1971

Fallen Spirits: Jay Sell, Brock Berry, 1996

Five Nine: Unknown

Got Your Hammer Hangin': Larry Duin, Jay Sell, Banny Root

Greyhound: Jay Sell, Bod Shultz, Brock Berry, 1995

Happy Hour: Steven Briggs, Brock Berry, 1997

Jonesin': Jay Sell, Brock Berry, 1996

Lady Dihedral: Larry Duin, Rob Bittner, Daryl Bodick

Larry's House: Chazz Spath, Brock Berry

Loading Dose: Liz Wilson-Sell, Jay Sell, 1996

Methadone: Jay Sell, Brock Berry, 1996

Moonshine: Jay Sell, Brock Berry, Bob Schultz, 1996

Our Lady of Fatima: Larry Duin, Jay Sell, 1991

Plaque Smear: Jay Sell, Chuch Brown, Daryl Bodick, 1991

Political Shots: Jay Sell, Brock Berry, 1996

Ripper Arete: Larry Duin, Jay Sell

Rockin' into the Night: Larry Duin, Jay Sell, 1996

Seven & Seven: Jay Sell, Brock Berry, 1996

Skid Row: Jay Sell, Brock Berry, 1995

Stir Fry: Jay Sell, Tim Bittner, 1991

Straight Jacket: Steven Briggs, Brock Berry, 1997

The Fossil: Jay Sell, Brock Berry, Bob Shultz

With Draws: Jay Sell, Brock Berry, 1996

Yards of Ale: Jay Sell, 1997

ECHO LAKES

3-D: Paul Crawford, Banny Root, October 1988

A Good Day to Die: Al Swanson, 1991

Aesop: Paul Crawford, September 1990

Aftermath: Mike Corbett, A. Doehring, 1979

Baby Jones: Dave Griffith

Black Panther: Dave Hatchett, Mike Hatchett

Blade Runner: Dan Osman, April 1988

Bolt Race: Paul Crawford, Craig Reason, 1986

Bookie: Mike Corbett, Charlene Serniuk, 1980

Boppy's Crack: Mike Corbett, Bill Serniuk, 1979

Bushfreak Corner: Unknown

Bushfreak Eliminate: Unknown

Chemical Warfare: Al Swanson, Dave Hatchett, Mike Hatchett, 1989

Chore Boy: Al Swanson, Dan Osman

Coin Toss: Al Swanson, Dave Hatchett, October 1988

Corkscrew: Unknown

Corner Pocket: Mike and Dave Hatchett, Ed Collins

Country Boy: Al Swanson, Dave Hatchett

Crack Babies: Dave Hatchett, Al Swanson

Crystalline Dream: Unknown

Death Tuna: Don Garret, Rick Van Horn, Paul Crawford, 1983

Dirty Deeds: Al Swanson, Charlene Serniuk

Dumbo: Paul Crawford, free solo, 1986

E.B.'s Wall: Kevin Nelson, Bill Todd, 1974

East Meat: Bill Serniuk, solo, 1979

Fight Fire with Fire: Al Swanson, Dave Hatchett, Bill Serniuk, 1987

First Stage: Val

Fit to Be Tied: Charlie Downs, Jon Bowlin, 1981

Flash the Blade: Dave and Mike Hatchett

Flu: Jay Sell, Jason Totallman

Fool's Gold: Jay Smith, 1991

Freon: Al Swanson, Mike and Dave Hatchett

Germ Warfare: Al Swanson, 1989

Gold Finger Arete: Al Swanson, 1991

Golden Shower: Al Swanson, 1991

Golden Years: Paul Crawford, Paul Tears, Fletcher Wilson, 1984

Great Golden Beaver: Jim Holden

Green Room: Al Swanson, John Nye

Grin and Bare It: Bill Todd, 1976

Hair Trigger: Al Swanson, October 1988

Hanus Anus: Dave and Mike Hatchett, Rick Lovelace

Hicks from the Sticks: Jay Smith, Paul Van Betten, Sal Mamusia

Hip Hop Hipe: Al Swanson, Cory Hicks

Hit and Run: Rick Cashner, Mike Corbett, Bill Serniuk, 1979

Hoster: Bill Serniuk and friends

I Cut My Hair: Paul Crawford (TR, no lead yet)

If I Had a Hammer: Al Swanson, Fred Cohen, Charlene Serniuk, 1985

Jam Session: Unknown

Kangaroo: John Bowlin, Jim Day, Jim Orey, 1979

Leapin' Lizards: Mike Corbett, Charlene Serniuk, 1979

Lelfie: Unknown

Little Sir Echo: (toprope) Paul Crawford, 1984; Kurt Rassmussen, September 1988

Magic Book: Mike Corbett, Bill Serniuk, Charlene Serniuk, 1979

Mangod: Al Swanson

Metal Blade: Dan Osman, July 1988

Metal Head: Ed Collins, Dave and Mike Hatchett

Metallica: Dan Osman, September 1990

Mind's Eye: John Collins, Al Swanson, Dave Hatchett, 1989

Negra Modelo: Dan Kametat, Tom Carter, 1993

New Jersey Turnpike: Jay Sell

Nurse's Aid: Unknown

Nye's Corner: John Nye

Odd Job: Al Swanson, Have Hatchett, John Collins, 1989

Offwidth Their Heads: Rick Cashner, Mike Corbett, 1979

Old Peculiar: Mike Corbett, Bill Serniuk, Charlene Serniuk, 1979

Pay Day: Bill Serniuk, solo, 1979

Pitchfork: Unknown

Power Stance: Dave Hatchett, Al Swanson

Puppet Master: Bill Serniuk and friends; variation by Al Swanson, Cory Hicks

Pyramid: Paul Crawford, Paul Obanheim, 1983

Rage for Order: Dave and Mike Hatchett, Dave Griffith, 1990

Rawl Wall: Al Swanson (solo); later lead by Cory Hicks, Jim Bittner, 1989

Rehumanize Yourself: John Akens, Jay Smith, Karl Jenkewitz, 1982

Right Parallel Crack: Banny Root, Bill Serniuk

Rock-A-Bye: Al Swanson, Charlene Serniuk, 1985

Rough and Ready: Unknown

Run 'n' Gun: Al Swanson

Salt Water Flush: Unknown

Samurai Psychologist: Dan Osman, Rick Allen

Sanitarium: Dave Hatchett, October 1988

Sayonara: Mike Corbett, Bill Serniuk, Charlene Serniuk, 1979

Show No Mercy: John Goodman, Dave and Mike Hatchett, 1990

Slave Driver: Al Swanson

Slip N' Slide: M. Francechini and friend, 1973

Slithering Slit: Bill Serniuk, solo

Smiley's People: Kurt Rassmussen, Mark Bauer

Snake Charmer: Paul Crawford, Jay Smith, 1982

Son of God: John Stock

Squeeze and Wheeze: Unknown

Summer Breeze: Mike Corbett, Bill Serniuk, 1979

Sun and Steel: Dave and Mike Hatchett, Rick Lovelace

Symo: Al Swanson, October 1988

Tempest: Dave Hatchett, Al Swanson, 1989

Testament: Mike and Dave Hatchett, John Goodman, 1990

The Crackler: John Collins, Al Swanson, Mike and Dave Hatchett

The Drill Press: Dave Hatchett

The Jon Bowlin Memorial: Jon Bowlin, Jim Orey, Charlie Downs, 1981

The Ramp: J. Bowlin, D. Johnson, J. Leonard, Jim Orey, A. Price, 1979

The Right Hand of God: John Stock

The Trooper: Dave Hatchett, Mike Hatchett, Ed Collins

Glaze-Her-Face: Paul Crawford, Jay Smith, Rick Van Horn, 1980

God of Thunder: Dario Gambetta, Tony Yaniro, 1978

Gods of Plunder: Petch Pietrolungo, 1996

Ham Sandwich: Unknown

Hands across the Water: B. Gallagher, J. Smart, 1979

Hannah's Hideout: Petch Pietrolungo, 1996

Hay Fever: Dan Osman, Banny Root

Haystack: Ken Edsburg, TM Herbert, Jerry Sublette, 1965

Hemorrhoids in Flight: Rick Cashner, Darrell Hatten, Rick Sumner, 1979

Here We Go Again: Eric Gable, Petch Pietrolungo, 1996

High Tour: Greg Dexter, Steve Miller, Jay Smith, 1977

Hornblower: Greg Dexter, Steve Miller, 1976

Hospital Corner: Unknown; FFA: Richard Harrison, Jay Smith, 1977

Hourglass Wall: Jeff Lowe, 1969; FFA: Paul Crawford, Bill Price, 1982

Hushed Passage: Dave Schultz (TR); lead bolts: Unknown, 1996

Incubus: Royal Robbins, Steve Roper, 1972

Jack in the Box: Brian Kay, Rochy, 1994

Jailbreak: T. Kesler, Rick Sumner, 1976

Jeff's Folly: M. Caldwell, R. Erdman, J. Fowler, C. Williams, 1969

Last Laugh: Richard Harrison, Jay Smith, 1977

Little Drive: Petch Pietrolungo, 1996

Lover's Chimney: Bruce Cooke, 1949

Magic Box: Jay Sell, Petch Pietrolungo, 1996

Magnum Force: Greg Dexter, Jay Smith, 1977

Main Line: Jay Smith, Bill Todd, 1976; FFA: John Bachar, Ron Kauk, 1978

Manzanita Exit: John Smart, Bill Gallagher, 1979

MDA: Jay Smith, Rick Sumner, 1976

More Madness: Karl McConachie, Paul Crawford, 1984

Mountain Surf: Gram Sanders (project)

North Country: Charley Jones, Victor Marcus, Jim Orey, C. Stanborough, 1975

North Face: K. Edsburg, J. Davidson, 1963; (aid pitch free) M. Andrews, Jim Orey; (first pitch var.) Paul Crawford, 1979

Novitiate's Nightmare: Unknown

Optimator: Petch Pietrolungo, 1996

Out to Lunge: Steve Miller, 1978

Ozzie: Paul Crawford, Richard Harrison, Nick Nordblum, 1982

Paramour: Eric Bjornstad, B. Hagen, 1968; FFA: Greg Dexter, Rick Sumner, 1975

Peanut Brittle: Gene Drake, H. Haymond, 1969

Piece of Mind: Edwin Drummond, Lanny Johnson, 1981

Pigs on the Wing: Jay Smith, Rick Sumner, 1977

Pillar of Society: Chris Clifford, Chris Pitman, 1984

Pop Bottle: Gene Drake, M. Haymond, Larry Morris, 1969

Power Box: Jay Sell, 1997

Preparation H: M. Haymond, Jim Hicks, 1969

Psychedelic Direct: Mike Creel, Chris Craig, 1990

Psychedelic Tree: Bruce Cooke, TM Herbert, 1968

Purple Haze: Richard Harrison, Jay Smith, 1977

Raspberry Bypass: D. Knight

Rated X Direct: Jim Orey, F. Van Overbeck, 1972; FFA: Karl McConachie, Jay Smith, 1984

Rated X: Eric Beck, Peter Haan, 1972

Rednecks: Rick Sumner, Bill Todd, 1976

Reds Delight: Red and friends

Roofer Madness: Jay Smith, Rick Sumner, 1977

Schnauzer: Jay Sell, Petch Pietrolungo, 1996

Scimitar: Mike Covington, Dick Erb, 1969; FFA: Jim Orey, F. Van Overbeck, 1972

Shady Lady: Jim Hicks, Ralph Regua, 1970

Shorts Only: Kevin Nelson, B. Chandler, 1980

Showtime: First pitch, Kadas and friends; second and third pitches, Jay Smith, 1990

Silly Willy Crack: Bill Price, 1982

Sinbad and the Devil: Petch Pietrolungo, D. Soldauini, K. Collins, 1995

Sinbad Takes a Taxi: Mark Nicholas, Petch Pietrolungo, 1996

Sinbad's High Sea Simulator: B. Kay, Circlehead, 1996

Sinbad: Eric Gable, Petch Pietrolungo, 1996

Skism: Mark Nicholas, 1996

Sky Rocket: Steve Miller, Rick Sumner, 1978

Smooth Sunshine: Petch Pietrolungo, Truck Cunneer, 1994

Snap, Crackle, Pop: Chris Smith, Spruce Schoenman, 1997

Special K: Spruce Schoenman, 1996

Stem Mister: Will Catrell, John Robinson, 1996

Stone Cold Crazy: Tony Yaniro, 1982

Stony End: Tony Yaniro, Max Jones, 1982

Stony God: Tony Yaniro, 1982

Stony Highway: Chris Clifford, 1984

Strawberry Overpass: Mark Nicholas, Brian Harrington, 1984

Sudden Death: (first two pitches) Rick Cashner, Rick Sumner, 1979; (upper pitches) Richard Harrison, Jay Smith, 1977

Surrealistic Direct: Jeff Lowe, J. Vives, 1969

Surrealistic Pillar: K. Edsburg, M. Edsburg, J. Sublette, 1963

The Banana: Unknown; FFA: Jim Orey, 1972

The Clonedike: Rick Sumner, Jeff Altenberg, Maggie Altenberg, 1981

The Crosstown Traffic: Karl McConachie, Paul Crawford, Jay Smith, 1981

The Farce: Unknown

The Gamoke: Richard Harrison, Jay Smith, 1977

The Groove: Rock Craft instructors, 1970

The Hourglass: Warren Harding, Dick Long, Jack Rankin, 1965; FFA: Greg Dexter, Rick Sumner, 1975

The Last Sandwich: Steve Miller, Will Cottrell, 1984

The Line: TM Herbert, Doug Tompkins, 1966; FFA: Tom Higgins, Frank Sarnquist, 1968

The Mixologist: Petch Pietrolungo, 1997

The Number: D. Ketchum, K. Ranen, 1971

The Slash: P. Berry, R. Linnett, 1958

Third Stone from the Sun: Richard Harrison, Steve Miller, Jay Smith, 1977

Tic-Tic-Tic: Ed Drummond

Tilted Milten: Petch Pietrolungo, Hippie Dan, 1997

Tombstone Terror: Gary Anderson, Steve Miller, Jay Smith, Rick Sumner, 1976

Traveler Buttress: (below Main Ledge) Steve Roper, Steve Thompson, Gordon Webster, 1966; (above Main Ledge) Unknown; FFA: Dick Long, Al Steck, 1965

Under the Big Top: Karl McConachie, Jay Smith, 1981

Unknown Soldier: Al Swanson, 1989

Up from the Skies: Paul Crawford, Paul Obanheim, Jay Smith, 1982

Vanishing Point: Gene Drake, Jim Orey, 1972

Wallflower: Paul Crawford, Jay Smith, Bill Todd, 1976

Wave Rider: Gene Drake, Jim Hicks, 1970

West Wall: K. Edsburg, A. McLane, 1965

White Scar: Petch Pietrolungo, Jay Sell, 1996

Wild Turkey: Richard Harrison, Jay Smith, 1977

Yankee Dog: Mark Nicholas, 1996

PHANTOM SPIRES

Abun-Daba: Kevin Rivett, David Babich, 1978

All Right: M. Nicholas, B. Mibach, June 1990

Ant Cracks: Unknown

Aunt Clara: Kurt Rassmussen, July 1988

Blue Note: Mike Kreal, Larry Von Wald, April 1989

Blue Tango: George Connor, Kevin Rivett, 1978

Burnt Offerings: Paul Crawford, Don Garret, 1982

Burrowing Owl: Kevin Rivett, 1974

Cabin Fever: Clint Cummins, Joel Ager, March 1990

Candy Ass: Dave Hatchett, Tom Burt, October 1988

Candyland: Eric Barrett, John Bowlin, Robert Oravetz, 1977

Cedar Crack: M. Nicholas, B. Mibach, May 1990

Chainsaw Willie: David Babich, 1982

Char-Broiled: Karl McConachie, Paul Crawford, 1984

Cheap Shot: Scott Loomis, 1989

Cockabooty: Unknown

Cornflakes: Robert Oravetz, Eric Barrett, Dave Starn, 1978

Corquett: Kevin Rivett, David Babich, 1978

Desperado Roof Variation: David Babich, George Connor, 1978

Dewlap: John Scott, Troy Croliss, August 1990

Dot to Dot: Al Swanson, Bill Serniuk, May 1988

Dr. Jeckel and Mr. Hyde: Tom Smith, Krista Smith, Larry Von Wald, 1984

East Arete: David Babich, Don Spitter, 1977; FFA: Jay Smith, Jo Bentley, Karl McConachie, 1986

East Face: George Connor, D. Chan, 1976

Electra: D. Hatchett, M. Hatchett, June 1990

Eraserhead: David Babich, Kevin Rivett, 1980

Fancy Dancin': Robert Oravetz, Eric Barrett, 1978

Fear of Rejection: M. Nicholas, B. Mibach, May 1990

Finders Keepers: Herb Leager, Bob Kamps, May 1990

Five Tendons: Will Chen, April 1990

French Letter: Mike Kreal, Larry Von Wald, April 1989

Gingerbread: George Connor, Robert Oravetz, 1975

Ham and Eggs: David Croy, Robert Oravetz, 1977

Hard Up Variation: Eric Barrett, D. Stam, 1977

Harding's Other Chimney: Warren Harding, John Ohrenschall, 1954

Hide and Seek: M. Nicholas, B. Mibach, June 1990

Jack Corner: David Babich, D. Spittler, 1976; FFA: Eric Barrett, Dave Stam, 1976

Joe Young: Eric Barrett, David Babich, 1977

Jugs Revisited: George Connor, Robert Oravetz, 1975

July: Kevin Rivett, David Babich, 1976

K.E. Cracks: George Connor, Robert Oravetz, 1976; FFA: Eric Barrett, David Stam, 1981

Ko-Ko Box: Kevin Rivett, David Babich, 1974

La Chute: George Connor, Kevin Rivett, 1979

Last Lockup: Dave Hatchett, Mike Hatchett

Lean and Mean: Bob Grow, J. Moore, 1976

Lemon Head: D. Hatchett, Joe Hedge, October 1988

Lil' Luke: Kevin Rivett, David Babich, 1978; FFA: Eric Barrett, John Bowlin, 1980

Lounge Lizard: Mike Kreal, Larry Von Wald, September 1990 (retrobolting and lead)

Love Knobs: D. Hatchett, Al Swanson, August 1988

Mean Moe: Robert Oravetz, George Connor, 1979

Mediator: M. Nicholas, September 1990

My Favorite Thing: Mike Kreal, Larry Von Wald, April 1989

Nahoul Wall: Inno Nagara, Troy Croliss, April 1990

Neckless Traverse: George Connor, D. Chan, 1977; FFA: George Connor, Robert Oravetz, 1979

North Face Lizard Head: Jay Smith, 1986

North Ridge: Unknown

Oedipus Rex: Kevin Rivett, David Babich, 1975

Oktober Fest: Paul Brown, David Babich, 1985

Over Easy: George Connor, Robert Oravetz

Panned Out: Bob Kridler, Mark Nicholas, Brian Mibach, May 1990

Phantom of the Opera: Mike Hatchett, Dave Hatchett, Rick Lovelace, June 1988

Platitude: David Coy, David Babich, Joe Metz, 1985

Price-Smith Route: Bill Price, Jay Smith, 1983

Quick Pullout: D. Hatchett, M. Hatchett, June 1990

Quickie: B. Mibach, M. Nicholas, May 1990

Rain Song: David Babich, 1980

Regular Route Lower Spire: R. Moreau, R. Hoopes, 1955

Regular Route Middle Spire: Unknown

Roadside Injection: M. Hatchett, D. Hatchett, R. Lovelace, Tom Thompson, June 1990

Robert's Crack: George Connor, Robert Oravetz, 1975; FFA: Eric Barrett, John Bowlin, 1979

Seduction: M. Nicholas, B. Mibach, May 1990

Singe City: Jay Smith, Karl McConachie, 1986

Sizzler: Jay Smith, Paul Crawford, 1986; Pro. placed on aid

Slowdancer: Eric Barrett and friends, 1978

Smoke House Brown: Al Swanson, Bill Serniuk, May 1988

Soot: Unknown

St. Nicholas: Mark Nicholas, April 1989

Stage Fright: Eric Barrett, Dave Stam, 1976

Steppin' Stone: Eric Barrett, George Connor, Dave Stam, 1978; FFA: D. Richardson and friends, 197

T-Bone: Paul Crawford, Jay Smith, Lanny Johnson, Mark Hudon, 1984

The Bowling Ball: Mike Kreal, Larry Von Wald, April 1989

The Clam: Unknown

The Clown: Kevin Rivett, David Croy, Robert Oravetz, 1979

The Go Man: Kevin Rivett, David Babich, 1978

The Siren: Dave Rubine, Will Chen, April 1990

The Slider: M. Nicholas, B. Mibach, May 1990

Trojan: M. Nicholas, B. Mibach, May 1990

Turning Point: Don Spittler, David Babich, 1976; FFA: Eric Barrett, George Connor, 1978

Twist and Shout: M. Nicholas, B. Mibach, May 1990

Tyro's Testpiece: Unknown

Up for Grabs: David Babich, Eric Barrett, 1978

Wally Gator: R. Lovelace, Dave Hatchett, M. Hatchett, June 1990

Well Done: Paul Crawford, Karl McConachie, 1984

Wet Dreams: Krista Smith, Tom Smith, 1984

Whole Slot of Trouble: Jay Smith, February 1991

Wraith: Paul Brown, Joel Moore, February 1991

Zoo Tramp: Kevin Rivett, David Babich, 1976

SUGARLOAF

Back in Black: Jay Smith, Karl McConachie, 1986

Beast of Burden: Chris Clifford and others, pro placed on rappel, 1984

Blind Faith: Jim Orey, John Bowlin, Charley Jones, 1973

Blue Velvet: Will Catrell and friends

Bolee Gold: Garry Anderson, Jay Smith, Rick Sumner, 1977

Captain Fingers: Gene Drake, Jim Hicks, 1970; FFA: Mark Hudon, Max Jones, 1979

Cry Uncle: Tom Herbert, Paul Crawford, 1987

Diagonal: Unknown

Dirty Dog: Unknown

Dog Fight: Al Swanson, John Nye

Dominion: Gene Drake, Dan Hart, Jim Orey, 1972

East Chimney: Unknown

East Corner: Gene Drake, Jim Hicks, 1969

East Face: Dan Patitucci, Joel Moore, June 1990

Expresso: Joel Moore, Paul Brown, September 1990

Farley: Eric Beck, Steve Roper, mid-1960s; knobby wall finish: Jim Orey, 1971

Fat Merchant's Crack: Royal Robbins, et al., 1967

Fingerlock: Jim Orey, 1972

Flight Deck: Blair Haffly, Paul Brown, 1985

Flytrap: Unknown

Gallows Pole: Paul Crawford, Rick Van Horn, 1982

Grand Delusion: Unknown; FFA: Chris Clifford

Grand Illusion: Unknown; FFA: Tony Yaniro, 1979

Hanging Jugs: Gene Drake, M. Haymond, 1969

Hard Right: Karl McConachie, Al Swanson, 1986

Harder Than It Used to Be: John Scott

Harding's Chimney: Warren Harding, John Ohrenschall, 1954

Hooker's Haven: Jim Orey, Charlie Jones, 1971; FFA: Mark Hudon, Max Jones, 1978

Hyperspace: Richard Harrison, Jay Smith, 1977

Lady Luck: Luke Freeman, Bill Todd, 1976

Lost in the Fog: Bill Todd, 1977

Lurch: Jim Hicks, Larry Morris, 1971

Mad Dog: Unknown

Make That Move Right Now Baby: M. Stumpf, B. Albonico, 1981

Only The Young Die Brave: Dave Kennedy, Will Chen, Mark Robinson, 1989

Opus: Paul Crawford, Jay Smith, 1987

Pan Dulce: Dan Patitucci, Joel Moore, September 1990

Pony Express: (first pitch) Dick Long, mid-1960s; (second pitch) Gene Drake, Jim Hicks, 1970

Rug Doctor: Al Swanson

Scheister: Unknown, probably in the 1950s

Scorpio: Jay Smith, Rick Sumner, J. Taylor, 1977

Stone: Greg Dexter, Steve Miller, 1976

Sugar Plum: Joel Moore, Bob Barnascomb, Paul Brown, Dan Patitucci, April 1989

Talking Heads: Jay Smith, Paul Crawford, 1982

Tapestry: Rick Sumner, Bill Todd, 1977

Taurus: Mark Hudon, Max Jones, 1977

Telesis: Jay Smith, Paul Crawford, 1987

The Fang: Jim Orey, M. Vincent, 1971

The Ghost in the Machine: Ed Drummond, Mark Robinson, 1984

The Hatchett: Dave Hatchett

The Man Who Fell to Earth: Paul Crawford, Dan Osman

The Southwest Corner: Steve Harvey, Mike Creel

TM Deviation: T. M. Herbert, Bruce Cooke, 1968

Trophy Hunter: Al Swanson

Twist and Shout: J. Moore, T. Phillips, May 1977

Under the Spreading Atrophy: Will Chen, Mark Robinson, 1989

Wintergreen: Paul Crawford, Jay Smith

RIVER ROCK

Africa Flake: Unknown

Deliverance on the Truckee: Aaron Silverman, 1995

Drunken Sporto's: Jason Howe, 1997

Improbable: Ron Anderson, 1978

Just to Watch Him Die: Unknown

Karl's Crack: Unknown

On Safari: Lon Harter, Kellé Harter, 1996

Project: Unknown

Project: Unknown

Spring Break: Unknown

The Old T.R.: Unknown

Total Recall: Unknown

UNR Crack: Unknown

PIG ROCK

American Graffiti: Tom Herbert, 1997

Bingo's Revenge: Doug Mishler

Blade Runner: Steve Glotfelty

Elastique: Doug Mishler

Le Boeuf: Steve Glotfelty

Plant Food: Steve Glotfelty, Doug Mishler

Rage in Eden: Steve Glotfelty

Son Be a Dentist: Doug Mishler, Steve Glotfelty

Splatomatic: Steve Glotfelty

Ton-Ton: Doug Mishler

Ultimate Violence: Steve Glotfelty

LAKE VIEW AND THE EGG

First ascent information not available.

DINOSAUR ROCK

Afternoon Corner: Paul Crafton, friends, 1976

Big Bang: Lon Harter, Mike Carville, 1996

Bloodshot: Lon Harter, Kellé Harter, 1992

Color Me Gone: Tom Sullivan, Bill Nagel, Ron Anderson, 1977

Deadman's Rappel: Bill Nagel, Ron Anderson, 1977

Edge of Doom: Dan Osman, 1982

End of Time: Unknown

Evolution of Man: Lon Harter, Kellé Harter, 1996

Flying Lizard: Unknown

Green Hell: Dan Osman, 1982

Lizard King: Jim Arnold

Nose Bleed: Ron Anderson

P.A. Corner: Ron Anderson, 1976

Quadzilla: Roger Borda, Lon Harter, 1992

Sauron's Nest: Lon Harter, Kellé Harter, 1996

The Gash: Ron Anderson, Greg Bergren, 1976

The Left Seam: Tom Sullivan, Bill Nagel, Ron Anderson, 1977

Tom's Traverse: Tom Sullivan, 1976

THE BOOK OF RED

First ascents were primarily by Dan Osman, Bill Griffin, and other Gardnerville climbers beginning in 1978.

Rated Route Index

5.9

5.10

5.10A

5.10B

5.10C

5.11D

Route Name Index

Area Climbing Stores, Instruction, and Gyms

CLIMBING STORES

Alpenglow Sports
415 North Lake Boulevard
Tahoe City, CA
(530) 583-6917

Sierra Mountaineer
10060 Bridge Street
Truckee, CA
(530) 587-2025

Sierra Mountaineer
1901 Silverada Boulevard
Reno, NV
(702) 856-4824

Reno Mountain Sports
155 North Moana Lane
Reno, NV
(702) 825-2855

Sports Ltd.
1032 Emerald Bay Road
South Lake Tahoe, CA
("Y" Shopping Center)
(530) 544-2284

CLIMBING SCHOOLS AND GUIDE SERVICES

Alpine Skills International (ASI)
At the Pass on Donner Pass Road (Old Highway 40)
Norden, CA
(530) 426-9801

CLIMBING GYMS

RockSport Climbing Center at
Sierra Mountaineer
1901 Silverada Boulevard
Reno, NV
(702) 352-7673

Gravity Works/Sports Exchange
10095 West River Street
Truckee, CA
(530) 582-4510

Headwall Café at Squaw Valley
1960 Squaw Valley Road (in the Tram Building)
Olympic Valley, CA
(530) 583-7673

GAD Gymnastic and Climbing Gym
867 Eloise Avenue, Suite B
South Lake Tahoe, CA
(530) 544-7314

ACCESS: It's every climber's concern

The Access Fund, a national, non-profit climbers organization, works to keep climbing areas open and to conserve the climbing environment. Need help with closures? land acquisition? legal or land management issues? funding for trails and other projects? starting a local climbers' group? CALL US! Climbers can help preserve access by being committed to Leave No Trace (minimum-impact) practices. Here are some simple guidelines:

• **ASPIRE TO "LEAVE NO TRACE"** especially in environmentally sensitive areas like caves. Chalk can be a significant impact on dark and porous rock—don't use it around historic rock art. Pick up litter, and leave trees and plants intact.

• **DISPOSE OF HUMAN WASTE PROPERLY** Use toilets whenever possible. If toilets are not available, dig a "cat hole" at least six inches deep and 200 feet from any water, trails, campsites, or the base of climbs. *Always pack out toilet paper.* On big wall routes, use a "poop tube" and carry waste up and off with you (the old "bag toss" is now illegal in many areas).

• **USE EXISTING TRAILS** Cutting switchbacks causes erosion. When walking off-trail, tread lightly, especially in the desert where cryptogamic soils (usually a dark crust) take thousands of years to form and are easily damaged. Be aware that "rim ecologies" (the clifftop) are often highly sensitive to disturbance.

• **BE DISCRETE WITH FIXED ANCHORS** *Bolts are controversial and are not a convenience* – don't place 'em unless they are *really* necessary. Camouflage all anchors. Remove unsightly slings from rappel stations (better to use steel chain or welded cold shuts). Bolts sometimes can be used proactively to protect fragile resources – consult with your local land manager.

• **RESPECT THE RULES** and speak up when other climbers don't. Expect restrictions in designated wilderness areas, rock art sites, caves, and to protect wildlife, especially nesting birds of prey. *Power drills are illegal in wilderness and all national parks.*

• **PARK AND CAMP IN DESIGNATED AREAS** Some climbing areas require a permit for overnight camping.

• **MAINTAIN A LOW PROFILE** Leave the boom box and day-glo clothing at home—the less climbers are heard and seen, the better.

• **RESPECT PRIVATE PROPERTY** Be courteous to land owners. Don't climb where you're not wanted.

• **JOIN THE ACCESS FUND!** To become a member, make a tax-deductible donation of $25 or more.

The Access Fund

Preserving America's Diverse Climbing Resources
PO Box 17010 Boulder, CO 80308
303.545.6772 • www.accessfund.org

FALCON GUIDES® Leading the Way™

FALCON GUIDES® are available for where-to-go hiking, mountain biking, rock climbing, walking, scenic driving, fishing, rockhounding, paddling, birding, wildlife viewing, and camping. We also have FalconGuides on essential outdoor skills and subjects and field identification. The following titles are currently available, but this list grows every year. For a free catalog with a complete list of titles, call FALCON toll-free at 1-800-582-2665.

BIRDING GUIDES

Birding Minnesota
Birding Montana
Birding Northern California
Birding Texas
Birding Utah

FIELD GUIDES

Bitterroot: Montana State Flower
Canyon Country Wildflowers
Central Rocky Moutnain
  Wildflowers
Great Lakes Berry Book
New England Berry Book
Ozark Wildflowers
Pacific Northwest Berry Book
Plants of Arizona
Rare Plants of Colorado
Rocky Mountain Berry Book
Scats & Tracks of the
  Pacific Coast States
Scats & Tracks of the Rocky Mtns.
Southern Rocky Mountain
  Wildflowers
Tallgrass Prairie Wildflowers
Western Trees
Wildflowers of Southwestern Utah
Willow Bark and Rosehips

FISHING GUIDES

Fishing Alaska
Fishing the Beartooths
Fishing Florida
Fishing Glacier National Park
Fishing Maine
Fishing Montana
Fishing Wyoming
Fishing Yellowstone Natl. Park
Trout Unlimited's Guide to
  America's 100 Best Trout
  Streams

PADDLING GUIDES

Floater's Guide to Colorado
Paddling Minnesota
Paddling Montana
Paddling Okefenoke
Paddling Oregon
Paddling Yellowstone & Grand
  Teton National Parks

ROCKHOUNDING GUIDES

Rockhounding Arizona
Rockhounding California
Rockhounding Colorado
Rockhounding Montana
Rockhounding Nevada
Rockhound's Guide to
  New Mexico
Rockhounding Texas
Rockhounding Utah
Rockhounding Wyoming

HOW-TO GUIDES

Avalanche Aware
Backpacking Tips
Bear Aware
Desert Hiking Tips
Hiking with Dogs
Mountain Lion Alert
Reading Weather
Route Finding
Using GPS
Wild Country Companion
Wilderness First Aid
Wilderness Survival
Zero Impact

WALKING

Walking Colorado Springs
Walking Denver
Walking Portland
Walking San Francisco
Walking St. Louis
Walking Virginia Beach

ROCK CLIMBING GUIDES

Rock Climbing Arizona
Rock Climbing Colorado
Rock Climbing Montana
Rock Climbing New Mexico
  & Texas
Rock Climbing Utah
Rock Climbing Washington

■ *To order any of these books, check with your local bookseller or call FALCON ® at **1-800-582-2665**.*
www.FalconOutdoors.com

FALCON®